Ask Me Smarter!

Brain Questions for Kids that are **FUN**-da-men-tal in Helping Them SOAR to Scholastic Success.

LANGUAGE ARTS AND LITERARY WORKS

Preschool – 5th Grade

By: Donna M. Roszak

Ask Me Smarter!

Brain Questions for Kids that are **FUN**-da-men-tal in Helping Them SOAR to Scholastic Success

LANGUAGE ARTS AND LITERARY WORKS

Preschool – 5th Grade

Published in the United States by: Zebra Print Press, LLC

Cover design by Donna M. Roszak
Cover creation by www.jimandzetta.com
Interior layout and typesetting by www.jimandzetta.com
Ebook conversion by www.jimandzetta.com

Library of Congress Control Number: 2017911082

ISBN: 978-0-9860801-2-8 (Trade Paperback)
        978-0-9860801-3-5 (Hardcover)

Printed in the United States of America

First Edition

Website: **www.askmesmarter.com**

To my son Lucas who has always believed in this book and is my biggest supporter, to my mother Dorothy, whom I hope would be proud, and to my-mother-in law Joan who has continued to encourage me throughout this endeavor.

Table of Contents

A Note to Parents, Guardians, and Teachers

This book is based on the premise that parents/guardians are their children's greatest and most influential teachers!

This book is designed as a **one-source tool** to help parents/guardians empower their children with a solid knowledge foundation, *based on traditional state content standards per grade level*, as they progress through their elementary school years. It is intended to enhance and reinforce the facts, ideas, and concepts that children are learning in school. This book serves to take away the guesswork, and to provide concrete questions that relate to the listed content standards per grade level. It is an oral approach to disseminating primarily rote information. It is a book based on the notion that learning is a life-long process, and that children learn differently and at different rates. Leaning is not always aligned with chronological age. It is a book that is sensitive to the fact that children come from diverse cultural upbringings and have diverse educational backgrounds and experiences.

What it is NOT: This book is *not* a school curriculum guide. It is *not* intended to be a quiz, a trivia game of random questions, or a competition venue. It is *not* a school textbook or workbook. It is *not* a manual for homeschoolers. It is *not* intended to be a substitute for fulfilling all school grade objectives and outcomes. It is *not* intended to promote the higher level thinking skills as outlined in Bloom's taxonomy. Further, it is *not* expected that children memorize and "master" all questions in all subjects at any given grade level before proceeding to the next.

Knowledge gained by answering *Language Arts* content questions is a sound learning strategy in that it is:

Specific
Measurable
Attainable
Results-oriented
Time framed by grade level
Empowering
Reinforcing

Preface

This book provides a **one-source** guide for parents/guardians/teachers to help their children learn important facts and concepts across the elementary levels that are child, grade, and age appropriate. All the grade levels are integrated together into one book to achieve a comprehensive approach that also accommodates different learning paces. It further allows for review and reinforcement based on child-readiness and retention capacity. Even though a child may learn one topic in one year does not guarantee the child will retain that same information and have the retention and recall capacity to build on that knowledge the following school year!

This oral approach is based on the premise that knowledge is acquired through the senses: sight, hearing, touch, smell, and taste. The more senses that are used in learning, the higher the retention rate will be. Children have different learning rates and different learning styles. If "speaking" is added to hearing and seeing, the learning will come even faster, and retention will be maximized. It can be concluded then, that learners have a higher retention of what they HEAR, and SAY than by what they *SEE* alone. Employing more than one sense in learning then, as this book aims to do, is what makes the learning permanent. When all is said and done, the key to long-term retention is sustained practice over time.

This book also provides a vacation or summer "bridge" tool for young learners when school is not in session. "Ask Me Smarter" may also prove to be a good companion during a long road trip!

Inherent in this simple question format is building a child's self-esteem with a *low-anxiety* verbal approach, empowering him or her with essential knowledge, facts, and insights.

This book is a result of my difficulty in comprehending my son's just published 5th grade social studies textbook that was so convoluted with facts and minute details that the understanding of the main idea was completely lost. After reading a particularly wordy passage on the Civil War, my son had no clue from that reading which leader was on which side and who ultimately won the war! It further stems from my frustration in locating a resource that did not read like a textbook, or one that was not specific to just one grade level or operate like a workbook. Further, many libraries and bookstores have an abundant selection of educational psychology books, how-to books, science experiment books, how to read books, colorful trivia decks, but I was not able to locate a single resource that provides a direct and comprehensive approach to asking specific questions to young learners across all core and non-core disciplines. Trivia cards and interactive websites while fun and educational, are somewhat random and hit or miss with regard to ensuring coverage of essential facts encompassing all the necessary academic subject areas. I felt compelled to write something that might help fill a niche I felt was lacking, and one that expands on current resources. To this end, it was my intent to compile several grade levels into one book.

How to Use This Book

It is important to use careful judgment in ascertaining which topics and how many questions should be asked of your child (children) at any one time. It is encouraged that questions be asked from different topics and questions that encompass different grade levels as appropriate. For example, a 1st grader may benefit from being posed "2nd grade" questions as well as being asked questions from the "kindergarten" section on any given topic. A 5th grader would similarly benefit from being asked a 3rd grade question! Some overlap with regard to the questions should be expected. Further, it is important to note that what may be deemed a "2nd grade" question in one state, may be regarded as a "3rd grade" question in another. In addition, some topics may be listed as a content standard in one state and not another. The question, "Why do you save money?" is posed as a pre-school question. That same question can be asked at any grade level. Theoretically, the older and more knowledgeable the child, the higher the level of response.

Core Questions: It is given that many questions in this book could represent a full week lesson, many worksheets, practice, application, and analysis. In many cases, a choice is offered after a question, but this choice could easily be eliminated if need be, or if the question is asked for the second or third time.

Language Arts: Many of these questions reflect words, spelling, readings, songs, and essential grammar facts. Many of the stories and novels mentioned are good to know, not necessarily **need** to know. What is important is that young learners be exposed to a wide variety of reading and writing experiences and genres.

Notable Literary Works Through the Ages: This chapter serves to expose children to a wide array of prominent authors and titles in world literature. Many of the books are regarded as "the classics." By no means are children expected to know every title, speech, or author. The reading of literature across all genres that is intellectually appropriate is the desired goal. The questions are arranged in chronological order by date of publication. It may behoove the interrogator to skim and scan this chapter, focusing on the questions that align with the learner's literary experiences. The first letter or words of the title are included as a prompt.

IMPORTANT: It should not be expected that children *master* a grade level before proceeding to the next! The emphasis is on the questions, *not* the grade level. As both a mother and an educator, one of the best pieces of advice I ever received was, "teach the child, not the grade or subject."

Questions are somewhat sequential and are inherently progressive as students gain knowledge. The questions are aimed to serve as a *representation* of what is listed as the prescribed "standards" or learning outcomes for the elementary grade levels in most states.

Parents/guardians/teachers are encouraged to *re-word* questions, repeat questions, and improvise. For example, if on one occasion you ask your child: "What is the opposite of "up?" Next time ask, "what is down the opposite of?"
Further, many questions have an inherent challenge in that they are posed with a choice, something that can, and should be omitted at the discretion of the interrogator.

If questions are asked at bedtime, an ideal time for the brain to process information and store it for future retrieval, ask your child some of the **same** questions the next morning for further reinforcement and empowerment. If the question has a choice of two or more answers, leave out the choice when asking the question again.

Some questions listed as curriculum content standards will and should illicit further discussion. Many questions may be posed as yes and no or true and false questions, simply to suggest a specific learning objective. For many of the questions it is suggested that *similar* types of questions be asked to promote further competence and awareness. For example, a preschooler may be asked to name something blue in his or her bedroom. You can follow up with, "What is found in nature that is blue?" A high level question posed may ask the learner to name all the colors in the rainbow. (ROY G BIV) Many questions are asked to promote multi-cultural awareness and ideally, cultural sensitivity as well.

The intention of the author is for this book to be used as an oral and auditory approach to learning and reviewing or discussing information, but it certainly would work well for a learner to read the questions and see how many questions he or she can answer correctly. It is intended to enhance and compliment what our children are already learning in school or at home. Its all-inclusive format and oral approach is what makes it unique, I believe.

If a child seems intrigued by a particular question or answer, I would highly encourage seeking out other resources from books, the Internet, pictures, etc. (See list of further resources.) We need to expand upon our children's great capacity to learn and feed their unwavering curiosity!

My hope is that your child will be engaged and challenged, and therefore empowered through this oral questioning format.

In assessing correctness, the answers are located in the appendices organized by chapter in numerical order.

Further Resources:
Library (School and Local)
Internet
Family Members
Field Trips
Field Experts
Authentic Learning Moments (Teaching fractions while cutting and serving pizza)
Real-time applications: (Conduct a science experiment; Follow a recipe; Hand-write a thank you note.)
"Wonder" Questions (What do you wonder about?)
Have your child ask YOU a question! If you are unable to answer it, suggest that you seek out the answer together.

It needs to be stated that information expands exponentially every day. Any given topic in and of itself could easily fill a library. One war may be an entire semester of study at the University level! Neither an entire library, nor the nearly infinite information capacity of a computer could ever fit into one manageable book. Given the limits and constraints of time and space, the inclusion of any topic or question is frequently at the expense or exclusion of another. If I was remiss in any regard, I invite the reader to fill in any perceived missing questions, as you deem appropriate. What follows is a compilation of questions that encompass a wide array of essential knowledge questions aimed at children 12 and under based on traditional state learning standards. The questions loosely "cover" the learning objectives listed under the curriculum guidelines for each respective grade level. Variations and expanding upon the questions is encouraged and expected.

There is definite overlap between grade levels. Because this is a question format, this approach in no way is intended to promote and develop a mastery of grade-level *skills* (socialization, cooperative learning, reading, writing, spelling, vocabulary acquisition, story-telling etc.) Nor can this format measure a child's proficiency with technology and research skills that are an integral part of learning outcomes per grade level. Any omission or perceived bias is completely unintentional. Ideally, this question and answer approach will serve to empower our children with essential and meaningful knowledge through these fact-based questions, and provide them with a strong foundation as they continue to learn, grow, and prepare for higher learning. In so doing, our children will become informed citizens and future contributing members of our global community.

Research shows that children learn in different ways and at different rates. This book is formatted to compliment the brain networks that play a key role in learning. The "Spacing Effect" is a sound strategy in that facts are learned best when they are studied at frequent intervals over a long time span. Long-term retention of facts and information is maximized through repeated retrieval. "Ask Me Smarter" aims to provide the opportunity for optimal learning to occur in that the emphasis is on the knowledge, not the grade level.

As you use this book as a supplemental learning tool, it is important to keep in mind:

1) Knowledge of **dates** is not essential in the primary grades.

2) Many of the questions, especially in grades 3, 4, and 5 have a choice of answers after the colon. The degree of difficulty is inherent in these questions in that the choice can be read or not, at the discretion of the person asking the questions, and the readiness of the learner.

3) Learners are always encouraged to learn the words to a poem or song, or seek out some new stories and novels, but are certainly not expected to be familiar with every book, poem or song mentioned.

4) Many questions are yes or no questions that reflect a specific learning standard per grade level. These questions are given the answer "Yes" if only to suggest the learning goal.

5) Many of the questions asked in the higher grades are admittedly a "stretch," but they are purposely included to challenge and engage the young learner.

"Knowledge is potential power?"

Now go ahead, ask them smarter!

Chapter 1 – Language Arts

Language Arts – Pre-School

1. What is your name?

2. What is your first name?

3. Do you know any of the letters in your first name?

4. Can you write any of the letters in your first name?

5. What is your middle name?

6. What is your surname, meaning your last name?

7. How old are you?

8. Who do you know that is older than you?

9. Who do you know that is younger than you?

10. Who do you know that is the same age as you?

11. When is your birthday?

12. What month are we in?

13. What day of the week is it today?

14. What day of the week is tomorrow?

15. What day of the week was yesterday?

16. Can you tell someone your needs and feelings?

17. Can you speak in sentences?

18. Can you have a conversation with an adult?

19. Can you ask me a question?

20. Can you answer my question, how do you feel today?

21. Can you describe what you did yesterday in order?

22. Can you listen to a book that is read to you out loud?

23. Can you answer questions about what is happening in a book?

24. Can you re-tell a story using pictures from the book to help you?

25. Can you show me in what direction we read a book?

26. Can you recite (say) any nursery rhymes from memory?

27. What words rhyme or sound alike in the nursery rhyme, "One two, buckle my shoe…?"

28. Can you finish the poem, "Rain, rain go away…?"

29. Can you finish the poem, "Diddle Diddle dumpling…?"

30. Can you finish the poem, "Wee Willie Winkie…?"

31. Can you finish the poem, "Peter, Peter Pumpkin Eater…?"

32. Can you finish the poem, "To market to market to buy…?"

33. Can you sing the song, "Kookaburra?"

34. Can you sing the song, "Pop Goes the Weasel?

35. Can you sing the song, "John Jacob Jingleheimer Schmidt?"

36. Can you sing the song, "Happy Birthday to You?"

37. Can you sing the song, "Twinkle, Twinkle Little Star?"

38. Can you sing the song, "Rock-A-Bye Baby?"

39. Can you sing the song, "Row, Row, Row Your Boat?"

40. Can you sing the song, "Old MacDonald Had a Farm?"

41. Can you sing the song, "Here We Go Round the Mulberry Bush?"

42. Can you sing the song and use motion for, "Ring Around the Rosie?"

43. Can you sing the song and use motion for, "This Little Piggy Went to Market?"

44. Can you sing the song and use motion for, "The Eensy, Weensy Spider?"

45. Can you sing the song and use motion for, "Five Little Monkeys?"

46. Can you sing the song and use motion for, "I'm a Little Teapot?"

47. Can you sing the song and use motion for, "Head, Shoulders, Knees, and Toes?"

48. Can you sing the song and claps for, "B-I-N-G-O?"

49. Can you sing the song and claps for, "If You're Happy and You Know It?"

50. What is the name of the story with the character "Goldilocks?"

51. What color is the little hen in the story about a hen?

52. How many pigs are there in the story?

53. What kind of animal tried to scare the three little pigs?

54. What three materials did the three pigs use to build their house with?

55. How does "The Three Little Pigs" end?

56. What is a name of another story that you know?

57. Can you draw a straight line?

58. What is the name of the tool that you use to cut paper?

59. Do you know how to use a scissors?

60. What are some rules to follow when you are in a store? (church) (school) (pool)

61. Do you follow the rules when you play a board game?

62. What is a board game that you know how to play?

63. What is your favorite toy to play with?

64. What is your favorite food?

65. Can you name two table manners when eating a meal?

66. What is a good word to use to show politeness when asking for something?

67. What do you say to show appreciation after you are given something?

68. How do you respond to the phrase, "Thank you?"

69. How would you say hello to a neighbor who is a man or the dad of the family?

70. How would you say hello to a neighbor who is a woman or the mom of a family?

71. Is it hot or cold today?

72. Is it day or night?

73. What time of the day is it when you wake up?

74. What time of the day is it when you go to bed?

75. What time of the day is it after lunch?

76. Is it morning, afternoon, or evening right now?

77. What is the name of the meal we eat in the morning?

78. What meal do we eat in the middle of the day?

79. What meal do we eat in the evening?

80. What season of the year are we in?

81. Are you a boy or girl?

82. How many brothers/sisters do you have? (Names)

83. Do you have a pet? (Name)

84. What do we need to do to take care of a (our) pet?

85. What part of your body do you run with?

86. What part of your body do you eat and talk with?

87. What part of the body do you wave with?

88. Which of your hands is your *left* hand? (Show how holding hand up with thumb at right angle to fingers forms the letter "L.")

89. Which of your hands is your *right* hand?

90. Are you right-handed or left-handed?

91. Can you dress all by yourself?

92. Can you zipper your jacket?

93. Can you button your shirt?

94. Can you tie your shoes?

95. What part of the body do you smell with?

96. What part of the body do you hear with?

97. What part of the body do you see with?

98. On what part of your body do you wear shoes, mittens, a hat, etc.?

99. Can you point to your knee, elbow, thumb, ankle, etc.?

100. What color is the grass?

101. What things can you name that are green?

102. What color is the sky?

103. What things can you name that are blue?

104. What color are your eyes?

105. What color is your hair?

106. What color is a ripe tomato?

107. What things can you name that are red?

108. What color is a ripe banana?

109. What things can you name that are yellow?

110. What things can you name that are orange?

111. What things can you name that are black?

112. What things can you name that are white?

113. What things can you name that are pink?

114. What things can you name that are purple?

115. What color is your room? (Etc.)

116. Can you say (sing) the letters of the alphabet?

117. What do letters that are combined spell out?

118. Can you point to the cover of this book?

119. Can you point to the back of this book?

120. Can you point out a page of this book?

121. Can you "pretend" to read a book?

122. Can you turn the pages of this book?

123. What kinds of things can transport us from place to place?

124. What is the name of the vehicle that transports sick or injured people to the hospital?

125. What is the name of the truck that transports dirt or rocks?

126. What is the name of the truck that hauls broken cars in for repair?

127. What is the name of the vehicle that transports children to school?

128. What is the name of the vehicle that arrives at a fire scene?

129. What types of liquids does a tanker truck carry?

130. What is the name of a type the transportation that floats on water?

131. What is the name of a motorized bicycle?

132. Is a bicycle a means of transportation?

133. What is the name of the type of transportation that runs on railroad tracks?

134. What is the name of the transportation that travels in the air?

135. What is the name of the transportation that is used on a farm?

136. What are the names of some tools?

137. What is the name of a farm animal?

138. What is the name of a zoo animal?

139. What is the name of a sea animal?

140. What is the name of a forest animal?

141. What is an example of an insect?

142. What are some animals that are pets?

143. Can you name an animal that has stripes?

144. Can you name an animal that has fins?

145. Can you name an animal that has wings?

146. Can you name an animal that has horns?

147. Can you name an animal that has paws?

148. Can you name an animal that has claws?

149. Can you name an animal that has fangs?

150. Can you name an animal that has long neck?

151. Can you name an animal that has long trunk?

152. What sound does a bird make?

153. What sound does a dog make?

154. What sound does a cat make?

155. What sound does a frog make?

156. What sound does a horse make?

157. What sound does a bear make?

158. What sound does a monkey make?

159. What sound does a cow make?

160. What sound does a chicken make?

161. What sound does a duck make?

162. Which is bigger: an elephant or a lion?

163. Which is smaller: a mouse or a dog?

164. Who is taller: you or me?

165. Which is shorter: a skyscraper building or a house?

166. Can you point *up*?

167. What is the opposite of *up*?

168. What is *in* your bedroom?

169. What is the opposite of *in*?

170. Where is the *front* of this book?

171. What is the opposite of *front*?

172. What is *on* your bed?

173. What is the opposite of *on*?

174. Is the television on or off?

175. What is *under* your bed?

176. What is the opposite of under?

177. Can you point to the *top* of this page?

178. What is the opposite of *top*?

179. Can you point to the *middle* of this page?

180. What is your *middle* name?

181. Can you point to the *bottom* of this page?

182. What is the opposite of *bottom*?

183. What is the opposite of *sad*?

184. What is the opposite of *night*?

185. What is the opposite of *behind*?

186. What is the opposite of *above*?

187. What is the opposite of *little*?

188. What is the opposite of *low*?

189. What is the opposite of *over*?

190. What is the opposite of *more*?

191. What is the opposite of *same*?

192. Can you name someone that is the same size as you?

193. What is *beside* (next to) your bed?

194. What is *inside* your dresser?

195. What is *outside* the house?

196. Is this book right side up or upside down?

197. What is a food that is *hot*?

198. What is a food that is *cold*?

199. Can you name an animal that is *fast*?

200. What is an animal that is *slow*?

201. Do people look the same or different?

202. Can you recognize and pronounce the common sight word "a?"(Show word!)

203. Can you recognize and pronounce the common sight word "and?"(Show word!)

204. Can you recognize and pronounce the common sight word "away?"(Show word!)

205. Can you recognize and pronounce the common sight word "big?"(Show word!)

206. Can you recognize and pronounce the common sight word "blue?"(Show word!)

207. Can you recognize and pronounce the common sight word "can?"(Show word!)

208. Can you recognize and pronounce the common sight word "come?"(Show word!)

209. Can you recognize and pronounce the common sight word "down?"(Show word!)

210. Can you recognize and pronounce the common sight word "find?"(Show word!)

211. Can you recognize and pronounce the common sight word "for?"(Show word!)

212. Can you recognize and pronounce the common sight word "funny?"(Show word!)

213. Can you recognize and pronounce the common sight word "go?"(Show word!)

214. Can you recognize and pronounce the common sight word "help?"(Show word!)

215. Can you recognize and pronounce the common sight word "here?"(Show word!)

216. Can you recognize and pronounce the common sight word "I?"(Show word!)

217. Can you recognize and pronounce the common sight word "in?"(Show word!)

218. Can you recognize and pronounce the common sight word "is?"(Show word!)

219. Can you recognize and pronounce the common sight word "it?"(Show word!)

220. Can you recognize and pronounce the common sight word "jump?"(Show word!)

221. Can you recognize and pronounce the common sight word "little?"(Show word!)

222. Can you recognize and pronounce the common sight word "look?"(Show word!)

223. Can you recognize and pronounce the common sight word "make?"(Show word!)

224. Can you recognize and pronounce the common sight word "me?"(Show word!)

225. Can you recognize and pronounce the common sight word "my?"(Show word!)

226. Can you recognize and pronounce the common sight word "not?"(Show word!)

227. Can you recognize and pronounce the common sight word "one?"(Show word!)

228. Can you recognize and pronounce the common sight word "play?"(Show word!)

229. Can you recognize and pronounce the common sight word "red?"(Show word!)

230. Can you recognize and pronounce the common sight word "run?"(Show word!)

231. Can you recognize and pronounce the common sight word "said?"(Show word!)

232. Can you recognize and pronounce the common sight word "see?"(Show word!)

233. Can you recognize and pronounce the common sight word "the?"(Show word!)

234. Can you recognize and pronounce the common sight word "three?"(Show word!)

235. Can you recognize and pronounce the common sight word "to?"(Show word!)

236. Can you recognize and pronounce the common sight word "two?"(Show word!)

237. Can you recognize and pronounce the common sight word "up?"(Show word!)

238. Can you recognize and pronounce the common sight word "we?"(Show word!)

239. Can you recognize and pronounce the common sight word "where?"(Show word!)

240. Can you recognize and pronounce the common sight word "yellow?"(Show word!)

241. Can you recognize and pronounce the common sight word "you?"(Show word!)

Language Arts – Kindergarten

242. Do you know think that "kindergarten" is a German word or a Spanish word?

243. What does "kindergarten" translates to in English: Children's Garden or A Kind Garden?

244. Can you sing the letters of the alphabet?

245. What sound does "a" make and what word besides **apple** starts with the letter "a?"

246. What sound does "b" make and what word besides **ball** starts with the letter "b?"

247. What sound does "c" make and what word besides **cat** starts with the letter "c?"

248. What sound does "d" make and what word besides **dog** starts with the letter d?"

249. What sound does "e" make and what word besides **egg** starts with the letter "e?"

250. What sound does "f" make and what word besides **fish** starts with the letter "f?"

251. What sound does "g" make and what word besides **gate** starts with the letter "g?"

252. What sound does "h" make and what word besides **hat** starts with the letter "h?"

253. What sound does "i" make and what word besides **igloo** starts with the letter "i?"

254. What sound does "j" make and what word besides **jar** starts with the letter "j?"

255. What sound does "k" make and what word besides **kite** starts with the letter "k?"

256. What sound does "l" make and what word besides **lemon** starts with the letter "l?"

257. What sound does "m" make and what word besides **man** starts with the letter "m?"

258. What sound does "n" make and what word besides **nest** starts with the letter "n?"

259. What sound does "o" make and what word besides **ocean** starts with the letter "o?"

260. What sound does "p" make and what word besides **pie** starts with the letter "p?"

261. What sound does "q" make and what word besides **queen** starts with the letter "q?"

262. What sound does "r" make and what word besides **rain** starts with the letter "r?"

263. What sound does "s" make and what word besides **Sun** starts with the letter "s?"

264. What sound does "t" make and what word besides **top** starts with the letter "t?"

265. What sound does "u" make and what word besides **under** starts with the letter "u?"

266. What sound does "v" make and what word besides **vase** starts with the letter "v?"

267. What sound does "w" make and what word besides **win** starts with the letter "w?"

268. What sound does "x" make and what word besides **x-ray** starts with the letter "x?"

269. What sound does "y" make and what word besides **yellow** starts with the letter "y?"

270. What sound does "z" make and what word besides **zipper** starts with the letter "z?"

271. What images can you see on an "**x-ray?**"

272. What is a word that rhymes with hat?

273. How do you spell cat?

274. How do you spell dad?

275. What is a word that rhymes with sad?

276. Can you finish the lines to the rhyme "Hickory, Dickory, Dock?"

277. Can you finish the lines to the rhyme "Diddle, Diddle Dumpling? "

278. Can you finish the lines to the rhyme "Little Bo Peep?"

279. Can you finish the lines to the rhyme "Little Boy Blue?"

280. Can you finish the lines to the rhyme "Baa, Baa, Black Sheep?"

281. Can you finish the lines to the rhyme "One, Two, Buckle My Shoe?"

282. Can you finish the lines to the rhyme "Rain, Rain, Go Away?"

283. Can you finish the lines to the rhyme "It's Raining, It's Pouring?"

284. Can you finish the lines to the rhyme "Roses Are Red?"

285. Can you finish the lines to the rhyme "Jack and Jill?"

286. Can you finish the lines to the rhyme "Jack Be Nimble?"

287. Can you finish the lines to the rhyme "Little Miss Muffet?"

288. Can you finish the lines to the rhyme "Mary Had a Little Lamb?"

289. Can you finish the lines to the rhyme "Old Mother Hubbard?"

290. Can you finish the lines to the rhyme "Old King Cole?"

291. Can you finish the lines to the rhyme "Three Blind Mice?"

292. Can you finish the lines to the rhyme "The Three Little Kittens?"

293. Can you finish the lines to the rhyme "There Was an Old Woman Who Lived in a Shoe?"

294. Can you finish the lines to the rhyme "Star Light, Star Bright?"

295. What do combined letters form: words or sentences?

296. What do combined words form: sentences or paragraphs?

297. What do sentences related to one main idea form: paragraphs or pages?

298. What kinds of things do we read?

299. What kinds of things do we write?

300. Do you write with your right hand or your left hand?

301. What electronic machine do we use with a keyboard that allows us to type text?

302. What is the title of this book?

303. What is the title of your favorite book?

304. What is the name of a person who writes a book?

305. What does an *illustrator* do?

306. What is the opposite of true?

307. Is a *fact* true or false?

308. If something is *fiction*, is it true or false?

309. Do we also read poems, letters, articles, stories, and fairy tales?

310. When we read a newspaper, is that a work of fiction or non-fiction?

311. What things can you find in a library?

312. What do you have to do to "borrow" books from the library?

313. What is the date called when you have to return your library books?

314. What is the name of the person who works in a library?

315. What is the term used if a library book is returned past the due date?

316. Do library books have barcode labels used for identification and checkout?

317. Which section of the library would you look to find a book about frogs: fiction or non-fiction?

318. Which section of the library would you look to find the story, "Goldilocks and the Three Bears:" fiction or non-fiction?

319. When would you read a *recipe*?

320. What is the name of the season when it is snowy and cold?

321. What is the name of the season when the leaves change color?

322. What is the name of the season when the plants and flowers start to grow and the birds and butterflies come out?

323. What is the name of the season when it is very warm and many people swim and camp?

324. What is the name of a baby dog?

325. What is the name of a baby cat?

326. Is a bowling ball light or heavy?

327. Is a feather light or heavy?

328. Did you eat supper before or after school?

329. What part of the day is it now?

330. What is the common shape of a clock?

331. How many numbers are on a clock?

332. On which number is the short hand?

333. On which number is the long hand? (Show clock/watch)

334. What is another name for 12:00 in the middle of the day?

335. What is another name for 12:00 at night?

336. What is the name of the chart we use to keep track of the date and day of the week?

337. How many days are there in one week?

338. Can you name the days of the week?

339. What are the two days of the weekend?

340. What is located to the **right** of your bed?

341. What is located to the **left** of your bed?

342. What is located **between** the bed and the door?

343. Can you name an object that is **far** from you?

344. What is something that is **close** to you?

345. What is the name of the tune that you *sing*?

346. Which song would you like to sing? (London Bridge; Old MacDonald; Twinkle, Twinkle Little Star; Ring around the Rosy; Row, Row, Row Your Boat; This Old Man; The Wheels on the Bus, etc.)

347. What is the name of a famous book or story?

348. Which of the following stories are you familiar with? (The Three Little Pigs; Goldilocks and the Three Bears; The Little Red Hen; The Ugly Duckling; Cinderella; King Midas and the Golden Touch; Snow White; The Velveteen Rabbit; or Johnny Appleseed?)

349. What is the name for stories that tell a lesson: fables or fairy tales?

350. Which fable are you familiar with: "The Lion and the Mouse" or "The Hare and the Tortoise?"

351. What would come next in this series: Long, longer, _?

352. What would come after big and before biggest?

353. What would come next in this series: Good, better, _?

354. What would come next in this series: Bad, worse, _?

355. Which is correct: "We watched the movie *quiet*." or, "We watched the movie *quietly*?"

356. Which is correct: "*Hope* we will go to the zoo," "*Hopely* we will go to the zoo," or, "*Hopefully* we will go to the zoo?"

357. What is the name of the precious metal that is yellowish in color and very valuable?

358. What is the color that is also like the metal that a quarter is made of?

359. What is the metal, also a color that a penny is made of?

360. How do you finish the saying, "Better safe than _?"

361. How do you finish the saying, "It's raining cats _?"

362. How do you finish the saying, "Look before you _?"

363. How do you finish the saying, "Where there's a will _?"

364. How do you finish the saying, "A dog is a man's _?"

365. How do you finish the saying, "Do unto others as you would have them _?"

366. Can you recognize and pronounce the common sight word "all?"(Show word!)

367. Can you recognize and pronounce the common sight word "am?"(Show word!)

368. Can you recognize and pronounce the common sight word "are?"(Show word!)

369. Can you recognize and pronounce the common sight word "at?"(Show word!)

370. Can you recognize and pronounce the common sight word "ate?"(Show word!)

371. Can you recognize and pronounce the common sight word "be?"(Show word!)

372. Can you recognize and pronounce the common sight word "black?"(Show word!)

373. Can you recognize and pronounce the common sight word "brown?"(Show word!)

374. Can you recognize and pronounce the common sight word "but?"(Show word!)

375. Can you recognize and pronounce the common sight word "came?"(Show word!)

376. Can you recognize and pronounce the common sight word "did?"(Show word!)

377. Can you recognize and pronounce the common sight word "do?"(Show word!)

378. Can you recognize and pronounce the common sight word "eat?"(Show word!)

379. Can you recognize and pronounce the common sight word "for?"(Show word!)

380. Can you recognize and pronounce the common sight word "get?"(Show word!)

381. Can you recognize and pronounce the common sight word "good?"(Show word!)

382. Can you recognize and pronounce the common sight word "have?"(Show word!)

383. Can you recognize and pronounce the common sight word "he?"(Show word!)

384. Can you recognize and pronounce the common sight word "into?"(Show word!)

385. Can you recognize and pronounce the common sight word "like?"(Show word!)

386. Can you recognize and pronounce the common sight word "must?"(Show word!)

387. Can you recognize and pronounce the common sight word "new?"(Show word!)

388. Can you recognize and pronounce the common sight word "no?"(Show word!)

389. Can you recognize and pronounce the common sight word "now?"(Show word!)

390. Can you recognize and pronounce the common sight word "on?"(Show word!)

391. Can you recognize and pronounce the common sight word "our?"(Show word!)

392. Can you recognize and pronounce the common sight word "out?"(Show word!)

393. Can you recognize and pronounce the common sight word "please?"(Show word!)

394. Can you recognize and pronounce the common sight word "pretty?"(Show word!)

395. Can you recognize and pronounce the common sight word "ran?"(Show word!)

396. Can you recognize and pronounce the common sight word "ride?"(Show word!)

397. Can you recognize and pronounce the common sight word "saw?"(Show word!)

398. Can you recognize and pronounce the common sight word "say?"(Show word!)

399. Can you recognize and pronounce the common sight word "she?"(Show word!)

400. Can you recognize and pronounce the common sight word "so?"(Show word!)

401. Can you recognize and pronounce the common sight word "soon?"(Show word!)

402. Can you recognize and pronounce the common sight word "that?"(Show word!)

403. Can you recognize and pronounce the common sight word "there?"(Show word!)

404. Can you recognize and pronounce the common sight word "they?"(Show word!)

405. Can you recognize and pronounce the common sight word "this?"(Show word!)

406. Can you recognize and pronounce the common sight word "too?"(Show word!)

407. Can you recognize and pronounce the common sight word "under?"(Show word!)

408. Can you recognize and pronounce the common sight word "want?"(Show word!)

409. Can you recognize and pronounce the common sight word "was?"(Show word!)

410. Can you recognize and pronounce the common sight word "well?"(Show word!)

411. Can you recognize and pronounce the common sight word "went?"(Show word!)

412. Can you recognize and pronounce the common sight word "what?"(Show word!)

413. Can you recognize and pronounce the common sight word "white?"(Show word!)

414. Can you recognize and pronounce the common sight word "who?"(Show word!)

415. Can you recognize and pronounce the common sight word "will?"(Show word!)

416. Can you recognize and pronounce the common sight word "with?"(Show word!)

417. Can you recognize and pronounce the common sight word "yes?"(Show word!)

Language Arts – 1st Grade

418. What is your first name and can you spell it?

419. What is your middle name?

420. What is your surname (last name) and can you spell it?

421. How many total letters are there in the alphabet?

422. Can you tell me a word that begins with each letter of the alphabet?

423. What are the five vowels in the alphabet?

424. What are all the other letters called that are not vowels?

425. How do you spell hat?

426. Can you name other words from the word family ending in -an that rhyme with can?

427. Can you name other words from the word family ending in -at that rhyme with cat?

428. Can you name other words that fit under the word family ending in –ap that rhyme with cap?

429. Can you name other words from the word family ending in –ab that rhyme with lab?

430. Can you name other words from the word family ending in –ad that rhyme with dad?

431. Can you name other words from the word family ending in -am that rhyme with ham?

432. Can you name other words from the word family ending in -ack that rhyme with back?

433. Can you name other words from the word family ending in -and that rhyme with sand?

434. Can you name other words from the word family ending in -ash that rhyme with cash?

435. Can you name other words from the word family ending in -ail that rhyme with nail?

436. Can you name other words from the word family ending in -ain that rhyme with rain?

437. Can you name other words from the word family ending in -air that rhyme with fair?

438. Can you name other words from the word family ending in -ate that rhyme with gate?

439. Can you name other words from the word family ending in -ake that rhyme with bake?

440. Can you name other words from the word family ending in -ale that rhyme with male?

441. Can you name other words from the word family ending in -ame that rhyme with game?

442. Can you name other words from the word family ending in -ay that rhyme with hay?

443. Can you name other words from the word family ending in -all that rhyme with ball?

444. Can you name other words from the word family ending in **-aw** that rhyme with paw?

445. Can you name other words from the word family ending in **-ar** that rhyme with jar?

446. Can you name other words from the word family ending in **-ark** that rhyme with bark?

447. Can you name other words from the word family ending in **-art** that rhyme with cart?

448. Can you name other words from the word family ending in **-ank** that rhyme with bank?

449. Can you name other words from the word family ending in **-int** that rhyme with sink?

450. Can you name other words from the word family ending in **-ed** that rhyme with bed?

451. Can you name other words from the word family ending in **-en** that rhyme with pen?

452. Can you name other words from the word family ending in **-et** that rhyme with jet?

453. Can you name other words from the word family ending in **-eck** that rhyme with neck?

454. Can you name other words from the word family ending in **-ell** that rhyme with bell?

455. Can you name other words from the word family ending in **-est** that rhyme with best?

456. Can you name other words from the word family ending in **-in** that rhyme with pin?

457. Can you name other words from the word family ending in **-ip** that rhyme with zip?

458. Can you name other words from the word family ending in **-it** that rhyme with sit?

459. What words rhyme with Sun?

460. What words rhyme with kite?

461. What words rhyme with book?

462. What words rhyme with tree?

463. What words rhyme with best?

464. What words rhyme with sleep?

465. Can you clap out the nursery rhyme "Twinkle, Twinkle Little Star" using one clap per syllable?

466. Are all of the following fairy tales or nursery rhymes: *Mary Had a Little Lamb; London Bridge; Old Mother Hubbard; Jack and Jill; Little Jack Horner; One, Two, Buckle My Shoe; Little Boy Blue; Baa, Baa Black Sheep; Three Blind Mice; Twinkle, Twinkle Little Star; There Was an Old Woman;* and *This Little Piggy Went to Market?*

467. Are the following stories considered fairy tales or nursery rhymes: *Snow White; Little Red Riding Hood; Sleeping Beauty; Pinocchio; The Little Red Hen;* and *Jack and the Beanstalk?*

468. Do all poems have to rhyme?

469. If a fable has a moral or teaches a lesson, which of the following is **not** a fable: *The Hare and the Tortoise; The Boy Who Cried Wolf; Chicken Little; The Goose and the Golden Eggs;* or, *The Three Little Pigs?*

470. What type of story did the Greek author named *Aesop* write that included animals to teach the moral or a lesson: fables or fairy tales?

471. Can you identify all of the following written forms: A story, a poem, an article, a report, a letter, text, a recipe, a journal, a sign, a list, a logo, a poster, a caption, an address, a thank-you note, a graph, and a map?

472. Can you identify visual media like a picture, a drawing, a sketch, an artwork, a video, a DVD, an audiotape, or an artifact?

473. How do you spell hop?

474. How do you spell hope?

475. How do you spell frog?

476. How do you spell stop?

477. How do you spell trip?

478. How do you spell ship?

479. How do you spell sea, like the ocean?

480. How do you spell see as in, "I see the boat?"

481. How do you spell book?

482. How do you spell tree?

483. If you spell how h-o-w, how do you spell cow?

484. If you spell pan p-a-n, how do you spell fan? (man, tan , can, ran, van)

485. What is the first letter in the word cat?

486. What is the middle letter in the word cat?

487. What is the last letter in the word cat?

488. What combination of letters does the word *cheek* begin with?

489. What combination of letters does the word *they* begin with?

490. What combination of letters does the word *when* begin with?

491. What combination of letters does the word *ship* begin with?

492. What combination of letters does the word *singing* end with?

493. What letter does *dogs* end with?

494. What combination of letters does *jumped* end with?

495. What combination of letters does *bigger* end with?

496. What combination of letters does *biggest* end with?

497. What combination of letters does *slowly* end with?

498. Is the vowel "a" in the word **cat** long or short?

499. Is the vowel "a" in the word **play** long or short?

500. Is the vowel "e" in the word **fed** long or short?

501. Is the vowel "e" in the word **feed** long or short?

502. Is the vowel "i" in the word **kit** long or short?

503. Is the vowel "i" in the word **kite** long or short?

504. Is the last "e" of the word **kite** silent or do you pronounce it?

505. Is the vowel "o" in the word **hop** long or short?

506. Is the vowel "o" in the word **hope** long or short?

507. Can you break the word *birthday* into two syllables?

508. What is the name of a word that is made up of two words put together: single or compound?

509. Is the word sailboat a compound word or a single word?

510. What are the two words in the compound word football?

511. Can you tell me other compound words?

512. What two words make up the contraction *can't*.

513. What is the punctuation mark called before the "t" that is a substitute for one or more letters?

514. What two words make up the contraction *it's*?

515. What is the contraction for *I am*?

516. What is the contraction for *I will*?

517. What is the contraction for *we will*?

518. What are the two words that make up the contraction *aren't*?

519. Which section of the dictionary would you look to find the word *there*?

520. Which section of the dictionary would you look to find the word *quick*?

521. What letter often comes after the letter "q?"

522. What would be the alphabetical order of the words cat, ant, and dog?

523. Which word would come first in the "b" section of a dictionary: *ball* or *brother*?

524. When you write a sentence, what must you include at the end of it that looks like a dot?

525. When you write a question, what must you include at the end of it?

526. What punctuation mark may be appropriate after writing, *I won*?

527. When writing a sentence, what kind of letter do you begin the sentence with?

528. Do all names start with a capital letter?

529. Is the second letter of a word written in upper case or lower case?

530. Is a *verb* considered a thing or an action word?

531. Is a *noun* considered a thing or an action word?

532. Can a noun be a person, place, or thing?

533. What is the *verb* in the sentence: I ran to the park?

534. What is the *noun* in the sentence: The park is pretty?

535. Do *adjectives* describe nouns?

536. What is the *adjective* in the sentence: The park is pretty?

537. Can you give your own example(s) of an adjective?

538. What is an example of something that is *fiction*?

539. What is an example of something that in *non-fiction*?

540. What is an example of a *fairy tale*?

541. What part of the book on the cover lets you know what the book is about?

542. What is the name of the person that wrote the book?

543. What is the name of the person that created and drew the pictures in a book?

544. In a non-fiction book, what is the list of topics called at the beginning that lets the reader know how the book is divided: The Table of Contents or The Index?

545. Does this book have a "**jacket**?"

546. What does a publisher do?

547. What is the **copyright** of this book?

548. Is there a dedication page in this book?

549. Do books have a **title page?**

550. What part of this book is the **text**?

551. Are there any **illustrations** in this book?

552. What is on the **cover** of this book?

553. What number would this book have on its spine if it were shelved in a library: call or file?

554. What is the **main idea** or plot in the story, "Goldilocks and the Three Bears?"

555. What is the **setting** of the story, "Goldilocks and the Three Bears?

556. Which came first: when Goldilocks tasted the porridge, or when she found the beds?

557. What name next, after Goldilocks tasted the porridge?

558. Can you tell me two **details** about the house in the story, "Goldilocks and the Three Bears?"

559. How would you describe Goldilocks?

560. Is the story "Goldilocks and the Three Bears" realistic or fantasy?

561. What is your favorite book or story?

562. What is the order (sequence) of events in the story, "The Three Bears?"

563. *Who* is the person that Cinderella marries?

564. *What* does Cinderella lose when she is running home after midnight?

565. *Where* is Cinderella going to, all dressed up in her Ball gown?

566. *At what time* must Cinderella return to her coach before it turns back into a pumpkin?

567. *Why* does Cinderella have to leave the Ball so quickly?

568. *How* does Cinderella get to the Ball?

569. If you say "I think Cinderella is pretty," is that a fact or is it your opinion?

570. If you say "The story Cinderella was written by the Grimm Brothers," is that a fact or your opinion?

571. What is a *fact* that you know about butterflies?

572. What is your *opinion* about butterflies?

573. What is your *opinion* about __?

574. Which is the correct form of *look* in the sentence: "I (look, looks, looking, or looked) at the book yesterday?"

575. Which is the correct form of *look* in the sentence: "I am (look, looks, looking,) at the book now?"

576. Which is the correct form of *look* in the sentence: "He (look, looks, looking,) at the book often?"

577. Which is the correct form of *look* in the sentence: "I (look, looks, looking,) at the book often?"

578. What is the past tense of listen?

579. What is the name of a short sentence or two under a picture: a caption or a description?

580. Which is correct: She *is, am,* or *are* tall?

581. Which is correct: They *is* tall, or they *are* tall?

582. Which is correct: I *is, am,* or *are* tall?

583. Which is correct: We *is, am,* or *are* tall?

584. Which is correct: She *has* a dog, or she *have* a dog?

585. Which is correct: They *has* a dog, or they *have* a dog?

586. Which is correct: I *has* a dog, or I *have* a dog?

587. Which is correct: We *has* a dog, or we *have* a dog?

588. Which is correct: The ducks *is* in the pond, or the ducks *are* in the pond?

589. Which is the correct use of to, too, two: I am going (t-o, t-o-o, or t-w-o) the zoo?

590. Which is correct: I have (t-o, t-o-o, or t-w-o) dogs?

591. Which is correct: I have (t-o, t-o-o, t-w-o) many carrots on my plate?

592. Which is plural: dog or dogs?

593. Which is singular: cat or cats?

594. What is the plural of witch?

595. What is the plural of beach?

596. What is the singular of babies?

597. What is the antonym or opposite of in?

598. What is the antonym or opposite of wet?

599. What is the antonym or opposite of far?

600. What is the antonym or opposite of cold?

601. What is the antonym or opposite of slow?

602. What is the antonym or opposite of shout?

603. What is the antonym or opposite of sour?

604. What is the antonym or opposite of old?

605. What is the antonym or opposite of empty?

606. What is the antonym or opposite of lose?

607. What is the antonym or opposite of poor?

608. What is the antonym or opposite of night?

609. What is the antonym or opposite of strong?

610. What is the antonym or opposite of tame?

611. What is the antonym or opposite of front?

612. What is the antonym or opposite of ugly?

613. What is the antonym or opposite of end?

614. When you tell time and say that it is 10:00 a.m., is that morning or evening?

615. When you tell time and say that it is 10:00 p.m., is that morning or evening?

616. Is a.m. (from Latin ante meridiem) before or after noon?

617. Is p.m. (from Latin post meridiem) before or after noon?

618. Can you finish the saying, "An apple a day keeps the Doctor …?"

619. Can you finish the saying, "April showers bring May …?"

620. Can you finish the saying, "If at first you don't succeed…?"

621. Can you finish the saying, "Practice makes..?"

622. Can you finish the saying, "The more the…?"

623. Can you finish the saying, "There's no place like…?"

624. What is the date today?

625. What day of the week was yesterday?

626. What are the 7 days of the week?

627. What are the 12 months of the year?

628. When is your birthday?

629. Can you recognize and pronounce the common sight word "after?"(Show word!)

630. Can you recognize and pronounce the common sight word "again?"(Show word!)

631. Can you recognize and pronounce the common sight word "an?"(Show word!)

632. Can you recognize and pronounce the common sight word "any?"(Show word!)

633. Can you recognize and pronounce the common sight word "as?"(Show word!)

634. Can you recognize and pronounce the common sight word "ask?"(Show word!)

635. Can you recognize and pronounce the common sight word "by?"(Show word!)

636. Can you recognize and pronounce the common sight word "could?"(Show word!)

637. Can you recognize and pronounce the common sight word "every?"(Show word!)

638. Can you recognize and pronounce the common sight word "fly?"(Show word!)

639. Can you recognize and pronounce the common sight word "from?"(Show word!)

640. Can you recognize and pronounce the common sight word "give?"(Show word!)

641. Can you recognize and pronounce the common sight word "giving?"(Show word!)

642. Can you recognize and pronounce the common sight word "has?"(Show word!)

643. Can you recognize and pronounce the common sight word "had?"(Show word!)

644. Can you recognize and pronounce the common sight word "her?"(Show word!)

645. Can you recognize and pronounce the common sight word "him?"(Show word!)

646. Can you recognize and pronounce the common sight word "his?"(Show word!)

647. Can you recognize and pronounce the common sight word "how?"(Show word!)

648. Can you recognize and pronounce the common sight word "just?"(Show word!)

649. Can you recognize and pronounce the common sight word "know?"(Show word!)

650. Can you recognize and pronounce the common sight word "let?"(Show word!)

651. Can you recognize and pronounce the common sight word "live?"(Show word!)

652. Can you recognize and pronounce the common sight word "may?"(Show word!)

653. Can you recognize and pronounce the common sight word "of?"(Show word!)

654. Can you recognize and pronounce the common sight word "old?"(Show word!)

655. Can you recognize and pronounce the common sight word "once?"(Show word!)

656. Can you recognize and pronounce the common sight word "open?"(Show word!)

657. Can you recognize and pronounce the common sight word "over?"(Show word!)

658. Can you recognize and pronounce the common sight word "put?"(Show word!)

659. Can you recognize and pronounce the common sight word "round?"(Show word!)

660. Can you recognize and pronounce the common sight word "some?"(Show word!)

661. Can you recognize and pronounce the common sight word "stop?"(Show word!)

662. Can you recognize and pronounce the common sight word "take?"(Show word!)

663. Can you recognize and pronounce the common sight word "thank?"(Show word!)

664. Can you recognize and pronounce the common sight word "them?"(Show word!)

665. Can you recognize and pronounce the common sight word "then?"(Show word!)

666. Can you recognize and pronounce the common sight word "think?"(Show word!)

667. Can you recognize and pronounce the common sight word "walk?"(Show word!)

668. Can you recognize and pronounce the common sight word "were?"(Show word!)

669. Can you recognize and pronounce the common sight word "when?"(Show word!)

Language Arts – 2nd Grade

670. Are reading, writing, speaking, and listening important in developing language skills?

671. Are reading, writing, speaking, and listening skills important in learning a *second* language?

672. Can you print all the upper and lower case letters A-Z?

673. What words do you know in another language?

674. What kinds of books do you like to read?

675. As you read a book are you able to sound out the words to yourself?

676. *Before* reading a book, what might help you predict what the book is about?

677. *After* reading a story, is it important to identify the main ideas?

678. Do stories often have a *main character*?

679. After reading a story, are you able to re-tell the story including many of the descriptive details?

680. After reading a story, can you identify the sequence of events? (What happened first, next, etc.?)

681. After reading a book, can you identify the genre or kind of written work it is like fiction, non-fiction, poetry, etc.?

682. If someone is reading a story to you, do you have an imagery of the story and the characters?

683. Do you think that both silent reading and reading out loud are important?

684. How would you compare the story, (Cinderella) with the story (Sleeping Beauty)? How are they alike? How are they different?

685. What is the purpose of doing research?

686. Where are some resources you could use to do research?

687. What is the name of the resource you would use if you want to look up the meaning of a word?

688. In what order is a dictionary organized: numerical or alphabetical?

689. What is the order of the following words in a dictionary: stop; sound; show; sand?

690. What is the alphabetical order of the words *sand* and *same*, both beginning with s-a?

691. Do you read both fiction and non-fiction books?

692. What magazines or newspapers do you read?

693. What is the name of our local newspaper?

694. Can you always believe everything you read in a newspaper or magazine?

695. Is the "a" in **fate** long or short?

696. Is the "a" in **fat** long or short?

697. Is the "o" in **hop** long or short?

698. Is the "o" in **hope** long or short?

699. How do you spell **was**?

700. How do you spell **were**?

701. How do you spell **says**?

702. How do you spell **said**?

703. How do you spell **who**?

704. How do you spell **why**?

705. How do you spell **light**?

706. How do you spell **night**?

707. How do you spell the compound word **bedroom**?

708. How do you spell **sometimes**?

709. How do you spell **sailboat**?

710. How do you spell **happy**?

711. How do you spell **silly**?

712. How do you spell **pretty**?

713. How do you spell **know**?

714. How do you spell **wrong**?

715. Is an antonym the same or opposite of a word?

716. What is the antonym or opposite of silent?

717. Does a synonym mean the same thing or the opposite of another word?

718. What is a synonym of big?

719. What is a synonym of small?

720. What is the word for something that is spelled the same but means something different: a homonym or a synonym?

721. What is a homonym of **lock** of hair?

722. What is a homonym of **right** hand?

723. What is the beginning part of a word called: a suffix or a prefix?

724. What is the ending part of a word called: a prefix or a suffix?

725. Is the ending -er in **bigger** the suffix or the prefix?

726. What would come next: small, smaller, __?

727. Which is the correct use of slow: The turtle crawled slow, slowly, slower?

728. Can you think of a word that ends with the suffix -*less*?

729. Can you think of a word that ends with the suffix -*able*?

730. Can you think of a word that starts with the prefix *re-?*

731. Can you think of a word that starts with the prefix *un-?*

732. What are a period, an exclamation mark, and a question mark: interrogation or punctuation?

733. What is the name of the marks you see at the beginning and the end of a sentence that indicate that a character is speaking directly: punctuation or quotation?

734. What is the correct use of sleep: The baby is sleep, the baby is sleeping, or the baby is slept?

735. What is the past tense of climb: I climb the tree yesterday, or I climbed the tree yesterday?

736. What is the past tense of finish? (Can you use it in a sentence?)

737. What is the past tense of do?

738. What is the past tense of eat?

739. What is the past tense of read?

740. What is the past tense of wear?

741. What is the past tense of dry?

742. What is the past tense of see?

743. What is the past tense of come?

744. What is the past tense of he is?

745. What is the past tense of they are?

746. What is the past tense of go?

747. What is the past tense of find?

748. What is the past tense of say?

749. What would you say in a book report about the last book you read?

750. Have you ever written a letter to someone? (To whom?)

751. In the development of a fiction story, there should be a beginning, middle, and what else?

752. In a non-fiction book, what is the page called that has a list of the sub-topics that shows how the book is organized: Table of Contents or Chapters?

753. In a non-fiction book, what is the name of the alphabetical list of all the main ideas and key concepts contained in the book located at the very end: Index or Dictionary?

754. Do you have a journal or diary that you write in?

755. Do you know of anyone who wrote a famous diary or kept a journal of important information?

756. Why do you think a scientist, an inventor, or another person might keep a journal?

757. Does good writing organization include a beginning, a middle part, and an ending?

758. Can you identify all the parts of a sentence like a subject and a verb and the punctuation marks?

759. Can you write a sentence?

760. Can you write a sentence that asks a question?

761. Can you write a sentence that ends with an exclamation?

762. Can you write a letter?

763. Can you write a thank you note?

764. Can you write a report?

765. Can you write a story?

766. Can you write a poem?

767. When should you write a thank you note?

768. Can you draft a paper by first writing your ideas down on paper?

769. What does it mean when you revise your writing?

770. What does it mean when you edit your writing?

771. When a written work is published does that mean it is shared with others?

772. Is it allowable to copy what others have written without giving credit to the person who wrote it?

773. Can you print and read both upper case and lower case letters?

774. Can you write a report on a book that you have read?

775. What are some resources in a library media center that might help you gather information or do research for a report?

776. What is an encyclopedia and how is it organized?

777. Can you identify all of the following parts of a book: title, title page; table of contents, copyright, chapter, index, and the glossary?

778. Can you identify and give an example of the following literary works: poetry, legend, and fable?

779. What is the name of the non-fiction book you would look at to read about a person's life and times and significant historical events: biography or memoir?

780. Who earns the annual *Caldecott* award in children's literature: the author or the illustrator?

781. Who earns the annual *Newbery* award in children's literature: the author or the illustrator?

782. What is the name of the resource either online or in book format that gives you information regarding almost any topic, person, place or thing: encyclopedia or biography?

783. Can you turn on a computer and monitor?

784. Can you identify a computer keyboard, monitor, and mouse?

785. Is typing or word processing something on the computer a good skill to develop?

786. Are you familiar with ways of searching for library resources by conducting online computer searches?

787. Do you think that everything that you find on the internet is factual and accurate?

788. What would be an **in**appropriate use of using the internet?

789. Can you conduct a computer search in the library media center by author, title, subject, or keyword?

790. Are you able to load software (insert a CD) onto the computer?

791. Can you recognize and pronounce the common sight word "always?"(Show word!)

792. Can you recognize and pronounce the common sight word "around?"(Show word!)

793. Can you recognize and pronounce the common sight word "because?"(Show word!)

794. Can you recognize and pronounce the common sight word "been?"(Show word!)

795. Can you recognize and pronounce the common sight word "before?"(Show word!)

796. Can you recognize and pronounce the common sight word "best?"(Show word!)

797. Can you recognize and pronounce the common sight word "both?"(Show word!)

798. Can you recognize and pronounce the common sight word "buy?"(Show word!)

799. Can you recognize and pronounce the common sight word "call?"(Show word!)

800. Can you recognize and pronounce the common sight word "cold?"(Show word!)

801. Can you recognize and pronounce the common sight word "does?"(Show word!)

802. Can you recognize and pronounce the common sight word "don't?"(Show word!)

803. Can you recognize and pronounce the common sight word "fast?"(Show word!)

804. Can you recognize and pronounce the common sight word "first?"(Show word!)

805. Can you recognize and pronounce the common sight word "five?"(Show word!)

806. Can you recognize and pronounce the common sight word "found?"(Show word!)

807. Can you recognize and pronounce the common sight word "gave?"(Show word!)

808. Can you recognize and pronounce the common sight word "goes?"(Show word!)

809. Can you recognize and pronounce the common sight word "green?"(Show word!)

810. Can you recognize and pronounce the common sight word "it's?"(Show word!)

811. Can you recognize and pronounce the common sight word "made?"(Show word!)

812. Can you recognize and pronounce the common sight word "many?"(Show word!)

813. Can you recognize and pronounce the common sight word "off?"(Show word!)

814. Can you recognize and pronounce the common sight word "or?"(Show word!)

815. Can you recognize and pronounce the common sight word "pull?"(Show word!)

816. Can you recognize and pronounce the common sight word "read?"(Show word!)

817. Can you recognize and pronounce the common sight word "right?"(Show word!)

818. Can you recognize and pronounce the common sight word "sing?"(Show word!)

819. Can you recognize and pronounce the common sight word "sit?"(Show word!)

820. Can you recognize and pronounce the common sight word "sleep?"(Show word!)

821. Can you recognize and pronounce the common sight word "tell?"(Show word!)

822. Can you recognize and pronounce the common sight word "their?"(Show word!)

823. Can you recognize and pronounce the common sight word "these?"(Show word!)

824. Can you recognize and pronounce the common sight word "those?"(Show word!)

825. Can you recognize and pronounce the common sight word "upon?"(Show word!)

826. Can you recognize and pronounce the common sight word "us?"(Show word!)

827. Can you recognize and pronounce the common sight word "use?"(Show word!)

828. Can you recognize and pronounce the common sight word "very?"(Show word!)

829. Can you recognize and pronounce the common sight word "wash?"(Show word!)

830. Can you recognize and pronounce the common sight word "wish?"(Show word!)

831. Can you recognize and pronounce the common sight word "work?"(Show word!)

832. Can you recognize and pronounce the common sight word "would?"(Show word!)

833. Can you recognize and pronounce the common sight word "write?"(Show word!)

834. Can you recognize and pronounce the common sight word "your?"(Show word!)

Language Arts – 3rd Grade

835. Are reading, writing, speaking, and listening important skills as you develop your first language?

836. Are reading, writing, speaking, and listening important skills in acquiring a second language?

837. Do you read silently?

838. Do you read out loud?

839. Are you able to sound out new words you are not familiar with?

840. How many letters are there in the alphabet?

841. What are the vowels in the alphabet?

842. Can the letter "y" sometimes be a vowel?

843. What sound does the consonant blend "th" make?

844. What sound does the consonant blend "st" make?

845. What sound does the consonant blend "bl" make?

846. What sound does the consonant blend "gr" make?

847. What sound does the consonant blend "sc" make?

848. Can you say a word that begins with the consonant blend br?

849. Can you say a word that begins with the consonant blend cr?

850. Can you say a word that begins with the consonant blend dr?

851. Can you say a word that begins with the consonant blend fr?

852. Can you say a word that begins with the consonant blend gr?

853. Can you say a word that begins with the consonant blend pr?

854. Can you say a word that begins with the consonant blend tr?

855. Can you say a word that begins with the consonant blend bl?

856. Can you say a word that begins with the consonant blend cl?

857. Can you say a word that begins with the consonant blend fl?

858. Can you say a word that begins with the consonant blend gl?

859. Can you say a word that begins with the consonant blend pl?

860. Can you say a word that begins with the consonant blend sl?

861. Can you say a word that begins with the consonant blend sc?

862. Can you say a word that begins with the consonant blend sk?

863. Can you say a word that begins with the consonant blend sm?

864. Can you say a word that begins with the consonant blend sn?

865. Can you say a word that begins with the consonant blend sp?

866. Can you say a word that begins with the consonant blend st?

867. Can you say a word that begins with the consonant blend sw?

868. Can you say a word that begins with the consonant blend scr?

869. Can you say a word that begins with the consonant blend squ?

870. Can you say a word that begins with the consonant blend str?

871. Can you say a word that begins with the consonant blend spr?

872. Can you say a word that begins with the consonant blend spl?

873. Is each letter listed separately in the dictionary?

874. Which word would come first in a dictionary: derby or deputy?

875. Which word would come first in a dictionary: primary or prince?

876. In what order are words listed in a dictionary?

877. What letter is "q" almost always followed by?

878. Is a hard "c" similar to the sound of the letter "k?"

879. Is a soft "c" similar to the sound of the letter "s?"

880. Does the word "cat" begin with a hard "c" or a soft "c?"

881. Does the word "cot" begin with a hard "c" or a soft "c?"

882. Does the word "cut" begin with a hard "c" or a soft "c?"

883. What word(s) can you think of that begin with a hard "c?"

884. Does the word "cent" begin with a hard "c" or a soft "c?"

885. Does the word "cycle" begin with a hard "c" or a soft "c?"

886. Does the word "city" begin with a hard "c" or a soft "c?"

887. What word(s) can you think of that begin with a soft "c?"

888. Is a soft "g" sound similar to the "j" sound?

889. Does the word "gate" begin with a hard "g" or a soft "g?"

890. Does the word "goat" begin with a hard "g" or a soft "g?"

891. Does the word "gum" begin with a hard "g" or a soft "g?"

892. Does the word "gem" begin with a hard "g" or a soft "g?"

893. Does the word "gym" begin with a hard "g" or a soft "g?"

894. Does the word "giant" begin with a hard "g" or a soft "g?"

895. When the letter "c" or the letter "g" is followed by an "e" (cent; gem) an "i" (city; giant) or a "y" (cycle; gym) do they often have a "soft" sound?

896. Can the letter "y" be a vowel as in the word "myth," and a consonant as in the word "yoke?"

897. When the letter "y" begins a word or a syllable, is it considered a consonant?

898. In the words yes, yellow, and yogurt, is the letter "y" a vowel or a consonant?

899. When the letter "y" does not begin the word or syllable, is it a vowel or a consonant?

900. In the words, gym, baby, and sky, is the letter "y" a vowel or a consonant?

901. Do we use "a" or "an" before a word beginning with a vowel sound?

902. Which is correct: "It is **a** <u>u</u>mbrella" or, "It is **an** <u>u</u>mbrella?"

903. Which is correct: "It is **a** <u>h</u>onor" or, "It is **an** <u>h</u>onor?"

904. Which is correct: "It is **a** <u>c</u>at" or, "It is **an** <u>c</u>at?"

905. Would you use "a" or "an" before the noun **owl**?

906. Would you use "a" or "an" before the noun **bird**?

907. Would you use "a" or "an" before the noun **elephant**?

908. Would you use "a" or "an" before the noun **chest**?

909. What is the purpose of a dictionary?

910. In what order are the words listed in a dictionary?

911. Can you look up the definition of a word in a dictionary?

912. Are you able to identify the correct meaning of a word in a dictionary that has more than one meaning?

913. What would be the alphabetical order of the following words: device; defend; declare; and destroy? (Alphabetize by third letter)

914. Which word comes first alphabetically: humble, human, humor, or hum?

915. Which word comes first alphabetically: lima bean, limb, lily, or lime?

916. What letter has the shortest section in the dictionary: "y" or "x?"

917. Do words have a single definition, or can they have multiple definitions?

918. Which pair of guide words would be on the same dictionary page where **name** is found: nail net or needle nine?

919. Which pair of guide words would be on the same dictionary page where **coat** is found: coast cocoa or coconut collaborate?

920. Which pair of guide words would be on the same dictionary page where **crawl** is found: cozy crash or crate credit?

921. Are upper case letters in the alphabet the same as capital letters?

922. What are words divided into: sections or syllables?

923. Are words divided into syllables in a dictionary?

924. How many syllables does the word *happy* have?

925. How many syllables does the word *happily* have?

926. How many syllables does the word *read* have?

927. How many syllables does the word *birthday* have?

928. How many syllables does the word *Mississippi* have?

929. Can you blend syllables together to make new words?

930. What word is formed from the syllables **ta** and **ble**?

931. What word is formed from the syllables **mon** and **key**?

932. Can you divide words into syllables?

933. What are the two syllables in the word **turtle**?

934. What are the three syllables in the word **snowboarding**?

935. What are the four syllables in the word **population**?

936. Is learning the spelling of a word important in the process of developing your reading skills?

937. Are all the letters in a word always pronounced?

938. What are the silent letters in the word high?

939. How do you spell the word **half**?

940. What is the silent letter in the word **half?**

941. How do you spell **tough**?

942. What are the letters in the word **tough** that sound like the letter "f?"

943. How do you spell **hop**?

944. How do you spell **hope**?

945. Is the letter "e" at the end of the word **hope** silent?

946. Does adding an "e" at the end of the word **hope** make the vowel "o" long or short?

947. How do you spell the word **pail** from the sentence: "I shovel the sand into the pail?"

948. How do you spell the word **pale** in the sentence: "The girl looked scared and her face was very pale?"

949. How do you spell the word **quit**?

950. How do you spell the word **queen**?

951. Which letter almost always follows the letter "q?"

952. What is the rule for the order of "i" and "e" when spelling words? "I" before "e" except after _

953. Does the letter "e" come before "i" when it makes a long "a" sound like the word "*vein*?"

954. What is the color similar to tan is called: **b-_ _g-e**?

955. What is the correct spelling in this sentence: "A leader of a tribe is a c-h-_ _f?"

956. What is the correct spelling in this sentence: "The puzzle is missing one p _ _c-e?"

957. What is the correct spelling in this sentence: "They did an experiment in s-c-_ _ n-c-e class?"

958. What is the correct spelling in this sentence: "Another way to "get" is to r-e-c-_ _v-e?"

959. What is the correct spelling in this sentence: "A person who robs is called a t-h-_ _f?"

960. What are words called that have two parts to them to form one word, like **sometimes**?

961. Can you spell the compound word **everything**?

962. Can you spell the compound word **yourself**?

963. How do you spell the compound word **butterfly**?

964. How do you spell the compound word **somewhere**?

965. How do you spell the compound word **sailboat**?

966. How do you spell the compound word **grandfather**? (grandmother)

967. What other compound words can you name?

968. Is a base word one that does not have a prefix nor a suffix?

969. Are you able to recognize the base of a word?

970. Which of the following words is a base word: dangerous, thankful, listen, or speaker?

971. What is the base word of **independently**?

972. Is a *prefix* located at the beginning or at the end of a word?

973. Are you able to recognize a prefix, or the beginning letters of a word?

974. What is the prefix to the word **unable**?

975. What is the prefix to the word **reinvent**?

976. What is the prefix in the word **misunderstood**?

977. What is the prefix in the word **unintentional**?

978. What is the prefix in the word **independently**?

979. What is the prefix for this sentence: "My sister isn't old enough for kindergarten, so she will attend __school?"

980. What is the prefix for this sentence: "Kaitlyn won the spelling bee when Adam __spelled *independence*?"

981. What is the missing prefix for this sentence: "A strong wave knocked over our sand castle, so now we have to _build it?"

982. Would you use dis, in, or un for this sentence: "She is __considerate and likes to interrupt?

983. Would you use dis, im, or un for this sentence: "Alex always __agrees with everything you say?"

984. Would you use dis, im, or un for this sentence: "It is __polite to talk with your mouth full?"

985. Would you use dis, im, or un for this sentence: "Some people feel __comfortable around babies?"

986. What is the suffix in the word **independently**?

987. What is a word called *without* a prefix or suffix?

988. What is the root or base of the word prettiest?

989. Are you able to recognize a suffix or ending letters of a word?

990. Is a suffix attached to the end or the beginning of a word?

991. Do common suffixes include "s," "ing," and "ed?"

992. What is the word when you add the suffix "s" to play?

993. What is the word when you add the suffix "ed" to play?

994. What is the word when you add the suffix "ing" to play?

995. What is the suffix in the word **mountainous**?

996. What is the suffix in the word **limitless**?

997. What is the suffix of the word **careful**?

998. What is the suffix of the word **fearless**?

999. What is the suffix of the word **happily**?

1000. What would you add to the word **care** to make it correct in the following sentence: "Callie was care_ when she carried the fish bowl?"

1001. What would you add to the word **power** to make it correct in the following sentence: "The knight lost his sword so now he feels power_ against his enemy?

1002. What suffix would you add to **e-d-i-t** to form a word that refers to a job: or, ian or ist?

1003. What suffix would you add to **a-r-t** to form a word that refers to a job: er, ian, or ist?

1004. What suffix would you add to **f-a-r-m** to form a word that refers to a job: er, ian, or ist?

1005. What suffix would you add to **d-e-n-t** to form a word that refers to a job: er, ian, or ist?

1006. What suffix would you add to **c-o-m-e-d** to form a word that refers to a job: er, ian, or ist?

1007. What suffix would you add to **p-o-l-i-t-i-c** to form a word that refers to a job: er, ian, or ist?

1008. Are synonyms words that mean the *same* thing or the *opposite* thing?

1009. What is a synonym for **big**?

1010. What is a synonym for **smart**?

1011. What is a synonym for **error**?

1012. What is a synonym for **risky**?

1013. What is a synonym for **wealthy**?

1014. What is a synonym for **completed**?

1015. What is a synonym for **stroll**?

1016. What is a synonym for **cautious**?

1017. What is a synonym for **scared**?

1018. What is a synonym for **assistant**?

1019. What is a synonym of **huge**?

1020. What is a synonym of **cry**: sob or laugh?

1021. What is a synonym of **wealthy**: poor or rich?

1022. What is a synonym of **damp**: dry or moist?

1023. Does an antonym mean the same as or the opposite of another word?

1024. What is an antonym of **wide**?

1025. What is an antonym of **smooth**?

1026. What is the antonym of **hard**: difficult or easy?

1027. What is the antonym of **hungry**: full or famished?

1028. What is the antonym of **build**: destroy or construct?

1029. What is an antonym for **deep**?

1030. What is an antonym for **sour**?

1031. What is an antonym for **over**?

1032. What is an antonym for **enemy**?

1033. What is an antonym for **dark**?

1034. What is an antonym for **poor**?

1035. What are two antonyms for **hard**?

1036. What is an antonym for **tame**?

1037. What is an antonym for **narrow**?

1038. What is an antonym for **awake**?

1039. What is the antonym for **most**?

1040. What is an antonym for **juicy**: wet, dry, tasty, or sweet?

1041. What is an antonym for **mend**: fix, sew, repair, or break?

1042. Is a homonym a word that is spelled the same, is pronounced the same, and has more than one meaning?

1043. What is the homonym of **right** and can you use each of them in a sentence?

1044. Is the word "**lock**" a homonym because it can used as" lock," as in the part of the door that you open and shut with a key, and "**lock**" as in a tuft of hair??

1045. What are the two meanings of the homonym "**bowl**?"

1046. What are the two meanings of the homonym "**yard**?"

1047. What are the two meanings of the homonym "**fly**?"

1048. What are the two meanings of the homonym "**duck**?"

1049. What are the two meanings of the homonym "**can**?"

1050. What are the two meanings of the homonym "**pitcher**?"

1051. What are the two meanings of the homonym "**ring**?"

1052. What are the two meanings of the homonym "**bat**?"

1053. What is the correct use of the word "**address**" in the following sentence according to its library definition: "The Gettysburg Address is well known by Abraham Lincoln?" A) The location of a house or building. B) The writing on an envelope that tells where it should be delivered. C) A speech

1054. What is the correct use of the word "**address**" in the following sentence according to its library definition: "When we moved, we got a new address?" A) The location of a building. B) The writing on an envelope that tells where it should be delivered. C) A speech

1055. What is the correct use of the word "**address**" in the following sentence according to its library definition: "The mail carrier couldn't read the address on the envelope." A) The location of a building. B) The writing on an envelope that tells where it should be delivered. C) A speech

1056. Is a homograph a type of homonym that is spelled the same, can be pronounced the same or differently, and has more than one meaning?

1057. Can the homograph **bass** refer to either a fish or a low, deep voice?

1058. Can the homograph **present** refer to a gift, or be used as a verb to introduce someone?

1059. Are *homophones* words that are pronounced the same but are spelled differently and mean different things?

1060. What is the homophone (and spelling) of f-l-o-w-e-r?

1061. What is the homophone (and spelling) of p-i-e-c-e?

1062. What are the two homophones of s-c-e-n-t?

1063. Are the words **by, bye,** and **buy** homophones?

1064. Which is correct: "I went to the park **b-y** the school." / "I went to the park **b-y-e** the school."/ "I went to the park **b-u-y** the school?"

1065. Which is correct: "I said **b-y** to my friends at noon." / "I said **b-y-e** to my friends at noon."/ "I said **b-u-y** to my friends at noon?"

1066. Which is correct: "I went to **b-y** an ice cream cone?" / "I went to **b-y-e** an ice cream cone?" / "I went to **b-u-y** an ice cream cone?"

1067. Are the words to, too, and two homophones?

1068. Which is correct: "I am going **t-o** the park." / "I am going **t-o-o** the park." / "I am going **t-w-o** the park?"

1069. Which is correct: "I am going **t-o**." / "I am going **t-o-o**." / "I am going **t-w-o**?"

1070. Which is correct: "I am going to the park with **t-o** friends." / "I am going to the park with **t-o-o** friends." / "I am going to the park with **t-w-o** friends?"

1071. Are the words there, their, and they're homophones?

1072. What is the homophone of r-i-g-h-t?

1073. Which is correct: "I am going t-h-e-r-e / t-h-e-i-r / t-h-e-y-'r-e tomorrow?"

1074. Which is correct: "I am going to t-h-e-r-e / t-h-e-i-r / or, t-h-e-y '-r-e house in 20 minutes."

1075. Which is correct: "T-h-e-r-e / t-h-e-i-r, / or, t-h-e-y-'r-e coming here from school?"

1076. Are the words s-e-i-z-e, s-e-a-s, and s-e-e-s homophones?

1077. Which is correct: "They are going to s-e-i-z-e, s-e-a-s, or s-e-e-s the chance to go on the ship?"

1078. Which is correct: "They are going to sail on the high s-e-i-z-e, s-e-a-s, or s-e-e-s?"

1079. Which is correct: He s-e-i-z-e, s-e-a-s, or s-e-e-s the ship on the horizon?"

1080. What is the homophone of s-c-e-n-t?

1081. What is the homophone of c-l-a-u-s-e?

1082. What is the homophone of t-a-l-e?

1083. What is the homophone of v-a-n-e?

1084. What is the homophone of p-e-e-k?

1085. What is the homophone of f-l-a-i-r?

1086. What is the homophone of p-o-l-e?

1087. What is the homophone of u-r-n?

1088. What is the homophone of b-o-u-g-h?

1089. What is the homophone of r-o-t-e?

1090. What is the homophone of b-r-e-a-d?

1091. What is the homophone of t-e-n-t-s?

1092. What is the homophone of h-e-i-r?

1093. What is the homophone of p-e-a-r?

1094. What is the homophone of t-o-a-d?

1095. Which is the correct homophone in the sentence: "How much is the plane f-a-i-r or f-a-r-e to Chicago?"

1096. Which is the correct homophone in the sentence: "I want to go to the county f-a-i-r or f-a-r-e this Saturday?"

1097. Which is the correct homophone: "The wind b-l-e-w or b-l-u-e away my hat?"

1098. Which is the correct homophone: "Sofia painted her room light b-l-e-w or b-l-u-e?"

1099. Which is the correct homophone: "I wear a belt around my w-a-i-s-t or w-a-s-t-e?"

1100. Which is the correct homophone: "It is important not to w-a-i-s-t or w-a-s-t-e paper?"

1101. Which is the correct homophone: "Mr. Anderson is the new principal: **p-a-l** or **p-l-e**?

1102. Which is the correct homophone: "Lincoln was a true man of principle: **p-a-l** or **p-l-e**?"

1103. Which is the correct homophone: "Paul t-h-r-e-w or t-h-r-o-u-g-h the ball t-h-r-e-w or t-h-r-o-u-g-h the basketball hoop?"

1104. Which is the correct homophone in the following sentence: "I will m-e-e-t or m-e-a-t you in the m-e-e-t or the m-e-a-t section of the supermarket?"

1105. Which is the correct homophone in the following sentence: "The Bears have o-n-e or w-o-n only o-n-e or w-o-n of their baseball games?"

1106. Do you know the difference between the singular form of a word and its plural form?

1107. Do you read different genres that might include fiction, non-fiction, and poetry?

1108. Can you identify fiction works like tall tales, folk tales, and fairy tales?

1109. What are "Paul Bunyan" and "Brer Rabbit examples of: tall tales or non-fiction?

1110. Is the story, "Why the Sea is Salt" an example of a folktale or a fairy tale?

1111. Is "Cinderella" an example of a fairy tale or a tall tale?

1112. Is a myth something that is real or made-up?

1113. What are the stories, "The Midas Touch" and "Helen of Troy" examples of: folktales or myths?

1114. Is it important to read a variety of materials to help build an understanding of the cultures of the United States and of the world?

1115. Are you able to make a *prediction* about what a book may be about before reading it?

1116. What part of a book can give you clues as to what the book is about?

1117. While you read a book, are you able to identify and re-tell the sequence of events like what happened first, next, last, then, and finally?

1118. After reading something in a textbook, are you able to state the main idea and other details?

1119. After reading something, are you able to write a short summary?

1120. After reading a factual reading, are you able to make a conclusion about what you read?

1121. After reading a story, are you able to identify the main idea, the characters, the setting, and the plot?

1122. What is the main idea in the story, "Cinderella?"

1123. What are the names of the characters in the story, "Cinderella?"

1124. What is the setting in the story, "Cinderella?"

1125. What is the plot of the story, "Cinderella?"

1126. When you read something, can you tell the difference between fact and opinion?

1127. Is the sentence, "A snake is a reptile." a fact or an opinion?

1128. Is the sentence, "Snakes are the scariest animals in the world." a fact or an opinion?

1129. Is a fact something that can be proven, or is it something that someone believes to be true?

1130. Is an opinion a personal judgment, or is it based on fact?

1131. When you read something in literature, are you able to understand the theme, the conflict, and the point of view?

1132. Can you identify a paragraph in a reading?

1133. How many spaces do we say that we "indent" the first sentence of a paragraph: three or five?

1134. Can you identify the major parts of a sentence like a noun and a verb?

1135. What three things can a noun be?

1136. What does the verb do in a sentence?

1137. What is the verb in the sentence: "I walked to the park today?"

1138. What are some examples of verbs?

1139. What is the noun in the sentence: "I walked to the park today?"

1140. What are some examples of nouns?

1141. What is the *proper noun* in the sentence: "Mrs. Smith walked to the park today?"

1142. What are some examples of proper nouns?

1143. Do nouns and verbs show agreement in a grammatically correct sentence?

1144. Which is correct: "The sky *are* falling." or "The sky *is* falling?"

1145. Which is correct: "The kids *have* bicycles." or "The kids *has* bicycles?"

1146. What does a pronoun do in a sentence: describes a noun or substitutes for a noun?

1147. What is the noun in the following sentence: "Maya is very pretty?"

1148. What is the subject pronoun that takes the place of the proper noun Maya?

1149. What is the subject pronoun that takes the place of the proper noun Joe?

1150. What is the pronoun that takes the place of the proper noun Chicago: it or the?

1151. What are some examples of pronouns?

1152. What does an adverb do in a sentence: describes a noun or describes a verb?

1153. What is the adverb in the following sentence: "The teacher slowly opened the door?"

1154. What two letters do adverbs often end in: ly or ty?

1155. What is the negative adverb of *always*?

1156. What are some examples of adverbs?

1157. Which of the three is the adverb: **t-o, t-o-o, or t-w-o?**

1158. What is another meaning of the adverb **t-o-o?**

1159. Which of the three is the preposition: **t-o, t-o-o, or t-w-o?**

1160. Which of the three is the adjective: **t-o, t-o-o, or t-w-o?**

1161. What is it called when you start the first sentence of a paragraph 5 spaces: invert or indent?

1162. What is the *first* sentence of a paragraph called: the topic sentence or the hook?

1163. Can you identify the punctuation marks in a sentence like a capital letter, comma, apostrophe, exclamation mark, question mark, quotation marks, colon, semi-colon, and period?

1164. What type of punctuation mark do we need to show possession: a comma or an apostrophe?

1165. How would you write the *books of John* as a possessive?

1166. How do you spell **it's** as in it is Friday?

1167. Is the word **it's** with an apostrophe "s" a contraction for *it is* or *it was*?

1168. What is the contraction for *is not*?

1169. What is the contraction for *do not*?

1170. What is the contraction for *I will*?

1171. What is the contraction for *they are*?

1172. Can you print all your letters in both upper case (capital A) and lower case (small a)?

1173. Are you beginning to write the letters of the alphabet in cursive in which you connect the letters together?

1174. When you write something, is it good practice to organize your writing with a distinctive beginning, middle, and an end?

1175. Which stage of the writing process is it if you are just jotting your ideas down on paper: drafting or revising?

1176. Which stage of the writing process is it if you are making changes to your writing: revising or drafting?

1177. Which stage of the writing process is it if you are looking for and correcting errors: editing or proofreading?

1178. What is the role of an editor of a newspaper?

1179. Is proofreading what you have written an important last step in the writing process before you submit your final piece?

1180. Which stage of the writing process is it when you are ready to share your final writing piece, or when a book is ready for the public: proofreading or publishing?

1181. What is the name of an expression that is commonly used that means something different than what it appears to mean: an idiom or a paraphrase?

1182. What does the idiom "a piece of cake" mean?

1183. Can you finish the idiom: "Actions speak louder than __?"

1184. Can you finish the idiom: "Beggars can't be __?"

1185. Can you finish the idiom: "When in Rome, do as the __?"

1186. Can you finish the idiom: "They are like two peas in a __?"

1187. Can you finish the idiom: "It cost me an arm and a ___?"

1188. Can you finish the idiom: "It was a secret until Sara spilled the ___?"

1189. Can you finish the idiom: "It is raining cats and__?"

1190. Can you finish the saying: "A feather in your __?"

1191. Can you finish the common saying: "Do unto others as you would have them…?"

1192. What letters in the alphabet are the same as capital letters: upper case or lower case?

1193. What is the name of the word in a sentence that tells whom or what the sentence is about: the subject or the topic?

1194. What is the *subject* in the following sentence, "Alex eats ice cream for dessert:" Alex or dessert?

1195. What is the part of the sentence that tells what the subject does, or what is done to the subject: the verb or the predicate?

1196. What is the *predicate* of the sentence, "Alex eats ice cream for dessert:" Alex or eats ice cream?

1197. What is the *predicate* of the sentence, "The cat purred softly:" the cat or purred softly?

1198. Which word of a sentence is always capitalized?

1199. Do proper nouns always begin with a capital letter?

1200. What is the proper noun in the sentence: "We live by a lake in Wisconsin?"

1201. Are titles like Doctor, Mr., and Mrs. capitalized?

1202. Are the names of places capitalized?

1203. Do you know the difference between the singular form of a word and its plural form?

1204. What is the singular form of the noun "cats?"

1205. What is the singular form of the noun "wives?"

1206. What is the singular form of the noun "teeth?"

1207. What is the singular form of the noun "geese?"

1208. What is the singular form of the noun "pennies?"

1209. What is the plural form of the noun "dog?"

1210. What is the plural form of the noun "turtle?"

1211. What is the plural form of the noun "echo?"

1212. What is the plural form of the noun "potato?"

1213. What is the plural form of the noun "tomato?"

1214. What is the plural form of the noun "hero?"

1215. What is the plural form of the noun "box?"

1216. What is the plural form of the noun "family?"

1217. What is the plural form of the noun "penny?"

1218. What is the plural form of the noun "quality?"

1219. What is the plural form of the noun "half?"

1220. What is the plural form of the noun "leaf?"

1221. What is the plural form of the noun "thief?"

1222. What is the plural form of the noun "wolf?"

1223. What is the plural form of the noun "self?"

1224. What is the plural form of the noun "knife?"

1225. What is the plural form of the noun "life?"

1226. What is the plural form of the noun "fish?"

1227. What is the plural form of the noun "deer?"

1228. What is the plural form of the noun "sheep?"

1229. What is the plural form of the noun "man?"

1230. What is the plural form of the noun "woman?"

1231. What is the plural form of the noun "person?"

1232. What is the plural form of the noun "child?"

1233. What is the plural form of the noun "mouse?"

1234. What is the plural form of the noun "foot?"

1235. What is the plural form of the noun "tooth?"

1236. What is the plural form of the noun "ox?"

1237. What is the singular form of the noun "copies?"

1238. What is the plural form of the noun "goose?"

1239. What is the singular form of the noun "flies?"

1240. What is the proper noun in the sentence: "The present is for Katie?"

1241. What is the proper noun in the sentence: "He lives in Arizona?"

1242. What is the proper noun in the sentence: "The museum will be closed on Thanksgiving Day?"

1243. How can you turn the noun **river** into a *proper* noun?

1244. How can you turn the noun **city** into a *proper* noun?

1245. How can you turn the noun **athlete** into a *proper* noun?

1246. How can you turn the noun **president** into a *proper* noun?

1247. How can you turn the noun **street** into a *proper* noun?

1248. How can you turn the noun **month** into a *proper* noun?

1249. How can you turn the noun **holiday** into a *proper* noun?

1250. How can you turn the noun **ocean** into a *proper* noun?

1251. How can you turn the noun **artist** into a *proper* noun?

1252. What is the noun in the sentence: "The leaves are turning colors?"

1253. In the sentence, "George Washington was the first President of the United States," what part of speech is 'United States?'

1254. What nouns can you name?

1255. Is a person's name a noun?

1256. What is the definition of a verb: it describes an action, or it describes a noun?

1257. What is the verb in the sentence: "The car drove by quickly."

1258. Which of the following is *not* an action verb: "run, swim, lake, collapse, walked, and saw?"

1259. What action verbs can you list?

1260. Are "is, am, are" considered verbs of *being*, or verbs of *belonging*?

1261. Which *being* verb is correct: "I **is, am,** or **are** watching television?"

1262. Which *being* verb is correct: "He **am, is,** or **are** watching television?"

1263. Which *being* verb is correct: "They **is, are,** or **am** watching television?"

1264. Which *being* verb is correct: "She **were** here yesterday" or "She **was** here yesterday?"

1265. Which *being* verb is correct: "Alyssa and Sam **was** here yesterday" or, "Alyssa and Sam **were** here yesterday?"

1266. Which verb is correct in the following sentence: "She **has** a new puppy" or, "She **have** a new puppy?"

1267. Which verb is correct in the following sentence: "Alex and Ben **has** a new puppy" or, "Alex and Ben **have** a new puppy?"

1268. Is the following sentence in the present, past or future tense: "Spencer **writes** his name on the board?"

1269. Is the following sentence in the present, past, or future tense: "Eva **jumped** on her bed?"

1270. Is the following sentence in the present, past, or future tense; "Ben **will sing** in the concert?"

1271. What is the past tense of the verb "play?

1272. What is the past tense of the verb "cry?"

1273. What is the past tense of the verb "go?"

1274. What is the past tense of the verb "eat?"

1275. What is the past tense of the verb "buy?"

1276. What is the past tense of the verb "make?"

1277. What is the past tense of the verb "feel?"

1278. What is the past tense of the verb "hear?"

1279. What is the past tense of the verb "think?"

1280. What is the past tense of the verb "see?"

1281. What is the past tense of the verb "keep?"

1282. What is the past tense of the verb "bring?"

1283. What is the past tense of the verb "is?"

1284. What is the past tense of the verb "do?"

1285. What is the past tense of the verb "know?"

1286. What is the past tense of the verb "break?"

1287. What is the past tense of the verb "begin?"

1288. What is the past tense of the verb "have?"

1289. What is the past tense of the verb "pay?"

1290. What is the past tense of the verb "give?"

1291. What is the past tense of the verb "cut?"

1292. What is the past tense of the verb "tell?"

1293. What is the past tense of the verb "speak?"

1294. What is the past tense of the verb "send?"

1295. What is the past tense of the verb "take?"

1296. What is the past tense of the verb "meet?"

1297. What is the past tense of the verb "teach?"

1298. What is the past tense of the verb "leave?"

1299. What is the past tense of the verb "find?"

1300. What is the past tense of the verb "read?"

1301. What is the past tense of the verb "fly?"

1302. What is the past tense of the verb "get?"

1303. What is the past tense of the verb "swim?"

1304. What is the present tense of the verb "said?"

1305. What is the present tense of the verb "shook?"

1306. What is the present tense of the verb "rang?"

1307. What is the present tense of the verb "stood?"

1308. What is the present tense of the verb "found?"

1309. What is the present tense of the verb "blew?"

1310. What is the present tense of the verb "gave?"

1311. What is the present tense of the verb "froze?"

1312. What is the present tense of the verb "slept?"

1313. What is the present tense of the verb "drank?"

1314. What is the definition of an adjective: it describes a noun or it describes a verb?

1315. What is the adjective in the sentence: "Rosa has curly hair?"

1316. What is the adjective in the sentence: "The pretty lady left the salon?"

1317. What is the adjective in the sentence: "The lady that left the salon is blonde?"

1318. What would the word "*American*" be considered: a proper adjective or a proper noun?

1319. What proper adjectives that are nationalities can you list?

1320. What would appearance words like elegant, plain, and drab be considered: descriptive adjectives or descriptive adverbs?

1321. Are all colors like blue, pink, and black considered adjectives or pronouns?

1322. Are feeling words like brave, lazy, and scary considered adjectives or adverbs?

1323. Are shape words like flat, shallow, and wide considered adjectives or adverbs?

1324. Are time words like ancient, quick, and brief considered adverbs or adjectives?

1325. Would spicy and juicy be considered taste or touch adjectives?

1326. Would rough and sticky be considered taste or touch adjectives?

1327. Are quantity words like empty, numerous, and many considered adjectives or adverbs?

1328. What sensory (smell, sound, sight, touch, taste) words would you use to describe an amusement park or a fair?

1329. What part of speech is the word "those" in the sentence, "Those shoes look nice on you:" a demonstrative adjective or a demonstrative pronoun?

1330. What adjectives can you add to the following sentence to make it more descriptive: "The girl walks through the park?"

1331. What adjectives can you add to the following sentence to make it more descriptive: "The boys rode their bicycles?"

1332. What adjectives can you add to the following sentence to make it more descriptive: "The lady baked a cake?"

1333. What is the plural of the adjective "this:" these or those?

1334. What is the plural of the adjective "that:" these or those?

1335. Which sentence would convey that you are referring to something close to you: "**This** house is big." or, "**That** house is big?"

1336. Which of the following best conveys what is farthest away from the speaker: "**That** tree is big," "**That** tree **over there** is big." or, "**This** tree is big?"

1337. Is the word "big" an adjective or a noun?

1338. What comparative ending would you add to "big" to mean "more big?"

1339. What superlative ending would you add to "big" to mean "the most big?"

1340. When making comparisons and you say small, smaller, smallest, so how would you finish "tall?

1341. Using comparisons, how would you finish "happy?"

1342. Using comparisons, how would you finish "peaceful?"

1343. Using comparisons, how would you finish "friendly?"

1344. Using comparisons, how would you finish "good?"

1345. Using comparisons, how would you finish "bad?"

1346. Using comparisons, how would you finish "many?"

1347. Using comparisons, how would you finish "little?"

1348. Using comparisons, how would you finish "far?"

1349. What is the name for the figure of speech used to compare two things using "like" or "as:" a simile or a metaphor?

1350. How would you finish the simile: "It is as dry as a _?"

1351. How would you finish the simile: "Easy as _?"

1352. How would you finish the simile: "Blind as a _?"

1353. How would you finish the simile: "Busy as a _?"

1354. How would you finish the simile: "Light as a _?"

1355. How would you finish the simile: "Gone like the _?"

1356. How would you finish the simile: "Sour like an _?"

1357. How would you finish the simile: "Big as an _?"

1358. Which part of speech describes a verb to tell **how** something is done: an adjective or an adverb?

1359. What is the adverb in the sentence: "Tom walked swiftly to his house."

1360. Does an adverb always end in "-ly?"

1361. Are the words "fast" and "slow" adverbs?

1362. Are the words "often," "always," and "never" adverbs of frequency or place?

1363. Are the words "very" and "really" adverbs?

1364. Are the words "there" and "here" adverbs of place or adverbs of frequency?

1365. Are "so that" and "in order to" adverbs of frequency or adverbs of purpose?

1366. Are "next," "last," "now," and "soon" adverbs of time or adverbs of frequency?

1367. What is the name for the word or a phrase that shows the relation of a noun or pronoun to other words in the sentence: conjunction or preposition?

1368. Do examples of prepositions include above, below, around, through, toward, over, in, at, to, for, and near?

1369. What is the preposition in the sentence: "Chris looked for his cat under the bed?"

1370. What can you name in your room that is **near** the bed? (below, over; under, between the bed and door, on, for, etc.)

1371. What is the definition of a pronoun: it takes the place of a noun or it modifies a noun?

1372. What is the pronoun in the sentence: "She rode her bike to school?"

1373. What pronoun would take the place of Marissa?

1374. What pronoun would take the place of Ben?

1375. What pronoun would take the place of Sara and Ben?

1376. What pronoun would take the place of Sara and me?

1377. What pronoun would I use if I were referring to myself?

1378. Which pronoun is correct in the following sentence: "John and **I** went to the theatre" or, "John and **me** went to the theatre?"

1379. Is the sentence "John and **I** went to the theatre" correct because "I" is the subject?

1380. Which pronoun is correct in the following sentence: "John invited **me** to the theatre" or, "John invited **I** to the theatre?"

1381. Is the sentence "John invited **me** to the theatre" correct because "me" is the object?

1382. Which pronoun is correct in the following sentence: "The bike belongs to **me**" or, "The bike belongs to **I**?"

1383. What is another way of saying, "The bike belongs to me:" The bike is _ or, It is _bike?

1384. What is another way of saying, "The bike belongs to her:" The bike is _ or, It is _bike?

1385. What is another way of saying, "The bike belongs to him:" The bike is _ or, It is _bike?

1386. What is another way of saying, "The bike belongs to you:" The bike is _ or, It is _bike?

1387. What is another way of saying, "The bike belongs to Nick and me:" The bike is _ or, It is _bike?

1388. What is another way of saying, "The bike belongs to Joey and Lucas:" The bike is _ or, It is _bike?

1389. Is the word t-h-e-i-r a possessive pronoun that shows ownership?

1390. What is the name for the spoken word that is used to express pain, delight, or surprise: interjection or exclamation?

1391. What is the interjection in the sentence: "Ouch! I stubbed my toe?"

1392. What is the interjection in the sentence: "Hooray! We won the contest?"

1393. What is the interjection in the sentence: "Oh my! I won the drawing contest?"

1394. What is the name for the part of speech that *connects* words, phrases, or sentences: interjection or conjunction?

1395. What is the conjunction in the sentence: "I wanted to go to the pool but I had to cut the grass?"

1396. What is the conjunction in the sentence: "He will go to college and he will become a doctor?"

1397. What is the conjunction in the sentence: "He will travel to Europe if he gets the job?"

1398. What is the name of a combination of two words with an apostrophe: contraction or conjunction?

1399. What is the contraction in the sentence: "The athlete didn't give up?"

1400. What does an apostrophe take the place of in a contraction: a letter or a word?

1401. What is the contraction of "I would?"

1402. What is the contraction of "I will?"

1403. What is the contraction of "would not?"

1404. What is the contraction of "they have?"

1405. What is the contraction of "have not?"

1406. What is the contraction of "you are?"

1407. What are the two words for the contraction **wouldn't**?

1408. What are the two words for the contraction **won't?**

1409. What type of sentence makes a statement: a declarative or an interrogative?

1410. What type of sentence asks a question: a declarative or an interrogative?

1411. Is the following sentence declarative or interrogative: "He is the president of the company?"

1412. Is the following sentence interrogative or exclamatory: "Is he the president of the company?"

1413. Which is correct to make the noun agree with the verb: "The sky **is** blue" or "The sky **are** blue?"

1414. Which is correct to make the noun agree with the verb: "The boys **is** tall" or "The boys **are** tall?"

1415. Are lower case letters in the alphabet the same as small letters?

1416. Can you write your words in upper case letters?

1417. Can you write words in lower case letters?

1418. When you write using upper and lower case letters, are you *printing* or writing in *cursive*?

1419. Can you write words in *cursive*?

1420. Are most signatures written in cursive?

1421. Can you sign your name in cursive?

1422. Can you identify and write upper case letters in cursive?

1423. Can you identify and write lower case letters in cursive?

1424. What is a group of words called that express a complete thought and contain a subject and a verb?

1425. Can sentences end with a period, a question mark, or an exclamation point?

1426. What is the cause and effect of the sentence: "Maria studied her spelling words and got an "A" on the test?"

1427. What is the cause and effect of the sentence: Matt called the tow truck because he had a flat tire?"

1428. What is the punctuation mark that you need at the end of a declarative sentence?

1429. What type of punctuation do you need between a series of words: a comma or a colon?

1430. What punctuation mark do you need after the number in a date?

1431. After which words would the commas go in the sentence: "Mrs. Smith enjoys singing, dancing, and cooking?"

1432. Where does the comma go in an address: after the city name or before the city name?

1433. What punctuation mark to you need at the end of a sentence that is asking something?

1434. What punctuation mark would you write to show emotion as if a character were shouting?

1435. What kind of marks do you need when you want to indicate that someone is speaking?

1436. Where would the quotation marks go in the sentence: Do you want strawberry or chocolate ice cream? asked Ryan?

1437. Where would the quotation marks go in the following: I love my new kitten! said Brittney. He is so playful?

1438. What kind of punctuation mark do you need to show possession as in: "the **boy's** mother?

1439. Does the apostrophe in *"**the girl's house**"* show possession?

1440. In "the **girl's** house," does the apostrophe go before or after the letter "**s**" in girls?

1441. How would you show possession to refer to: "the bike belonging to Marcos?"

1442. In the sentence, "I bought Jack's gift yesterday," which word in the sentence needs the apostrophe?

1443. In "The **elephants'** trunks are long," does the apostrophe go before or after the "s" in elephants?

1444. How would you show possession in *"the voices of the singers?"*

1445. Which is correct on the invitation: "**Y-o-u-apostrophe r-e** invited" or, "**Y-o-u-r** invited?"

1446. What is the shortened version of a word called: substitution or abbreviation?

1447. What type of punctuation mark does an **abbreviation or abbreviated word** have?

1448. What is the abbreviation of street?

1449. What is the abbreviation of avenue?

1450. What is the abbreviation doctor?

1451. What is the abbreviation of our state?

1452. What is the abbreviation for the United States?

1453. What is the abbreviation for Washington **D**istrict of **C**olumbia?

1454. What is the abbreviation for the month of October?

1455. What is the abbreviation of average?

1456. Can you create a series of at least 4 words that rhyme with *cat*?

1457. Can you identify the word that does not rhyme from the following: bat, cat, pig, sat?

1458. Can you say words from the word family ending in "-et?" (met)

1459. Can you say words from the word family ending in "-ight?" (night)

1460. Can you say words from the word family ending in "-old?" (sold)

1461. Can you say words from the word family ending in "-eat?" (seat)

1462. Which pair of words do **not** rhyme: **A**) how, low **B**) said, bet **C**) mother, other **D**) sign, line?

1463. In the sentence, "After misspelling the word in the spelling bee, Sam put his head down and sat down dejectedly," can you **infer** the meaning of the word '*dejectedly*?'

1464. Does an *inference* draw a conclusion after considering all the facts?

1465. When you read can you use context clues to determine the meaning of unfamiliar words?

1466. What is the context clue for the word *ferocious* in the sentence: "The **ferocious** dog growled at the cat?"

1467. Using context clues, what is the meaning of *flabbergasted* in the following sentence: "She was flabbergasted when she found out she won the contest:" angry, amazed, or tired?

1468. Using context clues, what is the meaning of *somber* in the following sentence: "Justin was in a **somber** mood when he heard the bad news:" excited, sad, or happy?

1469. Using context clues, what is the meaning of *concealed* in the following sentence: "The woman's large hat **concealed** her face:" revealed, showed, or hid?

1470. Using context clues, what is the meaning of *hazardous* in the following sentence: "Eating too much sugar can be hazardous to your health:" dangerous; great; or delightful?

1471. What is it called when you read or write a series of sentences connected by one main idea?

1472. What is it called when we space the first sentence five spaces that serves to identity the beginning of a new paragraph?

1473. What is the first sentence of a paragraph called: topic sentence or a leading sentence?

1474. What part of a paragraph indicates what the paragraph will be about: topic sentence or hook?

1475. What is the term for the sentences that support the topic sentence in a paragraph: supporting sentences or related sentences?

1476. What are some words that indicate a sequence or order to a series of events?

1477. Do the words, next, then, last, finally, also indicate sequential order?

1478. Can you name a story?

1479. Can you tell a story?

1480. Can you predict how a story will end?

1481. Can you use pictures and illustrations to gather story information and predict what a story will be about?

1482. Are the characters, setting, plot, and main idea all parts of a story?

1483. Who are the characters in the story "Snow White?"

1484. What are the two main settings in the story "Snow White?"

1485. What is the plot in the story "Snow White?"

1486. What is the main idea of the story "Snow White?"

1487. Can you recall other details in the story "Snow White?"

1488. What is the main purpose for reading non-fiction: to gain information, to learn different viewpoints, or to appreciate literature?

1489. Is the statement, "There are twenty four hours in a day" a fact or an opinion?

1490. Is the statement, "There are not enough hours in the day" a fact or an opinion?

1491. When we compare two cultures, are we communicating how they are similar and how they are different?

1492. When we contrast two cultures, are we focusing on how they are alike or how they are different?

1493. What are you reading right now?

1494. What genre, or kind of literature are you reading right now?

1495. What is the name of the genre that is an imaginary creation: non-fiction or fiction?

1496. What is the name of the genre that is based on facts and reality: fiction or non-fiction?

1497. Can you distinguish between fiction and non-fiction?

1498. How are books classified in a library: the Dewey Decimal System or by the author's last name?

1499. Which books in a library are shelved in alphabetical order according to the author's last name: fiction or non-fiction?

1500. What is the term for the series of numbers and letters on the spine of a book that indicate where the book is kept in the library, or how it is organized: call numbers or decimal numbers?

1501. What types of materials might you find in the reference section of a library?

1502. What is the name for the genre of literature that conveys information about a specific time period or some event more than 30 years ago: historical fiction or science fiction?

1503. Are fiction and non-fiction located in the same or different areas of the library?

1504. Can you distinguish fiction from fantasy?

1505. Can you distinguish fantasy from realism?

1506. What is a book called that is written about a prominent (important) person: biography or bibliography?

1507. What is a book called when an author writes about his or her own life: biography or autobiography?

1508. Can you distinguish between a biography and an autobiography?

1509. What is a literary work in the form of poems: poetry or prose?

1510. What are essays and short stories examples of: prose or narrative?

1511. What is name of a story that may express the beliefs of a group of people, relates an idea that many people believe, or is a story that gives reasons for something that happens in nature: a myth or a fable?

1512. Do you know of any myths?

1513. What is the name of the genre or literary works that tell stories about life in the future, or about stars, planets, and unknown worlds: science fiction or fantasy?

1514. What is the name of a written story handed down from one generation to the next that may be based on fact but are often not entirely true: legend or fable?

1515. What is the name of an oral story that is handed down from one generation to the next: a folktale or a fable?

1516. Do you know the titles of any legends?

1517. What is the name of a story that teaches a lesson that often has talking animal characters: folktale or fable?

1518. What genre are the stories, *The Boy Who Cried Wolf*, *The Goose That Laid the Golden Egg*, and *The Tortoise and the Hare*: fables or folktales?

1519. What fables are you familiar with?

1520. What is the name of the famous storyteller from ancient Greece that is most famous for the 600 fables that he wrote in his lifetime: Aesop or Apollo?

1521. What is the name of a story that is exaggerated or not true?

1522. Can you write a fictional story?

1523. Are all of the following involved in the writing process: plan, draft, revise, edit, print, and share?

1524. Can you write a report?

1525. Can you write a poem?

1526. Can you write a letter?

1527. What is the salutation of a letter: the greeting or the closing?

1528. Does a letter include a salutation, a body, and a closing?

1529. Can you write an address on a letter?

1530. Where does the address go on an envelope?

1531. Where is the return address located on an envelope: upper left corner or upper right corner?

1532. Where does the stamp go on an envelope: upper left corner or upper right corner?

1533. Can you write an invitation?

1534. What information is included on an invitation?

1535. Can you write a thank you note?

1536. What is an occasion for writing a thank you note?

1537. Can you fill out a form or an application?

1538. When might you need to fill out an application?

1539. Does an author generally write for a purpose?

1540. What does the author's writing reflect: a point of view or a style?

1541. Does an author have a distinct style?

1542. What are some resources you could use to seek further information about a topic?

1543. What are resources of information called: reference materials or resource materials?

1544. Can you write with pen and paper?

1545. Can you use the keyboard on a computer?

1546. Can you adapt, or adjust your writing for your audience?

1547. Would a letter written to your friend be formal or casual?

1548. Would a letter written to the president be formal or casual?

1549. Does an author generally write for a specific audience?

1550. What is the name of the prestigious award that a children's author may earn for his or her book: an Emmy award or a Newbery award?

1551. What does an illustrator do?

1552. What is the name of the prestigious award that a children's illustrator may earn for his or her illustrations: Caldecott or Newbery?

1553. What does a playwright write?

1554. Can many stories be acted out and presented as a play?

1555. What is the term for a conversation between two or more people: a dialogue or a drama?

1556. What is the reason for the revising a letter, article, or report?

1557. Can you write and present a book report?

1558. What is it called when you speak in front of an audience: a debate or a speech?

1559. When talking to others, are eye contact with your audience and hand gestures both considered forms of non-verbal communication?

1560. Can you make a short speech in front of an audience?

1561. How do you introduce yourself to others?

1562. Can you introduce a friend of yours to another friend?

1563. What important information would you need to write down when taking a telephone message?

1564. What is it called when you explain the content of a story or a report in your own words: re-wording or paraphrasing?

1565. Can you briefly *paraphrase* the story "The Three Pigs?" (Etc.)

1566. What is it called when you explain the main ideas of an informative article or report: paraphrasing or summarizing?

1567. Can you summarize a book or an article that you have read recently?

1568. What is the name of a diagram that indicates value with lines or bars: a graph or an x-ray?

1569. Can you read a chart, a table, and a graph?

1570. Where might you need to read a menu?

1571. Can you read a timeline?

1572. When might a timeline be a useful reference?

1573. What is the name of a planning tool that is often used to organize information by highlighting the main points: an outline or a list?

1574. What kind of materials include a dictionary, an atlas, the Internet, an encyclopedia, and a chart: resource or reference?

1575. Can you use reference materials to search for information?

1576. What reference material would you search to find the definition of a word?

1577. What reference material would you search to find other words that mean the same as **huge**: a dictionary or a thesaurus?

1578. When you look up "big" in a thesaurus, what words would be listed?

1579. What reference material would you search to find the location of Spain: an atlas or an almanac?

1580. What information would you find if you looked in an atlas?

1581. What is the name of the resource that is published once a year that contains statistics and facts about a wide variety of subjects: an almanac or an atlas?

1582. In what print resource organized by last name would you find the address of a neighbor?

1583. What reference material(s) would you use to search for information regarding George Washington?

1584. What reference material would you use to understand the population increases of a country per year: an atlas or an almanac?

1585. What resource would be most helpful if you need to find information about how to take care of a turtle: an almanac, an atlas, the Internet, or a telephone book?

1586. Can you skim and scan for information in a newspaper article?

1587. What kind of information would you find in a newspaper?

1588. What is the purpose of a *headline* in a newspaper?

1589. Does a news story contain the facts about a person or event, and explain who, what, when, where, and why?

1590. Can you write a news story?

1591. What is the name of the description underneath a picture in a newspaper: a headline or a caption?

1592. Can newspapers have more than one edition?

1593. Can you identify the parts of a book?

1594. What is the purpose of a *title* of a book?

1595. What are the sections called that novels and textbooks are divided into: chapters or units?

1596. What section of a book would you look at to find out the starting page for the chapter on the Civil War: the index or the table of contents?

1597. What is the alphabetical section at the end of a textbook called that lists each specific subject and page number: glossary or index?

1598. In what section of a textbook would you look up the meaning of the word "suffrage:" index or glossary?

1599. In a book about insects, where would you most likely find the page numbers for all the topics related to butterflies: the index, the glossary, or the table of contents?

1600. Does personal writing include writing an imaginative story or letter?

1601. What is the term for non-fiction text that provides information about people, places, things, or events: informational text or functional text?

1602. What would you write that would be considered informational text?

1603. If you were writing to persuade, would you include your opinion of the subject along with supporting data?

1604. What is the term for the writings that are used to help people perform a task, and include recipes, schedules, memos, and directions: informational text or functional text?

1605. What *functional* text writings do you read on a regular basis?

1606. Can you recognize and pronounce the common sight word "about?"(Show word!)

1607. Can you recognize and pronounce the common sight word "better?"(Show word!)

1608. Can you recognize and pronounce the common sight word "bring?"(Show word!)

1609. Can you recognize and pronounce the common sight word "carry?"(Show word!)

1610. Can you recognize and pronounce the common sight word "clean?"(Show word!)

1611. Can you recognize and pronounce the common sight word "cut?"(Show word!)

1612. Can you recognize and pronounce the common sight word "done?"(Show word!)

1613. Can you recognize and pronounce the common sight word "draw?"(Show word!)

1614. Can you recognize and pronounce the common sight word "drink?"(Show word!)

1615. Can you recognize and pronounce the common sight word "eight?"(Show word!)

1616. Can you recognize and pronounce the common sight word "fall?"(Show word!)

1617. Can you recognize and pronounce the common sight word "far?"(Show word!)

1618. Can you recognize and pronounce the common sight word "full?"(Show word!)

1619. Can you recognize and pronounce the common sight word "got?"(Show word!)

1620. Can you recognize and pronounce the common sight word "grow?"(Show word!)

1621. Can you recognize and pronounce the common sight word "hold?"(Show word!)

1622. Can you recognize and pronounce the common sight word "hot?"(Show word!)

1623. Can you recognize and pronounce the common sight word "hurt?"(Show word!)

1624. Can you recognize and pronounce the common sight word "if?"(Show word!)

1625. Can you recognize and pronounce the common sight word "keep?"(Show word!)

1626. Can you recognize and pronounce the common sight word "kind?"(Show word!)

1627. Can you recognize and pronounce the common sight word "laugh?"(Show word!)

1628. Can you recognize and pronounce the common sight word "life?"(Show word!)

1629. Can you recognize and pronounce the common sight word "long?"(Show word!)

1630. Can you recognize and pronounce the common sight word "much?"(Show word!)

1631. Can you recognize and pronounce the common sight word "myself?"(Show word!)

1632. Can you recognize and pronounce the common sight word "never?"(Show word!)

1633. Can you recognize and pronounce the common sight word "only?"(Show word!)

1634. Can you recognize and pronounce the common sight word "own?"(Show word!)

1635. Can you recognize and pronounce the common sight word "pick?"(Show word!)

1636. Can you recognize and pronounce the common sight word "seven?"(Show word!)

1637. Can you recognize and pronounce the common sight word "shall?"(Show word!)

1638. Can you recognize and pronounce the common sight word "show?"(Show word!)

1639. Can you recognize and pronounce the common sight word "six?"(Show word!)

1640. Can you recognize and pronounce the common sight word "small?"(Show word!)

1641. Can you recognize and pronounce the common sight word "start?"(Show word!)

1642. Can you recognize and pronounce the common sight word "ten?"(Show word!)

1643. Can you recognize and pronounce the common sight word "today?"(Show word!)

1644. Can you recognize and pronounce the common sight word "together?"(Show word!)

1645. Can you recognize and pronounce the common sight word "try?"(Show word!)

1646. Can you recognize and pronounce the common sight word "warm?"(Show word!)

Language Arts – 4th Grade

1647. What is the name of the general area that includes reading, writing, spelling, and composition: English or language arts?

1648. Can you read silently?

1649. Can you read aloud?

1650. Can you summarize out loud something that you have read?

1651. What is a short story that you have read?

1652. What is a chapter book that you have read?

1653. What is the name of a poem you have read?

1654. Do all poems have rhyme?

1655. What is the term for the division of lines in poetry: a stanza or a refrain?

1656. What is the name of the verse or phrase that is repeated often in a poem or a song: a refrain or a chorus?

1657. What is the term for the ordinary language that people use in speaking or writing that does not have the repeating rhythm that is used in verse: drama or prose?

1658. What is the name of the short, lyric poem that originated in Italy: sonnet or prose?

1659. How many lines does a sonnet have: twelve or fourteen?

1660. What famous English writer wrote many sonnets: William Shakespeare or Edgar Allan Poe?

1661. What is the name of a play you have read?

1662. Can you identify the title and the author of a book?

1663. Where is the table of contents located in a book?

1664. Where is the index located in a book?

1665. What do you use an index for: to look up the meaning of a word, or to find the page number that the topic is on?

1666. What is the name of the dictionary section of a textbook: an index or a glossary?

1667. What is the name of the beginning part that is written by the author to introduce the book: the foreword or the preface?

1668. What is the name given for the written addition at the end of the book: the preface or the appendix?

1669. Do you use a dictionary to look up the meaning of a word?

1670. What is another purpose for using a dictionary besides looking up the meaning of a word?

1671. What do you say when you answer the telephone?

1672. Can you make a prediction about what a story is about before reading it?

1673. Can you put all the events of a story in the proper sequence?

1674. Can you identify the main idea in a narrative text?

1675. Can you state the author's purpose when reading text?

1676. Can you state the supporting details when reading text?

1677. Can you compare two stories and say how they are similar?

1678. How do "Cinderella" and "Sleeping Beauty" compare?

1679. Can you contrast two stories and say how they are different?

1680. How do "Cinderella" and "Sleeping Beauty" contrast?

1681. What is the name for the action that occurs in a story that makes something else happen: compare and contrast or cause and effect?

1682. Which sentence is the cause and which sentence is the effect: "Pluto is one of the coldest planets." and, "Pluto is the farthest planet from the Sun?"

1683. What is the name of the reading genre that uses characters, plots, and settings to convey events that are **not** true?

1684. What is the name of the reading genre that uses real people, plots, and settings to convey actual events that are true?

1685. What is the name of the reading genre that uses animals who act and speak like people and that teaches a moral lesson: a fable or a folktale?

1686. Which author is famous for writing the fables: "The Tortoise and the Hare," and "The Boy Who Cried Wolf:" Aesop or Shakespeare?

1687. What is the name of the reading genre that is a made-up story with folk heroes like "Paul Bunyan," and "Pecos Bill," and is passed down from one generation to the next: a tall tale or a myth?

1688. What is the name for the story that is presented with dialogue and action: drama or prose?

1689. What is the name of an account of someone's life that is written by another person: a biography or a bibliography?

1690. What is the name of a traditional story that has been passed down from person to person like "Robin Hood," and has important meaning: a legend or a fairy tale?

1691. Is "Sleepy Hollow" by Washington Irving an example of a legend?

1692. Is "King Arthur and the Knights of the Round Table" an English legend?

1693. Is "Robin Hood" an English legend or an Irish legend?

1694. What is the name of a story that often includes gods and heroes as in "Zeus," and "Pandora's Box:" a myth or a legend?

1695. Is "Hercules" an example of a Greek myth or a Roman myth?

1696. What is the name of a narrative poem that has a refrain, tells a story, and is often sung: a ballad or a limerick?

1697. What is the name of a five-line humorous poem originating from Ireland whereby lines 1, 2, and 5 rhyme as in "There Once Was a Man from Nantucket:" a limerick or a sonnet?

1698. What is the name for the literary device found in many works of literature that uses ridicule or sarcasm aimed at someone or something, and is evident in many political cartoons: satire or epic?

1699. What is the name for the story in which the events and characters are symbols that stand for truths about something in life and teach a lesson as in "Moby Dick:" an allegory or a limerick?

1700. What is the name for an extended literary poem that has been passed down from ancient civilizations that celebrates the feats of a legendary hero as in, "The Iliad," "The Odyssey," "Beowulf," and Dante's "The Divine Comedy:" lyrical poem or epic?

1701. What is the term that includes plot, theme, characters, and setting: literary elements or story line?

1702. What is the literary term called when you use the clues in the text to get a sense of what will happen next: foreshadowing or predicting?

1703. What is the name of the literary term that is an extreme exaggeration of what something really is: allegory or hyperbole?

1704. What is the term for the figure of speech that compares two unlike things as in "cheeks like roses:" a simile or a metaphor?

1705. What is the term for the figure of speech that compares two unlike things *without* using the words like or as: a simile or a metaphor?

1706. Is the phrase, "*their cheeks were roses*" a simile or a metaphor?

1707. What is the literary term for a sentence in poetry where several of the words start with the same consonant as in **P**eter **P**iper **P**icked a **P**eck of **P**ickled **P**eppers: alliteration or onomatopoeia?

1708. What is the literary term given for the sound we say something makes as in "The snake hissed," "The bee buzzed," or, "The wolf howled at the moon: onomatopoeia or alliteration?

1709. What is the literary term when human qualities are given to objects or animals as in, "this city never sleeps," "the stars winked at me," and "lightning danced across the sky:" alliteration or personification?

1710. How do you finish the saying: "Beauty is only skin _?"

1711. How do you finish the saying: "The bigger they are, the harder they _?"

1712. How do you finish the saying: "Bull in a china _?"

1713. How do you finish the saying: "Bury the _?"

1714. How do you finish the saying: "Make ends _?"

1715. How do you finish the saying: "Don't put all your eggs in one _?"

1716. How do you finish the saying: "Don't count your chickens before they_?"

1717. How do you finish the saying: "One picture is worth a thousand _?"

1718. How do you finish the saying: "Two wrongs don't make a _?"

1719. How do you finish the saying: "Can't hold a candle _?"

1720. How do you finish the saying: "Seeing is _?"

1721. How do you finish the saying: "Half a loaf is better than _?"

1722. How do you finish the saying: "Haste makes _?"

1723. How do you finish the saying: "Lightning never strikes twice in the same _?"

1724. How do you finish the saying: "Once in a blue _?"

1725. How do you finish the saying: "An ounce of prevention is worth a pound of _?"

1726. How do you finish the saying: "When it rains it _?"

1727. How do you finish the saying: "Live and let_?"

1728. How do you finish the saying: "Through thick and_?"

1729. How do you finish the saying: "You can lead a horse to water, but you can't make it __?"

1730. What is etc. an abbreviation for, that means "and so on"?

1731. What is the French abbreviation that is often included on a written invitation when the person writing the invitation wishes for a response, and is short for, "**R**epondez **S**'il **V**ous **P**lait?"

1732. Can you print using both upper case and lower case letters?

1733. Are you developing your skill in writing in cursive?

1734. Can you write a letter to a friend or to a family member?

1735. Can you write an email?

1736. Can you write a poem?

1737. Can you write a report about a topic that interests you?

1738. If you use written ideas from a source, what do you need to include in your report that gives credit to the author of that source: a biography or a bibliography?

1739. What information would be included in a bibliography?

1740. What is the alphabetical order of the bibliography: author's first name or author's last name?

1741. Can you write a book report?

1742. Can you write a description of a holiday, an object, or a person?

1743. Can you write a thank you note?

1744. Can you outline the main points from something that you have read?

1745. Can you write a written summary of something that you have read?

1746. Can you write a summary of what you did today?

1747. What is the name of the process that includes pre-writing, drafting, revising, editing, and publishing: writing or proofreading?

1748. What is the name of your first attempt to write down all of your ideas in an essay format, after you have at put together all of your thoughts: rough draft or outline?

1749. What is the first sentence of a paragraph called that tells us what the main idea of the paragraph is: a thesis statement or a topic sentence?

1750. What is the sentence called at the end of a paragraph: a topic sentence or a concluding sentence?

1751. Can you write a concluding paragraph at the end of a report?

1752. What is the name of a story that you write that includes a plot, setting, point of view, conflict, and has a closing paragraph at the end: prose or drama?

1753. Do you use transitional words in your writing like next, finally, and in conclusion?

1754. Do you using several descriptive adjectives and verbs in your writing?

1755. Can you write something to persuade, inform, and entertain?

1756. What could you write about to persuade someone to do something?

1757. What could you write about to inform someone about something?

1758. What could you write about to entertain someone?

1759. Can you write a reflective *response* to literature, making a judgment about what you read?

1760. What resources could you use if you were writing a *research* paper?

1761. What resource would you look in to find basic information about frogs: an almanac, a thesaurus, or an encyclopedia?

1762. What resource would you look in to find a synonym for delicious: a dictionary or a thesaurus?

1763. What resource would you look at to find the meaning of concave: a dictionary or a thesaurus?

1764. What resource would you look at to find the longitude of Sweden: an atlas or an almanac?

1765. What resource would you look at to find information about the Aztec culture: an almanac or an online encyclopedia?

1766. Do you have basic computer keyboard skills for typing a paper or report?

1767. Does learning grammar include being familiar with the parts of speech?

1768. What is the name of the grammatical construction in which a noun is followed by another noun, e.g., "My uncle, the doctor…" that helps to explain it: apposition or alliteration?

1769. How many parts of speech are there in the English language: eight or twelve?

1770. What major part of speech is missing in the following list: Noun, adjective, pronoun, adverb, preposition, conjunction, and interjection?

1771. What part of speech refers to a person, animal, place, thing, or idea?

1772. What is the *noun* in the sentence: "The cheetah ran swiftly?"

1773. What part of speech describes or *modifies* a noun: a pronoun or an adjective?

1774. What is the *adjective* in the sentence: "Rusty is a smart dog?"

1775. What part of speech takes the place of a noun: a pronoun or a contraction?

1776. What is the pronoun is the sentence: "He is a smart dog?"

1777. What pronoun would take the place of *Alex*?

1778. What pronoun would take the place of *Rebecca*?

1779. What pronoun would replace *the car*?

1780. What pronoun would replace *Andrew and Zachary*?

1781. Are the words I, she, he, and it considered *personal* pronouns or *possessive* pronouns?

1782. Are the words mine, yours, his, hers, ours considered *personal* pronouns or *possessive* pronouns?

1783. What part of speech describes the main action in a sentence?

1784. What is the *verb* in the sentence: "I jumped over the rock?"

1785. Do all sentences have a subject and a verb?

1786. What part of speech tells how an action occurred: an adjective or an adverb?

1787. What is the *adverb* in the sentence: "He ran quickly to the park?"

1788. What is the *adverb* in the sentence: "Emily plays the piano well?"

1789. What is the name for the part of speech that shows location and links nouns, pronouns, and phrases to the other parts of a sentence: conjunction or preposition?

1790. Are the words *in, at, around, to, through, toward,* and *above* considered conjunctions or prepositions?

1791. What is the preposition in the sentence: "The alarm clock is beside the bed?"

1792. What is the preposition in the sentence: "My jacket is on the chair?"

1793. Are the phrases, "over the hill, behind the door, and outside the house" prepositional phrases or adverbial phrases?

1794. What part of speech joins words or phrases in a sentence: an interjection or a conjunction?

1795. What is the *conjunction* in the sentence: "I sold cakes and cookies?"

1796. What is the *conjunction* in the sentence: "I wanted to go but I had to study?"

1797. What part of speech is included in a sentence for effect and emphasis: an interjection or a conjunction?

1798. What is the *interjection* in this sentence: "Wow! That was a great show?"

1799. Does a *complete* sentence include a subject and a predicate?

1800. Does a *clause* contain both a subject and a verb?

1801. What is the subject in the sentence: "Jack loves ice cream?"

1802. What is the predicate in the sentence: "Jack loves ice cream?"

1803. What kind of sentence would you have if you left out a predicate or a subject: a run-on or a fragment?

1804. Is the sentence, "Visited Disneyworld last year" a fragment or a run-on?

1805. What word could you add to the beginning of "Visited Disneyworld" to make it a complete sentence?

1806. Is the sentence, "I went to Chicago it is a big city" a fragment or a run-on sentence?

1807. How can we divide the sentence, "I went to Chicago it is a big city" into two separate sentences?

1808. How would you combine the following run-on sentence to make one sentence: "Lisa made cookies. Michael made cookies?"

1809. What is the correct verb form in the sentence: "I am /are tall?"

1810. What is the correct verb form in the sentence: "He is/are funny?

1811. What is the correct verb form in the sentence: "They is/are outside?"

1812. What is the correct verb form in the sentence: "My friend Nathan live/lives in Ohio?"

1813. What is the correct verb form in the sentence: "A pack of wolves was/were running through the woods?"

1814. What kind of sentence is in the form of a statement: a declarative or an imperative?

1815. What kind of sentence is in the form of a question: an interrogative or a declarative?

1816. What kind of sentence expresses strong feelings: declarative or exclamatory?

1817. What kind of sentence gives instructions or expresses a command: declarative or imperative?

1818. What kind of sentence is, "It is windy today:" a declarative, an imperative, an interrogative, or an exclamatory sentence?

1819. What punctuation mark does a declarative sentence end with?

1820. What kind of sentence is, "Are you going to the party:" a declarative, an imperative, an interrogative, or an exclamatory sentence?

1821. What punctuation mark does an interrogative sentence end with?

1822. How do you say the sentence, "*The game is over.*" with an interrogative voice?

1823. How do you say the sentence, "*The game is over.*" with a declarative voice?

1824. What kind of sentence is, "We won the championship:" a declarative, an imperative, an interrogative, or an exclamatory sentence?

1825. What punctuation mark does an imperative sentence often end with?

1826. What kind of sentence is similar to a command or an order: declarative or imperative?

1827. What kind of sentence is, "Go walk the dog:" a declarative, an imperative, an interrogative, or an exclamatory?

1828. What punctuation mark tells a reader when to pause in a sentence?

1829. Where is the comma placed in the date *December 7 1949?*

1830. Where is the comma placed in the sentence, "*Yes you may go the park?*"

1831. Where is the comma placed when you address an envelope to *Orlando FL?*

1832. Is a comma placed before or after the quotation marks in the dialog phrase, "I have a surprise for you," said Brian?

1833. Is a comma placed before or after the conjunctions "and" or "but," when connecting two independent clauses?

1834. Where is the comma placed in the sentence, "Sticks and stones may break my bones but words can never hurt me?

1835. What separates items that are listed in a series of two or more: periods or commas?

1836. Where are the commas placed in the sentence, "Samantha brought cookies brownies and cupcakes to sell at the bake sale?

1837. What is the correct punctuation mark when introducing a list of ideas, or setting off a quotation: a comma or a colon?

1838. What is the punctuation mark that looks like a dot with a comma underneath it that is used to separate parts of a sentence, or to separate main clauses: a colon or a semi-colon?

1839. What is the punctuation mark that looks like two dots that is used to call attention to what follows such as a list or an explanation: a colon or a semi-colon?

1840. What punctuation mark do you use after the greeting *Dear Sirs* in a business letter: a semi-colon or a colon?

1841. What punctuation mark do you use after *Dear Krista* in a personal letter: a colon or a comma?

1842. What punctuation mark do you use between the hours and the minutes when writing the time six fifteen: a comma or a colon?

1843. What punctuation mark do you use between a title and a sub-title: a colon or a semi-colon?

1844. What is the name of the punctuation mark that is used to show possession: an apostrophe or a comma?

1845. Where is the apostrophe placed in the phrase: "My friends house?"

1846. Is the apostrophe placed before or after the "s" if the noun is already plural and ends in letter "s?"

1847. Where is the apostrophe placed in the sentence: "The girls (plural) room was a mess?"

1848. Where is the apostrophe placed in the phrase: "The dogs (singular) house?"

1849. What is the name of the punctuation mark used in a contraction: a comma or an apostrophe?

1850. What can an apostrophe take the place of in a contraction: a letter or a word?

1851. Where is the apostrophe placed to make the contraction meaning we are from *w-e-r-e*?

1852. What letter is the apostrophe replacing in the contraction *we're*?

1853. What letter is the apostrophe replacing in the contraction *isn't*?

1854. What is the contraction for the words *do not*?

1855. What is the contraction for the words *I would*?

1856. What is the contraction for the words *they are*?

1857. What two words make up the contraction *she's*?

1858. What two words make up the contraction *I'll*?

1859. What two words make up the contraction *you're*?

1860. What two words make up the contraction *didn't*?

1861. What two words make up the contraction *won't*?

1862. What do you call the punctuation marks that are used in text to indicate the *exact* words of the speaker?

1863. Are the titles of poems, articles, and short stories set off in quotation marks?

1864. Where would the quotation marks be placed in the following sentence: I have a game tonight, said Jordan?

1865. What is a word called that means the same thing as another word: a synonym or an antonym?

1866. What is a synonym of spotless?

1867. What is a synonym of buddy?

1868. What is a synonym of attempt?

1869. What is a synonym of lady?

1870. What is a synonym of strange?

1871. What is a synonym of happy?

1872. What is a word called that means the opposite of another word: a synonym or an antonym?

1873. What is an antonym of fail?

1874. What is an antonym of true?

1875. What is an antonym of cheap?

1876. What is an antonym of sunny?

1877. What is an antonym of liquid?

1878. What is an antonym of out-going?

1879. What is an antonym of wet?

1880. What is an antonym of near?

1881. What is an antonym of over?

1882. What is an antonym of soft?

1883. What is an antonym of rough?

1884. What are groups of letters called that are added to the beginning of a word to form a new word that has a different meaning: a suffix or a prefix?

1885. What is the meaning of the prefixes non-, im-, and in-: *not* or *wrong*?

1886. What is the prefix of the word *impossible*?

1887. What is the meaning of the word *impossible*?

1888. What is the prefix of the word *invisible*?

1889. What is the meaning of the word *invisible*?

1890. What is the prefix of the word *nonfiction*?

1891. What is the meaning of the word *nonfiction*?

1892. What is the meaning of the prefix **mis**: *not* or *wrong*?

1893. What is the prefix of the word *misbehave*?

1894. What is the meaning of the word *misbehave*?

1895. What is the meaning of the prefix **pre**: before or after?

1896. What is the prefix of the word *pregame*?

1897. What is the meaning of the word *pregame?*

1898. What is the meaning of the prefix **en**: out or in?

1899. What is the prefix of the word *endanger*?

1900. What is the meaning of the word *endanger*?

1901. Are suffixes added to the beginning or to the end of a word?

1902. What suffix is often used to form an adverb: -ly or -ful?

1903. What is the suffix in the adverb *swiftly*?

1904. What suffix can you add to the adjective *easy* to make it an adverb: -ly or -ily?

1905. What suffix can you add to the word *sleep* to make it an adjective: -ly or-y?

1906. What is the meaning of the suffix -ful: *capable of* or *full of*?

1907. What is the suffix in the word *playful*?

1908. What is the meaning of the suffix -able or -ible: *capable of* or *full of*?

1909. What is the suffix of the word *washable*?

1910. What is the suffix of the word *flexible*?

1911. Is the suffix *–ment* used to turn a verb into a noun or a noun into a verb?

1912. What suffix is added to the verb *agree* to make it a noun?

1913. By removing the suffix, how would you change the word *achievement* from a noun to a verb?

1914. What is the name of the word that does ***not*** have a prefix or suffix: a stem word or a Latin word?

1915. What is the stem of the word *undeniable*?

1916. What is the term given to a word that is spelled the same in both directions, e.g. eye, pop, kayak, madam, deed, level, radar, and racecar: a palindrome or a homogram?

1917. What is the term for a phrase whose meaning cannot be directly understood from the meaning of the words contained in it as in, "You are pulling my leg:" a homophone or an idiom?

1918. Would a person who does not speak fluent English have an easy or hard time understanding idioms?

1919. Can you recognize and pronounce the common sight word "action?" (Show word)

1920. Can you recognize and pronounce the common sight word "actually?" (Show word)

1921. Can you recognize and pronounce the common sight word "alive?" (Show word)

1922. Can you recognize and pronounce the common sight word "although?" (Show word)

1923. Can you recognize and pronounce the common sight word "amount?" (Show word)

1924. Can you recognize and pronounce the common sight word "area?" (Show word)

1925. Can you recognize and pronounce the common sight word "blood?" (Show word)

1926. Can you recognize and pronounce the common sight word "cause?" (Show word)

1927. Can you recognize and pronounce the common sight word "central?" (Show word)

1928. Can you recognize and pronounce the common sight word "century?" (Show word)

1929. Can you recognize and pronounce the common sight word "charcoal?" (Show word)

1930. Can you recognize and pronounce the common sight word "chart?" (Show word)

1931. Can you recognize and pronounce the common sight word "check?" (Show word)

1932. Can you recognize and pronounce the common sight word "club?" (Show word)

1933. Can you recognize and pronounce the common sight word "colony?" (Show word)

1934. Can you recognize and pronounce the common sight word "company?" (Show word)

1935. Can you recognize and pronounce the common sight word "condition?" (Show word)

1936. Can you recognize and pronounce the common sight word "court?" (Show word)

1937. Can you recognize and pronounce the common sight word "deal?" (Show word)

1938. Can you recognize and pronounce the common sight word "death?" (Show word)

1939. Can you recognize and pronounce the common sight word "describe?" (Show word)

1940. Can you recognize and pronounce the common sight word "design?" (Show word)

1941. Can you recognize and pronounce the common sight word "disease?" (Show word)

1942. Can you recognize and pronounce the common sight word "eleven?" (Show word)

1943. Can you recognize and pronounce the common sight word "equal?" (Show word)

1944. Can you recognize and pronounce the common sight word "experience?" (Show word)

1945. Can you recognize and pronounce the common sight word "factor?" (Show word)

1946. Can you recognize and pronounce the common sight word "favorite?" (Show word)

1947. Can you recognize and pronounce the common sight word "figure?" (Show word)

1948. Can you recognize and pronounce the common sight word "hospital?" (Show word)

1949. Can you recognize and pronounce the common sight word "include?" (Show word)

1950. Can you recognize and pronounce the common sight word "increase?" (Show word)

1951. Can you recognize and pronounce the common sight word "known?" (Show word)

1952. Can you recognize and pronounce the common sight word "least?" (Show word)

1953. Can you recognize and pronounce the common sight word "length?" (Show word)

1954. Can you recognize and pronounce the common sight word "loud?" (Show word)

1955. Can you recognize and pronounce the common sight word "measure?" (Show word)

1956. Can you recognize and pronounce the common sight word "molecule?" (Show word)

1957. Can you recognize and pronounce the common sight word "national?" (Show word)

1958. Can you recognize and pronounce the common sight word "necessary?" (Show word)

1959. Can you recognize and pronounce the common sight word "noun?" (Show word)

1960. Can you recognize and pronounce the common sight word "oxygen?" (Show word)

1961. Can you recognize and pronounce the common sight word "phrase?" (Show word)

1962. Can you recognize and pronounce the common sight word "property?" (Show word)

1963. Can you recognize and pronounce the common sight word "radio?" (Show word)

1964. Can you recognize and pronounce the common sight word "receive?" (Show word)

1965. Can you recognize and pronounce the common sight word "replace?" (Show word)

1966. Can you recognize and pronounce the common sight word "rhythm?" (Show word)

1967. Can you recognize and pronounce the common sight word "serve?" (Show word)

1968. Can you recognize and pronounce the common sight word "similar?" (Show word)

1969. Can you recognize and pronounce the common sight word "southern?" (Show word)

1970. Can you recognize and pronounce the common sight word "squirrel?" (Show word)

1971. Can you recognize and pronounce the common sight word "straight?" (Show word)

1972. Can you recognize and pronounce the common sight word "subtle?" (Show word)

1973. Can you recognize and pronounce the common sight word "suffix?" (Show word)

1974. Can you recognize and pronounce the common sight word "surely?" (Show word)

1975. Can you recognize and pronounce the common sight word "though?" (Show word)

1976. Can you recognize and pronounce the common sight word "thought?" (Show word)

1977. Can you recognize and pronounce the common sight word "touch?" (Show word)

1978. Can you recognize and pronounce the common sight word "twice?" (Show word)

1979. Can you recognize and pronounce the common sight word "used?" (Show word)

1980. Can you recognize and pronounce the common sight word "usually?" (Show word)

1981. Can you recognize and pronounce the common sight word "view?" (Show word)

1982. Can you recognize and pronounce the common sight word "weight?" (Show word)

1983. Can you recognize and pronounce the common sight word "wheat?" (Show word)

1984. Can you recognize and pronounce the common sight word "whom?" (Show word)

1985. Can you recognize and pronounce the common sight word "young?" (Show word)

Language Arts – 5th Grade

1986. What are poetry, drama, music, mystery, horror, romance, fantasy, science fiction, biography, and autobiography all considered: genres, literary works, or language arts?

1987. What are the two main genres in literature, one based on reality, the other imaginary?

1988. What is the name of the genre written for children 2-12 that often has big text and pictures: children's literature or youth literature?

1989. What is the name of the genre that involves an imaginary or magical theme, setting, and characters: fantasy or unrealistic fiction?

1990. What is the name of the genre that involves an unsolved murder or puzzle that the reader tries to figure out with the clues that are given: mystery or adventure?

1991. What is the name of the genre that involves scare tactics to reach the emotions of the reader: fantasy or horror?

1992. What is the name of the genre that involves a love story and finding happiness with another person: mystery or romance?

1993. What is the name of the genre that involves extraordinary situations that are full of suspense, action, and adventure: a thriller or a western?

1994. What is the name of the genre that is the written account of a person's life written by another person: a biography or an autobiography?

1995. What is the name of the genre that is the written account of a person's life as told by that person: a biography or an autobiography?

1996. What is the name of the genre that involves speaking or oral communication: a speech or a presentation?

1997. Are biographies, historical essays, and speeches considered fiction or non-fiction?

1998. What is the name of the fiction verse or prose often used for a theatrical performance, where emotion and conflict are expressed through dialogue and action: drama or poetry?

1999. What is the name of the verse format that may contain rhythm, emotion, and imagination, and is written to appeal to the reader's emotions: fantasy or poetry?

2000. What is the name of the genre that is a story about the extraordinary or supernatural, where animals often speak as humans: fable or fairy tale

2001. What is the name of the wonder tale that may be a type of fable or folktale often about fairies or other creatures, and are aimed at children: fantasy or fairy tale?

2002. What is the name of the genre based on science that is often set in the future, or on another celestial body: realistic fiction or science fiction?

2003. What is the name of a story that can actually happen and is true in real life: realistic fiction or folklore?

2004. What is the genre name given for songs, myths, and stories that are often passed down the generations by word of mouth: folklore or fable?

2005. What is the genre name given to a story with characters and events in a historical setting: realistic fiction or historical fiction?

2006. What is the genre given to a story that is shocking or terrifying in which the characters and events create feelings of fear for the reader: fantasy or horror?

2007. What is the genre name given to a humorous story full of exaggerations, with characters that do the impossible: legend or tall tale?

2008. What is the genre name given to a fact-based story about a folk hero, and often includes imaginative details as well: tall tale or legend?

2009. What is the genre name given to a type of legend that is often based on historical events that is expressed with symbolism and the actions of gods: legend or mythology?

2010. Are narratives, essays, biographies, history, and speeches fiction or non-fiction?

2011. What is the term for a short composition on a specific topic that reflects an author's viewpoint: an essay or a narrative?

2012. What is the general term for factual text that deals with an actual subject?

2013. What is the general term for literary works that are not based on fact, and are invented or imagined stories?

2014. What is the literary term for a story or song-like poem that tells a story: a poem or a ballad?

2015. What is the literary term for a poem that tells a story from a narrative point of view: a narrative poem or a lyric poem?

2016. What is the literary term for a rhyming poem that expresses the author's feelings: a lyric poem or a narrative poem?

2017. What is the literary term for a poem that is an original work with no rhyme or pattern syllable repetition: a lyric poem or free verse?

2018. What is the term for a grouping of related lines in a poem: a paragraph or a stanza?

2019. What is the term in poetry for the pattern of rhyming words within each stanza such as ABAB or ABBA: rhyme scheme or rhyme pattern?

2020. What is the term in poetry for the regular beat that is a measure of how your voice rises and falls when you read a poem: stress or meter?

2021. What is the term in poetry for the rhyme established by a poem: stress or meter?

2022. What was the most common meter in English poetry consisting of an unstressed syllable followed by a stressed syllable, and was used extensively by Shakespeare in his poems: syllable verse or iambic pentameter?

2023. What is the term for a certain kind of stanza that was popular in England during the 17th and 18th centuries that consists of two lines that rhyme with one another: a duet or a couplet?

2024. What is the literary term for a five line humorous poem whereas lines 1, 2, and 5 rhyme and lines 3 and 4 rhyme: a limerick or a cinquain?

2025. What is the literary term for a five-line poem that does not rhyme, line 1 is a noun, line 2 has two adjectives, line 3 has three "-ing" words, line 4 has four statement words, and line 5 has a synonym for the noun in line 1: a limerick or a cinquain?

2026. What is the literary term for a four-line poem that repeats a rhyme pattern: a quatrain or a cinquain?

2027. What is the literary term given for a Japanese three-line poem that celebrates something in nature, and has a syllable pattern containing five, seven, and five syllables respectively: a limerick or haiku?

2028. What is the name of the greatest storyteller and oral poet of ancient Greece who told the two famous epics called "The Iliad" and "The Odyssey," about great heroes and famous deeds: Homer or Apollo?

2029. What is the literary term given to a work that has spoken lines, and is performed for an audience by actors: a musical or a play?

2030. Can songs that rhyme be considered a form of poetry?

2031. Do all poems have to rhyme?

2032. Was Henry Wadsworth Longfellow, author of "The Arrow and the Song" and "Paul Revere's Ride," a famous American songwriter or a famous American poet?

2033. What famous English poet is the author of "The Road Not Taken" and "Fire and Ice:" Robert Frost or Ralph Waldo Emerson?

2034. What famous American poet is the author of "The Snow Storm" and "Ode to Beauty:" Ralph Waldo Emerson or Walt Whitman?

2035. What famous American poet is the author of "I Hear America Singing," "Leaves of Grass," and "Song of Myself:" Walt Whitman or Emily Dickenson?

2036. What famous African-American poet is the author of "Narcissa" and "We Real Cool:" Gwendolyn Brooks or Emily Dickenson?

2037. What famous American poet is the author of "A Bird Came Down the Walk" and "I'm Nobody! Who are You?:" Elizabeth Browning or Emily Dickenson?

2038. What famous English poet is the author of "The Tyger" and "A Poison Tree:" William Blake or Walt Whitman?

2039. What famous English author wrote the poems "Jabberwocky" and "The Hunting of the Snark," as well as the novels, "Alice's Adventures in Wonderland" and "Through the Looking Glass:" Robert Frost or Lewis Carroll?

2040. What famous English romantic poet wrote "Ode to a Nightingale" and "To My Brother George:" John Keats or Ralph Waldo Emerson?

2041. What American writer and poet is most famous for his book "Walden," a reflection of living a simple life in natural surroundings, as well as the essay "Civil Disobedience:" Henry David Thoreau or John Keats?

2042. What American author and poet was most famous for his short stories that included *The Pit and the Pendulum, The Masque of the Red Death,* and *The Tell-Tale Heart,* as well as the poems, *The Haunted Palace* and *The Raven*: Ralph Waldo Emerson or Edgar Allan Poe?

2043. What English poet wrote "She Walks in Beauty" and "When We Two Parted," as well as his renowned narrative poem, "Don Juan:" Lord Byron or Edgar Allan Poe?

2044. What is the name of the blind 17ᵗʰ century English poet who is best known for his epic poem "Paradise Lost," that was originally published in 1667 in ten books, and has over 10,000 lines of verse: John Milton or Lord Byron?

2045. What is the name of one of the most prominent poets of the Victorian era who is famous for her poems and sonnets including the love sonnet, "How do I love thee? Let me count the ways:" Emily Dickenson or Elizabeth Barrett Browning?

2046. What is the name of the contemporary (1928-2014) African-American poet and author regarded as a global renaissance woman, who authored several books and poems including the poems, "And Still I Rise" and "I Know Why the Caged Bird Sings:" Maya Angelou or Elizabeth Browning?

2047. What is the name of a 14-line verse that may be Italian, English, or Shakespearean, and has a fixed rhyme scheme: a sonnet or a sonata?

2048. What is the literary term given to a short work of literature that can be read in one sitting and typically has a simple storyline: a short story or a novel?

2049. What is the literary term given for a short non-fiction work on a specific topic, written in a magazine or a newspaper that is written to inform: an essay or an article?

2050. What is the literary term given for a long story that usually involves a setting, plot, and many characters: a short story or a novel?

2051. What is the literary term given to describe the written or oral communication between at least two people, where several questions are asked and answered: an autobiography or an interview?

2052. What are the two main divisions of books in a library?

2053. What are the different formats that books can be available in?

2054. Who might benefit from books written in large print?

2055. What is the name of the classification system used in a library to shelve books according to their subject or author?

2056. What is the name of the person who writes a story, poem, article, or novel?

2057. What is the name of the person who writes a drama: an author or a playwright?

2058. What is the name of a book or story called?

2059. What is the term given either to a literary work that has a secondary title, or the printed translation of the dialog of a foreign language film: caption or sub-title?

2060. What is the name of the person who draws the pictures for a story or book?

2061. What is the name of the sections or divisions that a novel is divided into?

2062. What is the name of the section at the beginning of a non-fiction work that outlines the different topics contained in the book and their corresponding page numbers?

2063. What is the name of the section at the end of a non-fiction book or textbook that contains an alphabetical list of *terms* contained within the book along with its definition?

2064. What is the name of the section at the end of a non-fiction book or textbook that facilitates reference in that it contains an alphabetical list of names, places, and subjects in the work, giving the page or pages on which each item is mentioned?

2065. What is the name of the legal right that is granted to an author, composer, playwright, or publisher to keep the exclusive right to produce and control the content of the work?

2066. What is the name of the person or company that is listed at the beginning of a book that is responsible for printing and distributing the book, newspaper, or magazine?

2067. What is the name of the alphabetical compilation of sources cited by an author at the end of a book that were referred to in the text, giving credit to those works: bibliography or autobiography?

2068. Does a bibliography of a book source include the author's name, the book's title, the place of publication, the publisher, the date, and the page or pages where the information was found?

2069. What is the name for a reference providing an alphabetical list of words with guide words at the top of each page that may include the word's meaning, syllable divisions, pronunciation, or translation?

2070. What is the name for a reference providing an alphabetical list of synonyms, words that are similar in meaning?

2071. What is the name for the reference tool that is a collection of maps?

2072. What is the name for the annual publication that contains a calendar, weather forecasts, tides, and other weather and astronomical data: atlas or almanac?

2073. What is the name for the satellite-based electronic navigation tool: a GPS or a GSP?

2074. Does GPS stand for **G**lobal **P**ositioning **S**ystem?

2075. What is the term for "GPS," that is an abbreviation using the first letters of each word: an antonym or an acronym?

2076. Are FBI, CIA, and NCAA antonyms or acronyms?

2077. What acronyms can you name?

2078. Is ALA an acronym for the American Library Association?

2079. What is the literary term that tells the events of a story in a logical order, and includes an introduction, rising action, climax, falling action, and a final outcome: the plot or the setting?

2080. What is the name of an essential part of a plot that can be either internal or external, and may be man vs. man, man vs. society, man vs. circumstances, or man vs. himself: the storyline, the conflict, or the characters?

2081. What is the literary term for where the story takes place, and may include place, historical period, weather conditions, social conditions, and mood: the location or the setting?

2082. What is the literary term given for the people, animals, or imaginary creatures in a story: the characters or the actors?

2083. What is the name of the main character of a story: the protagonist or the antagonist?

2084. What is the name of the person that is the opposer of the main character: the protagonist or the antagonist?

2085. What is the literary term given for the angle from which a story is told: point of view or opinion?

2086. What is the point of view in a story if it is told through the eyes of the protagonist or main character, using pronouns "I," "me," and "my:" first person or third person?

2087. What is the point of view in a story that is narrated by the author in the third person using pronouns "they," "she," "he," or "it:" third person or omniscient?

2088. What is the literary term for the central or controlling idea in a piece of fiction like, "love is blind," or, "things are not always as they appear to be:" the plot or the theme?

2089. What is the literary term given for the reason an author decides to write about a specific topic either to entertain the reader, or to persuade the reader to believe in something: the author's purpose or the author's style?

2090. What is the literary term given to the thing that reveals the unique personality and voice of the author through the author's word choice, dialog, tone, mood, and either formal or informal language: the author's style or the author's point of view?

2091. What is the name of the renowned children's award in the United States that honors the author who has made the most distinguished contribution to American literature for children, and is awarded by the American Library Association: the Newbery or the Caldecott?

2092. What is the name of the literary medal that honors the best children's picture book of the year: the Newbery or the Caldecott?

2093. What is the name of the prestigious prize that is awarded annually to an outstanding contributor not only in the field of literature, but also has recognized achievement since 1901 in physics, chemistry, medicine, peace, and economics: the Pulitzer or the Nobel?

2094. What is the name of the prestigious prize that is awarded annually to the thirteen best achievements in American journalism, literature, and music: the Pulitzer or the Nobel?

2095. What is the term given to a popular, top-selling book that is recognized by many outlets, including the weekly and monthly lists provided by the New York Times newspaper?

2096. How are best-seller books divided: by language or by genre?

2097. What is it name of the process of changing the words of one language into another like English to Spanish or Spanish to English: translation or interpretation?

2098. Does a translator translate the written or spoken words from one language to another?

2099. Does an interpreter translate the written or spoken words from one language to another?

2100. What language or languages do you speak?

2101. Does the United States have an official language?

2102. What is the second most common language spoken in the United States?

2103. What is the term for a person that speaks one native language: monolingual or bilingual?

2104. What is the term for a person that can fluently speak two languages: bilingual or multi-lingual?

2105. What is the term for a person that can fluently speak more than two languages: bilingual or multi-lingual?

2106. What is the most commonly spoken language in the world: Mandarin Chinese or English?

2107. What language comes after Mandarin Chinese and Hindi in terms of how many people in the world speak that language: English or Spanish?

2108. What is the language spoken by many people of North America, South America, Central America, and Spain, that ranks right after English in terms of the amount of people that speak it?

2109. Do you think some distinct ethnic groups and tribes in the United States and the world still speak and communicate in their own native language?

2110. Do you think some languages are dying out, because fewer and fewer people speak them?

2111. What is your estimate on the number of living languages, not including dialects that are still spoken today: 3,000 or 7,000?

2112. What is the most widely published language: Chinese, English, or Spanish?

2113. What is the study of the structure of a language called: linguistics or phonetics?

2114. Do we have linguistic diversity in the United States?

2115. Do many of our English words have Greek and Latin roots?

2116. What does the Greek root "aero" mean, as in aerodynamics, aerate, or aerobics?

2117. What does the Greek root "ast" mean, as in astronaut, asteroid or astronomy?

2118. What does the Greek root "biblio" mean, as in Bible or bibliography?

2119. What does the Greek root "bio" mean, as in biography or biology?

2120. What does the Greek root "cosm" mean, as in cosmos, cosmic, or cosmopolitan?

2121. What does the Greek root "cycl" mean, as in cycle, cyclone, or bicycle?

2122. What does the Greek root "geo" mean, as in geology, geometry, and geologist?

2123. What does the Greek root "hydr" mean, as in hydrant, hydrogen and hydroelectric power?

2124. What does the Greek root "meter" mean, as in thermometer, diameter, centimeter, or barometer?

2125. What does the Greek root "mega" mean, as in megaphone or megabucks?

2126. What does the Greek root "micro" mean, as in microscope and microfilm?

2127. What does the Greek root "mono" mean, as in monologue or monarch?

2128. What does the Greek root "phon" mean, as in phoneme and telephone?

2129. What does the Greek root "photo" mean, as in photographs or photocopier?

2130. What does the Greek root "poly" mean, as in polygon and polymer?

2131. What does the Greek root "proto" mean, as in prototype or protozoan?

2132. What does the Greek root "psyche" mean, as in psychologist or psych?

2133. What does the Greek root "tele" mean, as in television or telephone?

2134. What does the Greek root "thermo" mean, as in thermometer, thermal, or thermostat?

2135. What does the Greek (and Latin) root "tri" mean, as in trilogy, triangle, and tricycle?

2136. What does the Latin root "annus" mean, as in annual and anniversary?

2137. What does the Latin root "ante" mean, as in antebellum and antecedent?

2138. What does the Latin root "aqua" mean, as in aquatic and aquarium?

2139. What does the Latin root "bi" mean, as in bicycle, bisect, and bipartisan?

2140. What does the Latin root "centum" mean, as in percent, century, and cent?

2141. What does the Latin root "decem" mean, as in decade and decimal?

2142. What does the Latin root "dico" mean, as in dictation and dictator?

2143. What does the Latin root "duo" mean, as in duo and duplicate?

2144. What does the Latin root "fortuna" mean, as in fortunate or fortune?

2145. What does the Latin root "heres" mean, as in heir, heirloom, or inheritance?

2146. What does the Latin root "labor" mean, as in laborer, laboratory, and collaborate?

2147. What does the Latin root "magnus" mean, as in magnificent or magnify?

2148. What does the Latin root "minus" mean, as in five minus two and minor?

2149. What does the Latin root "navigare" mean, as in navigate, navigator and navy?

2150. What does the Latin root "omni" mean, as in omniscient and omnipotent?

2151. What does the Latin root "post" mean, as in posterity or posthumous?

2152. What does the Latin root "pre" mean, as in prefix, predict, and preview?

2153. What does the Latin root "primus" mean, as in primary or primitive?

2154. What does the Latin root "quartus" mean, as in quarter or quartet?

2155. What does the Latin root "uni" or "unus" mean, as in unit or unanimous?

2156. What does the Latin root "video" or "visus" mean, as in video or visual?

2157. What does the Latin root "vita" mean as in vitality and vitamin?

2158. What is the name for the study of and the origin of words: etymology or lingualism?

2159. Does a dictionary often have the etymology, or origin of that word?

2160. What is the foreign origin of banana, mumbo, safari, and zombie: African or Arabic?

2161. What is the foreign origin of algebra, coffee, magazine, and zero: African or Arabic?

2162. What is the foreign origin of boomerang, dingo, kangaroo, and koala: African or Australian?

2163. What is the foreign origin of gung ho, kung fu, soy, tea, tofu, and typhoon: Chinese or Japanese?

2164. What is the foreign origin of cookie, pickle, sled, golf, snack, and wagon: Czech or Dutch?

2165. What is the foreign origin of jungle, pajamas, shampoo, cheetah, and veranda: East Indian or Chinese?

2166. What is the foreign origin of ballet, boulevard, bouquet, carousel, chic, crepe, croissant, depot, fiancé, garage, mayor, Mardi Gras, turquoise, and resume: French or Italian?

2167. What is the foreign origin of diesel, Fahrenheit, frankfurter, bratwurst, hamburger, kindergarten, sauerkraut, and strudel: French or German?

2168. What is the foreign origin of bar mitzvah, kosher, menorah, and shalom: Greek or Hebrew?

2169. What is the foreign origin of bog, clock, galore, shamrock, and leprechaun: Scottish or Irish?

2170. What is the foreign origin of bologna, carnival, confetti, fiasco, finale, gondola, macaroni, pasta, piano, spaghetti, and volcano: Spanish or Italian?

2171. What is the foreign origin of bonsai, futon, judo, karate, ninja, origami, samurai, sushi, tsunami, and tycoon: Korean or Japanese?

2172. What is the foreign origin of chipmunk, powwow, skunk, totem, and wigwam: East Indian or Native American?

2173. What is the foreign origin of aloha, hula, lei, and taboo: Polynesian or Hawaiian?

2174. What is the foreign origin of cosmonaut, czar, Kremlin, mammoth, parka, and sputnik: Russian or Polish?

2175. What is the foreign origin of kielbasa, polska, babka, and kloty: Russian or Polish?

2176. What is the foreign origin of adobe, alfalfa, alpaca, armada, avocado, bronco, burro, cafeteria, canoe, canyon, cargo, chaps, condor, conquistador, corral, Colorado, coyote, fiesta, guacamole, Florida, hacienda, hurricane, iguana, jalapeño, macho, matador, mesa, Montana, mosquito, mustang, nacho, Nevada, papaya, patio, piñata, plaza, poncho, potato, pueblo, quesadilla, quinoa, ranch, rodeo, rumba, salsa, savannah, sierra, siesta, silo, stampede, stockade, taco, tamale, tango, tapioca, tobacco, tomato, tortilla, tornado, tuna, vanilla, vigilante, and Zorro: Spanish or Italian?

2177. What is the foreign origin of coffee, kiosk, sherbet, shish kebab, and yogurt: Yiddish or Turkish?

2178. What is the English word for hallo, bonjour, hola, ciao, and shalom?

2179. What is the English word for auf wiederschen, au revoir, adios, arrivederci, and sayonara?

2180. What is the English word for bitte, s'il vous plait, and por favor?

2181. What is the English word for danke, merci, gracias, and grazie?

2182. What is the English word for ja, oui, si, and ya?

2183. What is the English word for nein, non, and nao?

2184. What is the English animal name for katze, chat, katt, and gato?

2185. What is the English animal name for kuh, vaca, and ku?

2186. What is the English animal name for hund, chien, and perro?

2187. What is the English animal name for frosch, rana and groda?

2188. What is the English animal name for cheval, caballo, or ferd?

2189. What is the English animal name for schwein, cerdo or porco?

2190. What is the English animal name for schlange, serpiente, or culebra?

2191. What is the French phrase commonly used in English writing when ordering an individual item on a menu: a la carte or a la mode?

2192. What is the French phrase commonly used in English writing that means served with ice cream: a la carte or a la mode?

2193. What is the French phrase commonly used in English writing that means goodbye, or until we meet again: adios or au revoir?

2194. What is the French phrase commonly used in English writing that means enjoy your meal: buen provecho or bon appétit?

2195. What is the French phrase commonly used in English writing that means hello: hola or bonjour?

2196. What is the French phrase commonly used in English writing that means have a good trip: bon voyage or buen viaje?

2197. What is the French phrase commonly used in English writing that means the end of a street, or a dead end: cul de sac or boulevard?

2198. What is the French phrase commonly used in English writing that means on the route, or on the way: en route or en masse?

2199. What is the French phrase commonly used in English writing that means a social mistake: faux pas or error?

2200. What is the French phrase commonly used in English writing that means appetizer: appetit or hors d'oeuvre?

2201. What is the French phrase commonly used in English writing that means the attitude or practice that we should not meddle in the affairs of others: faux pas or laissez-faire?

2202. When would you see the French acronym RSVP?

2203. What does etiquette require you to do if you see RSVP, French for *repondez s'il vous plait* on an invitation?

2204. What is the Latin phrase for *seize the day*: carpe diem or bona fide?

2205. What is the Latin phrase for *in good faith:* carpe diem or bona fide?

2206. What is the Latin phrase for *and so on*: et cetera or ibid?

2207. What is the Latin phrase for *my fault*; carpe diem or mea culpa?

2208. What is the Latin phrase for *the way things are*: quid pro quo or status quo?

2209. What is the Latin phrase for conversely, or in the reverse order: et cetera or vice versa?

2210. What is the term for a set of letters that can be attached to the front of a word to make a new word: prefix or suffix?

2211. What does the prefix *anti* mean, as in antibacterial and antibodies: away or against?

2212. What does the prefix *inter* mean, as in international, interview, and interstate: between or beneath?

2213. What does the prefix *co* mean, as in co-exist and co-captions: together or against?

2214. What does the prefix *mid* mean, as in midnight and midair: middle or high?

2215. What does the prefix *fore* mean, as in forefather and foresight: before or ahead?

2216. What does the prefix *post* mean, as in postgame and postseason: before or after?

2217. What do the prefixes *il, ir, in,* and *im* mean, as in illegal, irregular, intolerant, and immature: not or is?

2218. What does the prefix *semi* mean, as in semicircle and semiannual: whole or partial?

2219. What is the term for a set of letters that can be attached to the end of a word to make a new word: prefix or suffix?

2220. What suffixes can be added to adjectives to make them adverbs: -ly or –ness?

2221. How can you make the adjective **slow** into an adverb by adding the suffix -ly?

2222. How can you make the adjective **happy** into an adverb by adding the suffix -ily?

2223. What suffix is used to describe what somebody does or believes, like an artist or a biologist?

2224. What suffix is added to nouns to make them into adjectives, as in fool and foolish, or style and stylish?

2225. What suffix indicates the state, condition, or quality of something, as in redness or sadness?

2226. What two suffixes are often used to make verbs into nouns, as in act to action, or run to runner?

2227. What does the suffix –ish mean, that can turn a noun into an adjective, as in fool to foolish, red to reddish, or style to stylish: rather or slightly?

2228. Is a literary work built using, letters, words, sentences, and paragraphs?

2229. What do you need to do the first sentence of a new paragraph to make it stand out?

2230. What do you always need to do to the first letter of a word in a sentence?

2231. Do you always capitalize the pronoun "I?"

2232. Do you capitalize the names of specific people, places, events, dates, and documents?

2233. Do you capitalize the names of languages, races, religions, and the names of Gods?

2234. Do you capitalize titles of respect like Dr. Judge, Mr., and Mrs.?

2235. Do you capitalize the names of organizations and trade names like Nike and Coca-Cola?

2236. Do you capitalize important words in the titles of stories, books, newspapers, and magazines?

2237. Do you capitalize abbreviations and acronyms?

2238. What punctuation mark goes at the end of a sentence that makes a statement?

2239. What punctuation mark goes at the end of a sentence that asks a question?

2240. What punctuation mark goes at the end of a sentence that is exclaimed or shouted?

2241. What punctuation mark do you use when you want to separate items in a list?

2242. What punctuation mark do you use after yes and no in a sentence?

2243. Where is the comma placed when writing the month, day, and year?

2244. Where is a comma inserted when writing an address on an envelope?

2245. What is the name of the noun or noun phrase that renames another noun right beside it: an appositive or an acronym?

2246. What is the appositive in the following sentence: "My friend, Sara Smith, is visiting us from Arizona?

2247. What is the appositive in the following sentence: "Rusty, my Goldendoodle, is getting a haircut today?

2248. What punctuation looks like two periods stacked on top of one another?

2249. What punctuation mark is used in the following sentence: "I had to choose one of three clubs: dance, chorus, or jazz band," because it introduces a list?

2250. What is the term for writing letters in a word in a slant to the right: italics or bold?

2251. What should you do when you write down the title of a book: underline it, italicize it, or either?

2252. What would you use to set off a title if you're writing about a poem, a song, or a magazine article: italicize the title or place the title inside quotation marks?

2253. Where would the quotation marks be in the following sentence: "We sang The Star Spangled Banner before the game?"

2254. What is the term given for the following eight things: noun, pronoun, adjective, verb, adverb, conjunction, preposition, and interjection: language devices or parts of speech?

2255. What two parts of speech does a sentence need to be complete?

2256. What is the part of speech that names a person, place, thing, or idea?

2257. What is an example of a noun?

2258. What kind of noun names a specific person, place, or thing and is always capitalized: a common noun or a proper noun?

2259. What is an example of a proper noun?

2260. What is the proper noun in the following sentence: "Many famous monuments are located in Washington, D.C?"

2261. What kind of noun is not specific and is not capitalized unless it is at the beginning of a sentence: a common noun or a proper noun?

2262. What are the *common* nouns in the following sentence: "New York is famous for its parks, museums, restaurants?"

2263. What is an example of a common noun?

2264. What is a word that takes the place of a noun: an adjective or a pronoun?

2265. Do we use personal pronouns to make sentences longer or shorter?

2266. Does the personal pronoun agree in case, gender, and number with the noun it replaces?

2267. What pronouns can you use to refer to yourself besides "I?"

2268. Are the personal pronouns I, me, my, or mine interchangeable, or does the form of the pronoun depend on how it is used in a sentence?

2269. Does the particular form a pronoun takes called the "case" of the noun, and does it have to agree with the noun it replaces?

2270. Are nominative, objective, and possessive considered gender or cases?

2271. What pronoun would replace "the girl" in the sentence: "The girl held the doll:" the nominative case "she," or the objective case "her?"

2272. What pronoun would replace "the dolls" in the sentence: "The girl held the dolls:" the nominative case "they," or the objective case "them?"

2273. What are the personal pronouns I, we, you, he, she, it, and they: nominative or objective?

2274. What are the personal pronouns me, us, you, him, her, it, and them: nominative or objective?

2275. Which sentence illustrates the correct use of the personal pronoun: "My sister and **me** are going to the park" or, "My sister and **I** are going to the park?

2276. Which sentence illustrates the correct use of the personal pronoun: "Dad is taking Ryan and **I** to the zoo" or, "Dad is taking Ryan and **me** to the zoo?"

2277. What is an example of a pronoun?

2278. What is the part of speech that describes or modifies a noun and gives more detail?

2279. What are the adjectives in the following sentence: "The blue shirt is expensive?"

2280. Can you add adjectives to the following sentence to make it more detailed and specific: "The bike rode down the path"

2281. What is an example of an adjective?

2282. What is a word that shows action or a state of being?

2283. What is an example of a verb?

2284. Can verbs be expressed in different *tenses* like present, past, and future?

2285. How would you change the verb in the following sentence from the present to the past tense: "The dog **eats** the bone?"

2286. How would you change the verb in the following sentence from the past to the future tense: "The dog **ate** the bone?"

2287. How would you change the verb in the following sentence from the future to the present tense: "The dog **will eat** the bone?"

2288. What is the part of speech called that modifies a verb and tells how an action is performed?

2289. What is the adverb in the following sentence: "Marissa turned the key slowly?"

2290. Do all adverbs end in -ly?

2291. What is the adverb in the following sentence: "Soon the plane will land?"

2292. What is the adverb in the following sentence: "He ran very fast?"

2293. What is the adverb in the following sentence: "He played the game well?"

2294. What is an example of an adverb?

2295. Can you add an adverb to the following sentence to make it more specific: "The clerk set down the glass vase?"

2296. What are some adverbs you can name like slowly or quickly that tell us *how*?

2297. What do the adverbs like, never, and after tell us: when or where?

2298. What do the adverbs *here* and *there* tell us: when or where?

2299. What do the adverbs *quite* and *very* tell us: when or to what extent?

2300. What is the comparative adverb of *badly*: worse or the worst?

2301. What is the superlative adverb of the series: tall, taller, _?

2302. What is the superlative adverb of the series: little, less, _?

2303. What is the superlative adverb of the series: much, more, _?

2304. What is the superlative adverb of the series well, better, _?

2305. What is the part of speech called that joins words, phrases or clauses: a contraction or a conjunction?

2306. What part of speech are the words and, or, nor, for, but, yet, and so?

2307. How can you use the conjunction "so" to make a complete sentence from the following run-on: "The chicken took a long time to bake, you should start cooking it right away?"

2308. What is an example of a conjunction?

2309. What is the part of speech called that shows the relationship of a noun or pronoun to another word or words in the sentence: a conjunction or a preposition?

2310. What is an example of a preposition?

2311. What is the part of speech called that is used to express strong emotion: an exclamation or an interjection?

2312. What is the interjection in the following sentence: "Yikes! I'm late for school?"

2313. What is the interjection in the following sentence: "What! We have a test today?"

2314. What is an example of an interjection?

2315. What is the term for the part of speech that is the noun or pronoun that the verb "does" something to, the *who* or *what* that the verb is acting on: the direct object or the indirect object?

2316. What is the direct object in the following sentence: "Diego Rivera painted murals in Mexico's National Palace?"

2317. *What* was being painted in the sentence: "Diego Rivera painted murals in Mexico's National Palace?"

2318. What is the direct object in the following sentence: "Harriet Tubman led slaves to freedom?"

2319. *Who* was being led in the sentence: "Harriet Tubman led slaves to freedom?"

2320. If a sentence has a direct object, can it also have an indirect object?

2321. What is the term for the person or the thing that receives the direct object from the subject and answers *to whom* or *for whom*: the indirect object or the predicate?

2322. What is the indirect object in the following sentence: "Joe threw Zach the Frisbee?"

2323. *To whom* did Joe throw the Frisbee in the sentence: "Joe threw Zach the Frisbee?"

2324. What is the indirect object in the sentence: "Paul made his friends a pizza?"

2325. *For whom* did Paul make the pizza in the sentence: "Paul made his friends a pizza?"

2326. Is "friends" the direct or indirect object of the verb in the following sentence: "Paul made his friends a pizza?"

2327. What is the *subject* in the following sentence: "Paul made his friends a pizza?"

2328. What is the *verb* in the following sentence: "Paul made his friends a pizza?"

2329. What is the *direct object* in the following sentence: "Paul made his friends a pizza?"

2330. Can you identify the subject of a sentence by asking who or what is doing what the verb describes?

2331. What is the subject in the following sentence: "The baby smiled at his mother?"

2332. *Who* smiled at his mother in the sentence: "The baby smiled at his mother?"

2333. Is "baby' or "mother" the subject of the sentence, "The baby smiled at his mother" because it answers "who" about the verb?

2334. Do the subject and a verb always have to agree in a sentence?

2335. What form of the verb do you use if your subject is singular: singular or plural?

2336. What form of the verb do you use if your subject is plural: singular or plural?

2337. How would you say the following sentence using subject and verb agreement: "He teach science," or, "He teaches science?"

2338. How would you say the following sentence using subject and verb agreement: "The deer ran through the forest," or "The deer runs through the forest?"

2339. Which of the verbs would you use to complete the sentence: "A flock of birds **fly** or **flies** overhead?"

2340. Which of the verbs would you use to complete the sentence: "A band of musicians **was** or **were** singing for us?"

2341. Which of the verbs would you use to complete the sentence: "One of my cousins **like** or **likes** to jump rope?"

2342. Which of the verbs would you use to complete the sentence: "Two of my cousins **like** or **likes** to jump rope?"

2343. What voice is a sentence like "The dog chased the ball" written in if the subject of the sentence performs the action: active or passive?

2344. How is a sentence written if the subject of the sentence is acted upon by some other agent, and usually includes the verb form *was* or *were* as in, "The ball was chased by the dog:" active voice or passive voice?

2345. Which voice is more lively and interesting to a reader: active or passive?

2346. Is the following sentence written in active voice or passive voice: "William Shakespeare wrote *Romeo and Juliet*?"

2347. In what voice is "*Romeo and Juliet* was written by William Shakespeare:" active or passive?

2348. What is a sentence called when it is missing a subject or a verb: a fragment or a run-on?

2349. What is it called when two or more sentences are written as one sentence and are often separated by commas: a fragment or a run-on?

2350. Is the following sentence a fragment, a run-on, or a complete sentence: "I made chicken for supper?"

2351. Is the following sentence a fragment, a run-on, or a complete sentence: "Very tasty?"

2352. Is the following sentence a fragment, a run-on, or a complete sentence: "The chicken takes a long time to bake, you should start cooking it right away?"

2353. What word can you add to fix the following run-on: "The chicken takes a long time to bake, you should start cooking it right away?"

2354. What is the term for the part of a sentence that states something about the subject, always includes the verb, and can be long or short: the theme or the predicate?

2355. What is the predicate in the following sentence: "The police officer directed traffic at the intersection?"

2356. What is the predicate in the following sentence: "Evan cried?"

2357. What is the predicate in the following sentence: "I carried books in my backpack to read whenever I went on errands with my mom?"

2358. Is the predicate typically placed before or after the subject of the sentence?

2359. What is the subject in the following sentence: "The garbage left a horrible smell?"

2360. What is the predicate in the following sentence: "In the brisk wind were flying fifty kites?"

2361. Is it important to keep the rules for the parts of speech in mind when writing?

2362. What have you written a short story about?

2363. Can you write a description of a person or a place?

2364. Can you write a summary of what you did yesterday?

2365. What have you written a report on?

2366. What have you written an essay about?

2367. What is the term for the first paragraph of an essay or report: the attention-getter or the introduction?

2368. What is the term for the middle paragraphs of an essay or report: the middle or the body?

2369. What is the term for the last paragraph of an essay or report: the conclusion or the ending?

2370. What is the name of the sentence in an introductory paragraph that prepares the reader for the main focus of the paper, or the position of the author in the paper: the topic sentence or the thesis statement?

2371. When you write or say exactly what you mean, what language are you using: figurative or literal?

2372. Should a "figure of speech" be taken literally or not?

2373. Is the following sentence written in literal or figurative language: "The leaf floated in the pond?"

2374. Is the following sentence written in literal or figurative language: "The dancer floated across the stage?"

2375. What type of language do scientists often use to be as precise as they can: literal or figurative?

2376. What type of language do story-tellers and poets often use in their writings to heighten our emotions and imagination, and to help us see things in a different way: literal or figurative?

2377. What is the term for a figure of speech where there are two contradictory terms right next to each other: an octagon or an oxymoron?

2378. Which of the following would be considered an oxymoron: jumbo shrimp or baby shrimp?

2379. What would all of the following be considered: awful good, bitter sweet, civil war, icy hot, good grief, lead balloon, freezer burn, pretty ugly, steel wool, small crowd, silent scream, and wise fool?

2380. What is the term for what writers use to help the reader create pictures of images of something: imagination or imagery?

2381. What is the term for the figure of speech that makes a comparison using extreme exaggeration for emphasis or effect: imagery or hyperbole?

2382. What are the following sentences examples of: "I have a ton of homework" or, "I have a million things to do" or, "My shoes are killing me:" hyperbole or literal language?

2383. Can *you* say a phrase or a sentence that would be considered hyperbole?

2384. What figure of speech compares two unlike things using "like" or "as:" a simile or a metaphor?

2385. What is the phrase "float like a butterfly:" a simile or a metaphor?

2386. What is the phrase "quiet as a mouse:" a simile or a metaphor?

2387. What figure of speech compares unlike things *without* using "like" or "as:" a simile or a metaphor?

2388. Which of the following is a metaphor: "She is as stubborn as a mule," or, "She is a mule?"

2389. Which of the following is a simile: "The snow blanketed the field," or, "Her face was as white as a sheet?"

2390. What is the *snow* being compared to in after following sentence: "The snow blanketed the field?"

2391. What is the literary term for something that stands for or suggests something other than itself: a symbol or a stamp?

2392. What is one symbol of the United States of America?

2393. What do the 50 stars on the American flag symbolize or represent?

2394. What does a heart symbolize?

2395. What do skull and crossbones symbolize on a bottle of bleach?

2396. Can a symbol mean different things to different people?

2397. What is the symbolism of the two paths in the woods in Robert Frost's, "The Road Not Taken?"

2398. What is the literary term when a thing or an animal is given qualities or abilities of a human being: alliteration or personification?

2399. What is the literary term that is present in the following sentences: "This city never sleeps," and, "Callie heard the last piece of cake calling her name:" alliteration or personification?

2400. What is the Greek work for a special effect that writers use when a word imitates the sound that it makes: alliteration or onomatopoeia?

2401. What words related to water might be examples of onomatopoeia?

2402. What thing might produce the onomatopoeia sound of "hiss?"

2403. What is the onomatopoeia word that is often used in literary pieces when something explodes?

2404. What words might capture the sound of bacon frying?

2405. What sound does a race car make that would be an example of onomatopoeia?

2406. What sound does a dog make that would be an example of onomatopoeia?

2407. What sound does a cat make that would be an example of onomatopoeia?

2408. What sound does a duck make that would be an example of onomatopoeia?

2409. What sound does a bird make that would be an example of onomatopoeia?

2410. What sound does a sheep make that would be an example of onomatopoeia?

2411. What sound does a frog make that would be an example of onomatopoeia?

2412. What is the literary term for the special effect used by writers and poets when several words in a row start with the same sound: personification or alliteration?

2413. What literary term is "Peter Piper picked a peck of pickled peppers" an example of?

2414. What is the literary term for the genre that is essentially a play that is acted out on a stage in a theater?

2415. What is another term for the author of a drama: a poet or a playwright?

2416. What is the name of the funny, happy play first developed by the Greeks: tragedy or comedy?

2417. What is the name of the tragic, sad play first developed by the Greeks: tragedy or comedy?

2418. What symbol did the Greeks use to stand for comedy and tragedy in drama: masks or wands?

2419. What is the name of perhaps the most famous English dramatist from the early 1600's?

2420. What was the name of the theater in London where many of William Shakespeare's plays were performed: the London Theater or the Globe Theater?

2421. Where do the famous phrases "To be or not to be," and "All's well that ends well" come from: Shakespeare's plays or Shakespeare's poems?

2422. Were Shakespeare's subtle but humorous plays, "A Midsummer Night's Dream," and "Much Ado about Nothing:" comedies or tragedies?

2423. Were Shakespeare's plays "Antony and Cleopatra," "Romeo and Juliet," "Hamlet," and "Macbeth" comedies or tragedies?

2424. What does an act in a play contain: several scenes, or several acts?

2425. What is the literary term for a 14-line poem that Shakespeare was famous for writing: a sonnet or a quatrain?

2426. Do lines in poems have to be in sentence format?

2427. Do lines in poems have to rhyme?

2428. Do different kinds of poems have different rhyme patterns, like ABAB or ABBA?

2429. Can you write a poem?

2430. Can you write a letter?

2431. What is the meaning of a salutation in a letter: a greeting or a closing?

2432. What is another word for the name and return address: a greeting or a heading?

2433. What kind of a letter would include a return address, date, casual greeting, body, closing, and signature line: a personal letter or a business letter?

2434. What kind of a letter would include a return address, date, person and title to whom the letter is being addressed, greeting, body, closing, signature line, and title: a personal letter or a business letter?

2435. Can a business letter be written in either block form or indented form?

2436. Is "Dear Mr. Smith" a greeting or a closing?

2437. Is "Sincerely" a greeting or a closing?

2438. What is a closing line on a business letter besides "Sincerely?"

2439. Do different cultures have certain sayings and phrases?

2440. Does "que sera sera" mean *what will be will be* in French or Spanish?

2441. Does "asi es la vida" mean *such is life* in French or Spanish?

2442. Does "c'est la vie" mean *such is life* in French or Spanish?

2443. Do we have several sayings and idioms in our English language?

2444. How do you finish the saying: "All for one and one for _?"

2445. How do you finish this saying: "Beauty is only skin_?"

2446. How do you finish this saying: "All's well that ends_?"

2447. How do you finish this saying: "A bird in the hand is worth two in the_?"

2448. How do you finish this saying: "Don't look a gift horse in the_?"

2449. How do you finish this saying: "A fool and his money are soon_?"

2450. How do you finish this saying: "Good fences make good_?"

2451. How do you finish this saying: "He who hesitates is_?"

2452. How do you finish this saying: "He who laughs last laughs_?"

2453. How do you finish this saying: "Money is the root of all_?"

2454. How do you finish this saying: "Necessity is the mother of _?"

2455. How do you finish this saying: "It's never over till it's_?"

2456. How do you finish this saying: "Once bitten, twice_?"

2457. How do you finish this saying: "Pot calling the kettle_?"

2458. How do you finish this saying: "The proof of the pudding is in the_?"

2459. How do you finish this saying: "Rome wasn't built in a_?"

2460. How do you finish this saying that infers a guideline: "Rule of_?"

2461. How do you finish this saying: "A stitch in time saves_?"

2462. How do you finish this saying: "Strike while the iron is_?"

2463. How do you finish this saying: "There's more than one way to skin a_?"

2464. How do you finish this saying: "Truth is stronger than_?"

2465. How do you finish the saying: "Birthday _?"

2466. How do you finish this saying: "Bite the hand that feeds_?"

2467. How do you finish this saying: "Catch forty_?"

2468. How do you finish this saying: "Chip on your_?"

2469. How do you finish this saying: "Don't count your chickens before they _?"

2470. How do you finish this saying that is an idiom for humiliation: "Eating_?"

2471. How do you finish this saying: "Every cloud has a silver_?"

2472. How do you finish this saying: "Few and far_?"

2473. How do you finish this saying: "The grass is always greener on the other_?"

2474. How do you finish this saying: "Kill two birds with one_?"

2475. How do you finish this saying: "Lock, stock, and _?"

2476. How do you finish the saying: "Make a mountain out of a _?"

2477. How do you finish this saying: "A penny saved is a penny_?"

2478. How do you finish this saying: "Read between the_?"

2479. How do you finish this saying: "Steal my_?"

2480. How do you finish this saying: "Take the bull by the_?"

2481. How do you finish this saying: "Till the cows come_?"

2482. How do you finish this saying: "Time heals all_?"

2483. How do you finish this saying: "Tom, Dick, and_?"

2484. How do you finish this saying: "Vice_?"

2485. How do you finish this saying: "A watched pot never _?"

2486. How do you finish this saying: "What will be will _?"

2487. What is the word a person might say when somebody scores a point against us in a discussion: touché or andale?

2488. Can you recognize and pronounce the common sight word "ache?" (Show word)

2489. Can you recognize and pronounce the common sight word "amphibian?" (Show word)

2490. Can you recognize and pronounce the common sight word "antique?" (Show word)

2491. Can you recognize and pronounce the common sight word "audience?" (Show word)

2492. Can you recognize and pronounce the common sight word "bawl?" (Show word)

2493. Can you recognize and pronounce the common sight word "beach?" (Show word))

2494. Can you recognize and pronounce the common sight word "biceps?" (Show word)

2495. Can you recognize and pronounce the common sight word "binoculars?" (Show word)

2496. Can you recognize and pronounce the common sight word "boarder?" (Show word)

2497. Can you recognize and pronounce the common sight word "break?" (Show word)

2498. Can you recognize and pronounce the common sight word "canoes?" (Show word)

2499. Can you recognize and pronounce the common sight word "capit<u>a</u>l?" (Show word)

2500. Can you recognize and pronounce the common sight word "capit<u>o</u>l?" (Show word)

2501. Can you recognize and pronounce the common sight word "conservation?" (Show word)

2502. Can you recognize and pronounce the common sight word "cylinder?" (Show word)

2503. Can you recognize and pronounce the common sight word "deceive?" (Show word)

2504. Can you recognize and pronounce the common sight word "decimal?" (Show word)

2505. Can you recognize and pronounce the common sight word "diagnose?" (Show word)

2506. Can you recognize and pronounce the common sight word "diagonal?" (Show word)

2507. Can you recognize and pronounce the common sight word "dialogue?" (Show word)

2508. Can you recognize and pronounce the common sight word "drought?" (Show word)

2509. Can you recognize and pronounce the common sight word "earthquake?" (Show word)

2510. Can you recognize and pronounce the common sight word "equal?" (Show word)

2511. Can you recognize and pronounce the common sight word "equator?" (Show word)

2512. Can you recognize and pronounce the common sight word "equivalent?" (Show word)

2513. Can you recognize and pronounce the common sight word "exclamation?" (Show word)

2514. Can you recognize and pronounce the common sight word "expedition?" (Show word)

2515. Can you recognize and pronounce the common sight word "expense?" (Show word)

2516. Can you recognize and pronounce the common sight word "extinguish?" (Show word)

2517. Can you recognize and pronounce the common sight word "extraordinary?" (Show word)

2518. Can you recognize and pronounce the common sight word "extrasensory?" (Show word)

2519. Can you recognize and pronounce the common sight word "extraterrestrial?" (Show word)

2520. Can you recognize and pronounce the common sight word "fir?" (Show word)

2521. Can you recognize and pronounce the common sight word "guard?" (Show word)

2522. Can you recognize and pronounce the common sight word "inquire?" (Show word)

2523. Can you recognize and pronounce the common sight word "judicial?" (Show word)

2524. Can you recognize and pronounce the common sight word "knight?" (Show word)

2525. Can you recognize and pronounce the common sight word "loose?" (Show word)

2526. Can you recognize and pronounce the common sight word "microphone?" (Show word)

2527. Can you recognize and pronounce the common sight word "mourn?" (Show word)

2528. Can you recognize and pronounce the common sight word "neighbor?" (Show word)

2529. Can you recognize and pronounce the common sight word "night?" (Show word)

2530. Can you recognize and pronounce the common sight word "paraphrase?" (Show word)

2531. Can you recognize and pronounce the common sight word "pause?" (Show word)

2532. Can you recognize and pronounce the common sight word "peace?" (Show word)

2533. Can you recognize and pronounce the common sight word "petition?" (Show word)

2534. Can you recognize and pronounce the common sight word "piece?" (Show word)

2535. Can you recognize and pronounce the common sight word "pour?" (Show word)

2536. Can you recognize and pronounce the common sight word "preamble?" (Show word)

2537. Can you recognize and pronounce the common sight word "prejudice?" (Show word)

2538. Can you recognize and pronounce the common sight word "prospector?" (Show word)

2539. Can you recognize and pronounce the common sight word "punctuation?" (Show word)

2540. Can you recognize and pronounce the common sight word "usually?" (Show word)

2541. Can you recognize and pronounce the common sight word "quail?" (Show word)

2542. Can you recognize and pronounce the common sight word "qualify?" (Show word)

2543. Can you recognize and pronounce the common sight word "quality?" (Show word)

2544. Can you recognize and pronounce the common sight word "quantity?" (Show word)

2545. Can you recognize and pronounce the common sight word "quarrel?" (Show word)

2546. Can you recognize and pronounce the common sight word "quiet?" (Show word)

2547. Can you recognize and pronounce the common sight word "quite?" (Show word)

2548. Can you recognize and pronounce the common sight word "quotation?" (Show word)

2549. Can you recognize and pronounce the common sight word "quotient?" (Show word)

2550. Can you recognize and pronounce the common sight word "request?" (Show word)

2551. Can you recognize and pronounce the common sight word "retract?" (Show word)

2552. Can you recognize and pronounce the common sight word "route?" (Show word)

2553. Can you recognize and pronounce the common sight word "sequence?" (Show word)

2554. Can you recognize and pronounce the common sight word "sketch?" (Show word)

2555. Can you recognize and pronounce the common sight word "sleigh?" (Show word)

2556. Can you recognize and pronounce the common sight word "surround?" (Show word)

2557. Can you recognize and pronounce the common sight word "thermometer?" (Show word)

2558. Can you recognize and pronounce the common sight word "toe?" (Show word)

2559. Can you recognize and pronounce the common sight word "unique?" (Show word)

2560. Can you recognize and pronounce the common sight word "vertebrates?" (Show word)

2561. Can you recognize and pronounce the common sight word "veto?" (Show word)

2562. Can you recognize and pronounce the common sight word "wade?" (Show word)

2563. Can you recognize and pronounce the common sight word "weighed?" (Show word)

2564. Can you recognize and pronounce the common sight word "whether?" (Show word)

2565. Can you recognize and pronounce the common sight word "view?" (Show word)

2566. Can you recognize and pronounce the common sight word "whole?" (Show word)

2567. What is the literary term for an alternate name or pseudonym adopted by an author for various reasons: a pen name or an alias?

2568. Do most writers publish works using their own name or a pen name?

2569. What is the pen name of Samuel Clemens author of "The Adventures of Tom Sawyer:" Mark Twain or Huckleberry Finn?

2570. What was the pen name of Theodor Geisel, the author of "Green Eggs and Ham," and "The Cat in the Hat:" Dr. Seuss or Mr. Grinch?

2571. What is the name of the best-selling book of all time written in two parts, and contains chapters and verses that have been translated into more than 1200 languages?

2572. What is the term for exemplary novels that have stood the test of time, and serve as literary models in American, British, and World literature: classics or bestsellers?

Chapter 2 – Notable Literary Works Through the Ages

1. What is the name of the ancient Greek epic poem written in approximately 800 BC by Homer that relates the battles and events during the ten-year Trojan War between Greece and Troy: "The I_?"

2. What is the name of the ancient Greek epic poem written around 800 BC by Homer that centers on the challenges facing the Greek warrior Odysseus after the fall of Troy, and his quest to return home and reestablish himself as King: "The O_?"

3. What is the name of the author and Greek storyteller of a collection of over 650 fables from 600 BC that often involve animals, and in the end teach a moral or lesson: Aesop or Hans Christian Anderson?

4. What is the name of Aesop's fable number 87 that tells a story of a goose that magically creates something gold and teaches the moral, *being greedy never pays*: "The Goose that Laid the __?

5. What is the name of Aesop's fable number 147 about two animals that attack another animal and collapse from being worn out, as another animal watching the action *grabs* this animal and runs off with it thus teaching the moral, *one might have all the work but another all the profit:* "The Lion, the Bear, and the _?"

6. What is the name of Aesop's fable number 150 that tells the story of one large animal and a much smaller one and teaches the moral, *little friends may prove to be great friends*: "The Lion and the _?"

7. What is the name of Aesop's fable number 210 that tells the story of a shepherd boy named Peter who repeatedly tricks the people of his village by convincing them that his sheep are being attacked by a dog-like animal, until one day this animal really does attack and eats his flock after his calls for help go unnoticed thus teaching the moral, *asking for help when one does not need it may result in others not believing you when you really do need it:* "The Boy Who Cried _?"

8. What is the name of Aesop's fable number 226 that centers on a turtle that challenges a rabbit to a race that teaches the moral, *slow and steady wins the race*: "The Tortoise and the _?"

9. What is the name of Aesop's fable number 352 about two rodent cousins that go to visit each that try to convince each other that its place to live is better than the others, thus teaching the moral, *better a little in safety than in abundance surrounded by danger*: "The Town Mouse and the Country _?"

10. What is the name of Aesop's fable number 373 about two insects, one of whom sings away the summer, while the other works hard to store food for the winter, thus teaching the moral, *it is best to prepare for the days of necessity*: "The Ant and the _?"

11. What is the name of Aesop's fable number 563 about a slave who escaped from his master and hid out in a cave that turned out to be an animal's den, pulled a thorn from this animal's paw, was shown

gratitude and friendship by this animal, was then captured by his former master but then set free when this animal refused to attack him in an open arena, thus teaching the moral, *gratitude is the sign of noble souls*: "Androcles and the _?"

12. What is the title of the Greek tragedy written by Euripides first performed in Athens in 425 BC, dramatizing the life of a slave named Andromache and her relationship with Hermoine, the wife of her master: "A_?"

13. What is the name of the Greek tragedy written by Sophocles and first performed in 429 BC and tells the life of a man named Oedipus and his path to become king of Thebes: "Oedipus the _?"

14. What is the name of the Latin epic poem from 19 BC written by Virgil that tells the story of how the Trojan Aeneas who traveled to Italy and essentially founded Rome: "The A_?"

15. What is the name of the epic Anglo-Saxon poem guessed to have existed in the year 1000, about a Scandinavian hero who fights the demon Grendel in a wrestling match: "B_?"

16. What is the name of the 1215 political charter, drafted by the powerful barons of England and signed by King John, that outlined the political and civil liberties of all classes, served to limit the powers of the King, and provided the foundation for the British constitution and English citizen's rights: "The Magna _?"

17. What is the name of 1475 collection of short stories by English author Geoffrey Chaucer, written during the Hundred Years War, that aim to showcase English society and the church as told by 29 pilgrims on their journey to a shrine in Canterbury: "The Canterbury _?"

18. What is the Latin name of the Latin narrative poem by the Roman poet Ovid, first published in English in 1498 and also called "Books of Transformations," that outlines the history of the world since its creation to the anointing of Julius Caesar: "M_?"

19. What is the title of the 1532 book by the Italian historian Niccolo Machiavelli, the most translated book from the Italian language, that serves as a guide for ruling a kingdom, attaining political power, establishing principalities, the qualities of a strong leader, and provides a perspective on what constitutes a strong Italian leader: "The P_?"

20. What is the name of the epic poem written by Italian author Dante Alighieri in 1555 about the soul's journey toward God, and the afterlife: "The Divine _?"

21. What is the title of the 1597 tragedy by William Shakespeare that centers on two feuding families in Verona, the Montagues and the Capulets, and the two main characters that are prevented from declaring their love for one another, ending tragically for both characters: "Romeo and _?"

22. What is the title of the 1599 tragedy by William Shakespeare with the famous speech by Marc Antony in Act 3, Scene 2 that begins with the often quoted opening line, "Friends, Romans, Countrymen, lend me your ears: "Julius _?

23. What is the title of the 1603 Greek tragedy by William Shakespeare, his longest play and still one of

the most-performed even today, set in Denmark, and tells the story of a Prince who takes revenge on his uncle Claudius for murdering his father, the King: "H_?"

24. What is the title of the 1603 tragedy by William Shakespeare that is based on an Italian story called "A Moorish Captain," and centers on a Moorish general in the Venetian army, his wife Desdemona, his lieutenant Cassio, and his infantry officer Lago, and has been adapted for film and opera: "O_?"

25. What is the name of the 1605 novel by Miguel de Cervantes about an idealist knight and his realist companion Sancho Panza and their adventures in Spain on a horse and a donkey: "Don Quixote de la _?"

26. What is the title of the 1606 tragedy written by English author William Shakespeare about an aging King who is left to divide up his kingdom among his three daughters, is ultimately betrayed by two of them, leaving the future of the kingdom in great jeopardy: "King _?"

27. What is the famous opening line of the English poet William Shakespeare's Sonnet 18, first published in 1609 as part of a collection of 154 sonnets that starts with the author comparing someone he loves to the summer season, declaring that *thou art more lovely*: "Shall I Compare Thee to a Summer's _?"

28. What is the name of the collection of books representing both Christianity and Judaism, has been translated into more than 500 languages, has a Christian version that includes the Old Testament and the New Testament, has a Hebrew version that is regarded as the sacred book of Judaism, was first published in English as the version of King James, and first printed on the Gutenberg press: "The _?"

29. What is the name of the first five books of the Hebrew Scriptures: "The Old Testament" or "The Torah?"

30. What is the name of the poem contained in William Shakespeare's comedy play *As You Like It*, first published in 1623, that gets its name from the first line in the poem: All the World's a _?"

31. What is the name of the poem first published in 1639 by Walt Whitman as part of his Holy Sonnets where the author argues against the power of death and in the end, suggests that death itself will die: "Death Be Not _?"

32. What is the name of the 1667 epic poem by John Milton, filling ten books and having over ten thousand lines, that centers on the Biblical account of the fall of man and the temptation of Adam and Eve: "Paradise _?"

33. What is the title of the 1678 Christian novel by Paul Bunyan written while the author was in prison, that follows a man named Christian and his religious journey from this world to heaven, the Celestial City: "The Pilgrim's _?"

34. What is the name of the 1697 French fairy tale by Charles Perrault about a tom cat who earns power, wealth, and a princess through trickery, ending up as a lord of his own kingdom: "Puss in _?"

35. What is the name of the 1697 French fairy tale by Charles Perrault about a little girl in a red coat who meets a wolf in the forest on her way to her grandmother's cottage, and is later saved by a lumberjack after the wolf disguises himself as her grandmother: "Little Red Riding _?"

36. What is the other name of the 1706 collection of 42 Asian folk stories first compiled in Arabic entitled "Arabian Nights," and include *Aladdin and the Wonderful Lamp* and *Ali-Baba and the Forty Thieves*: One Thousand and One _?"

37. What is the full title of the 1719 fictional autobiography by William Defoe about a castaway who lives on a remote tropical island near Trinidad for 28 years and his island confrontations before he is finally rescued: "Robinson _?

38. What is the full title of the 1726 novel by Irish author Jonathan Swift about the voyages and discoveries of the protagonist as he travels to several remote nations of the world, and is a satire on human nature: "Gulliver's _?

39. What is the full title of the 1729 novel by Charles Perrault that is a collection of literary fairy tales: "Tales of Mother _?

40. What is the name of the 1755 British nursery rhyme about a house that is connected to other people and other things, and shows how all these things are connected together in this progressively-told rhyme: "This is the House that Jack _?"

41. What is the full title of the 1757 fairy tale adaptation by Jeanne-Marie Le Prince de Beaumont about a girl named Belle who is obligated as part of a deal to live with a monster in a castle, leaves for a week, and sheds tears to find him near death upon her return to the castle, tears that transform him from a monster to a handsome prince: "Beauty and the _?"

42. What is the name of the 1775 speech by Patrick Henry to the Virginia Convention telling the colonists that the Revolutionary War had begun, and calling for arms and the support of all: "Give Me Liberty or Give Me _?"

43. What is the title of pamphlet written in the summer of 1776 by Thomas Paine, written in plain and simple English that served as the inspiration and motivation for the people of the Thirteen Colonies to declare and fight for their independence from Great Britain: "Common _?"

44. What is the name of the official 1776 document, drafted by Thomas Jefferson along with John Adams and Benjamin Franklin, signed by 56 members including John Hancock, was presented to the Continental Congress in Philadelphia, officially adopted on July 4, 1776, and served to explain why the colonies were choosing to separate themselves from Great Britain: The Declaration of _?"

45. What is the name of the 1794 poem by the Scottish writer William Blake about the beauty of a wild striped beast that is both beautiful and ferocious at the same time: "The T_?"

46. What is the name of the poem by the Scottish author Robert Burns in 1794 based on song of the same name, comparing the writer's love for a lady to a red flower that symbolizes love: "A Red, Red _?"

47. What is the name of the 1807 English fairy tale as told by Benjamin Tabart, about a young boy who plants a magic bean that grows to the sky, and when the boy climbs up the stalk, he meets a giant who greets him with the words *fee-fi-fo-fum*: "Jack and the _?"

48. What is the name of the 1807 poem by William Wordsworth about a cluster of lovely yellow spring

flowers growing alongside a lake in the English countryside, that the author admired while out on a walk with his sister Dorothy: "D_?"

49. What is the title of the 1808 tragic play by Johann Wolfgang Goethe, based on a German legend, and tells the story of a man and his quest to find true meaning and harmony in life and with nature: "F_?"

50. What is the title of the 1811 romance novel by Jane Austen set in London during the years between 1792 and 1797 that centers on the lives and romantic relationships of sisters Elinor and Marianne Dashwood: "Sense and _?"

51. What is the full title of the 1812 novel by Johann Rudolf Wyss about a family that is shipwrecked in the East Indies en route to Australia, and build a raft and a tree house during their stay on the island: "The Swiss Family _?

52. What is the name of the German authors of a collection of fairy tales published in 1812 that include the classics *Cinderella, Sleeping Beauty, Rapunzel, Hansel and Gretel, Snow White, Rumpelstiltskin, Little Red Riding Hood, and The Golden Goose*: the Grimm brothers or the Anderson brothers?

53. What is the title of the 1813 novel by Jane Austen that centers on the lives of five sisters, Jane, Elizabeth, Mary, Kitty, and Lydia Bennett in rural 19th-century England, and how their lives are affected when a wealthy man named Mr. Bingley and his friend Darcy arrive in town: "Pride and _?"

54. What is the title of the 1814 lyric poem written by Lord Byron about an elegant, beautiful lady: "She Walks in _?"

55. What is the name of the 1815 novel by Jane Austen and tells the story of a young, spoiled English woman, and the effects of her matchmaking and meddling in others' affairs: "E_?"

56. What is the name of the 1818 horror novel by Mary Shelley about a mad scientist who creates a monster while conducting a laboratory experiment: "Franken_?"

57. What is the name of the 1819 satiric poem by Lord Byron that is based on the legend of a Spanish nobleman that is easily distracted by all the women he meets: "Don _?"

58. What is the full title of the 1820 novel by Washington Irving that tells the tale of Ichabod Crane and includes a ghost that appears as a Headless Horseman: "The Legend of Sleepy _?"

59. What is the full title of the 1820 novel by Washington Irving about a man who lived near the Catskill Mountains who wandered off one day and slept for twenty years: "Rip Van _?"

60. What is the name of the historical novel from 1820 by Sir Walter Scott that portrays the tensions between the Saxons and the Normans in England during the reign of King Richard I: "Ivan_?"

61. What is the name of the 1820 poem by John Keats one of Keats's *1819 odes*, inspired by the beautiful colors he noticed while on a walk one fall evening in Winchester, England: "Ode to _?"

62. What is the name of the 1820 poem by John Keats where the author appears to be interested in the timeless drawings on a piece of classical Greek art, as well as what those pictures, forever imprinted in stone, represent: "Ode on a Grecian _?"

63. What is the full title of the 1823 collection by Jacob and Wilhelm Grimm that include "Snow White" and "Hansel and Gretel:" Grimm's Fairy _?"

64. What is the full title of the 1826 historical novel by James Fenimore Cooper that is set during the Seven Years War when France and Great Britain were battling for control over North America the Native American allies that helped the French, and provides a convincing portrayal of a disappearing race and way of life: "The Last of the _?"

65. What is the full title of the 1831 French Gothic novel by Victor Hugo that tells the story of Quasimodo, a deformed hunchback and bell-ringer at Notre Dame Cathedral in Paris, who falls in love with the gypsy Esmeralda, and is forever at odds with his adoptive father Claude Frollo, the Archdeacon of Notre Dame: "The Hunchback of Notre _?"

66. What is the full title of the 1837 fairy tale by Robert Southey about a young blond girl who stumbles upon a cottage belonging to a family of bears: "Goldilocks and the Three _?"

67. What is the full title of the 1837 tale by Hans Christian Anderson about two weavers to promise a new set of clothes to an Emperor that are invisible to all those unfit for their positions, and is being complimented by all the citizens at a procession before an innocent child comments that he is not wearing *any* clothing: "The Emperor's New __?"

68. What is the full title of the 1838 novel by Charles Dickens about a young orphan boy who unknowingly finds himself in London involved with pickpockets and other criminals, but rises above that life of corruption: "Oliver _?"

69. What is the name of the 1842 short story by Edgar Allan Poe that tells the story of Prince Prospero who hides in a walled abbey in order to escape a dangerous plague, holds a masquerade party with seven colored rooms, and in the end meets his fate when he encounters a mysterious masked figure in the scarlet room: "The Masque of the Red _?"

70. What is the name of the 1842 story by Edgar Allan Poe about a man who is taken prisoner during the Spanish Inquisition and his attempts to survive both a fire pit and an approaching swinging object hanging above him: "The Pit and the _?"

71. What is the name of the 1843 story by Edgar Allan Poe about the narrator who tries to convince the reader that his murder of an old man was justified, how he hid him under the floorboards of his house, and how his guilt got the better of him when he heard the heartbeat of his victim through those floorboards: "The Tell-Tale _?"

72. What is the full title of the 1843 novel by Charles Dickens that tells of the transformation of Ebenezer Scrooge after he is visited by the Ghosts of Christmas past, present, and yet to come: "A Christmas _?"

73. What is the full title of the 1843 literary tale by the Danish author Hans Christian Anderson about a homely little barnyard bird that withstands the ridicule of others, endures some challenges along the way, and is finally accepted by a flock after it transforms into a beautiful swan: "The Ugly _?"

74. What is the full title of the 1844 novel by Alexandre Dumas that is set in France, and tells of the

adventures of d'Artagnan after he travels to Paris to join the Guard, and his three friends Athos, Porthos, and Aramis who are bonded with the motto, *all for one, one for all*: "The Three _?"

75. What is the full title of the 1845 novel by Alexandre Dumas about a man who goes to prison, escapes, and goes after those who wrongfully put him in prison: "The Count of Monte _?"

76. What is the name of the 1845 narrative poem by Edgar Allan Poe about a man who is sad about the loss of his love Lenore, who receives a visit one night from a talking black bird that replies *"nevermore"* when he asks the bird when he will see her again: "The R_?"

77. What is the name of the 1845 short story by the Danish author Hans Christian Anderson about a poor, dying girl who tries to sell matches one New Year's Eve, uses the matches to keep herself warm, sees visions of her grandmother in heaven as she lights each match, and in the end, her soul rises to join her grandmother: "The Little Match _?"

78. What is the full title of the 1846 collection by Danish author Hans Christian Anderson that include "The Princess and the Pea;" "The Little Mermaid;" and "The Emperor's New Clothes:" "Fairy _?"

79. What is the name of the 1846 short story by Edgar Allan Poe about the narrator Montressor who tells how he took revenge on his friend Fortunado who had insulted him, by tricking him to go down to the wine cellar of an Italian palazzo to try a fine vintage of wine called Amontillado, and then traps him in a niche: "The Cask of _?"

80. What is the name of the 1847 novel by William Makepeace Thackeray that makes fun of the society in 19th century Britain, centering on themes of love and fortune as it follows the adventures of Amelia Sedley and Becky Sharp: "Vanity _?"

81. What is the name of the 1847 novel by Charlotte Bronte about the title character living in England from her childhood as an orphan, her education, her time as a governess, and her marriage to Rochester: "Jane _?"

82. What is the name of the 1847 novel by Emily Bronte about the love between Catherine Earnshaw and Heathcliff, and how their unresolved love destroys them and those around them: "Wuthering _?"

83. What is the name of the short 1848 publication by Karl Marx and Friedrich Engels, regarded as one of the world's most important political documents, that outlines the actions necessary for replacing a capitalist society with a Communist one, and asserts that only a revolution would be effective in eliminating all social classes: "Communist _?"

84. What is the full title of the 1850 novel by Charles Dickens that traces the life of a young boy who escapes an unhappy childhood in England to his adventures as an adult, his marriage, and his life as a successful author: "David _?"

85. What are the famous first lines from sonnet number 43 by Elizabeth Barrett Browning, published in 1850 as a collection of 44 love sonnets: "How do I love thee? Let me count the _?"

86. What is the name of the 1850 novel by Nathanial Hawthorne set in Puritan Boston, Massachusetts, that tells the story of Hester Prynne who committed a great sin, the red symbol she must now wear on her

dress for all to see as a reminder of her sin, and how she struggles to rise above it and her shame: "The Scarlet _?"

87. What is the name of the 1851 novel by Herman Melville that tells the story of Captain Ahab and his crew, and his pursuit of a ferocious great white whale that had destroyed his ship on a previous voyage off the coast of Japan, and begins with the line, *Call Me Ishmael*: "Moby _?"

88. What is the title of the 1851 romance novel by Nathaniel Hawthorne about the Pyncheon family living in a gabled house in New England that has served to provide mystery and intrigue for many generations: The House of the Seven _?"

89. What is the full title of the 1851 speech given by civil rights activist Sojourner Truth at the Women's Convention in Ohio, named for the line that she repeated throughout the speech: "Ain't I A _?"

90. What is the full title of the 1852 speech given by abolitionist Frederick Douglass to the citizens of Rochester, New York on the Fourth of July, who criticized the nation for celebrating freedom while nearly four million people were still working as slaves: "The Hypocrisy of American _?"

91. What is the title of the 1852 anti-slavery novel by abolitionist and writer Harriet Beecher Stowe, regarded as instrumental in promoting the anti-slavery movement leading to the American Civil War that depicts the life of a black slave as the *Uncle Tom*, a character portrayed as someone who is a dutiful servant to his master: "Uncle Tom's _?"

92. What is the title of the 1854 autobiography by Henry David Thoreau that is reflection of a man who immerses himself in nature, and comes to appreciate the simple things in his natural surroundings while living in a cabin near Walden pond for one year: "Walden: Life in the _?"

93. What is the name of the 1855 collection of over 400 poems by Walt Whitman that included *Song of Myself,* one of the original twelve poems in the first edition, and *I Hear America Singing*, included in one of the later editions: "Leaves of _?"

94. What is the full title of the 1856 novel by French writer Gustave Flaubert that tells the story of a doctor's wife, Emma Bovary, a romantic soul, who has grown bored with her dull life and so turns to the company of others to find fulfillment in her otherwise empty life: "Madame _?"

95. What is the full title of the 1859 novel by Charles Dickens that depicts the lives of the lower class peasantry and the upper class aristocracy in both Paris and London right before the French Revolution: "A Tale of Two __?"

96. What is the rest of the opening line of the 1859 Charles Dickens novel "A Tale of Two Cities:" *"It was the best of times, it was the _?"*

97. What is the name of the 1861 poem written by American poet Henry Wadsworth Longfellow, that celebrates the famous horseback journey of 1775 by American patriot Paul Revere from Boston to Lexington to warn Samuel Adams and John Hancock of a British attack, after leaving a code for the Sons of Liberty that lanterns were to be placed in the bell tower of the Old North Church, *one if by land, and two if by sea*: "Paul Revere's _?"

98. What is the full title of the 1861 novel by Charles Dickens that tells the story of an orphaned boy named Pip and the Blacksmith's family that adopts him: "Great _?"

99. What is the title of the 1862 French historical novel by Victor Hugo set during a time of political unrest in Paris, that centers on the character Jean Valjean who is imprisoned for 19 years for stealing a loaf of bread, his life on the run from a police inspector who is pursuing him, the young, motherless girl Cosette he befriends, and his continuous struggle to fit in to society as an ex-convict and attain redemption: "Les _?"

100. What is the name of the 1863 speech delivered by President Abraham Lincoln during the Civil War when he referred to the Declaration of Independence with the opening line of his speech with his words *"Four score and seven years ago:"* "The Gettysburg __?"

101. What is title of the 1865 novel by Lewis Carroll that follows the adventures of a seven-year old girl and the new world she finds herself in after falling down a rabbit hole: "Alice's Adventures in _?"

102. What is the name of the 1865 poem by Walt Whitman written as a tribute to Abraham Lincoln after his death, honoring an American President with whom Whitman shared his opposition to slavery, and his commitment to the Union: "O Captain, My _?"

103. What is the name of the 1866 novel by Russian author Fyodor Dostoyevsky and set in St. Petersburg Russia, that centers around an ex-student named Raskolnikov who plots to kill a pawnbroker for the cash, believing all along that he can justify the murder with all the good deeds he will carry out with the money, but in the end is persuaded to confess his terrible crime: "Crime and _?"

104. What is the full title of the 1868 novel by Louisa May Alcott that follows the lives of four sisters, Meg, Jo, Amy, and Beth as they mature through life, and their struggle with poverty: "Little _?"

105. What is the name of the 1869 epic novel by the Russian author Leo Tolstoy that provides an overview of the events of the 1812 French invasion of Russia under Napoleon, includes insights to the war from the perspective of five aristocratic Russian families, but illustrates the effects of the war on *all* classes of society: "War and _?"

106. What is the full title of the 1870 novel by Jules Verne that relates the adventures of Captain Nemo and his submarine Nautilus: "Twenty Thousand Leagues Under the _?"

107. What is the full title of the 1871 novel by Lewis Carroll that continues the adventures of Alice and her life compared to chess game after she looks into a mirror above the fireplace mantel: "Through the Looking _?"

108. What is the name of the 1871 nonsense poem by Lewis Carroll in his novel "Through the Looking Glass" about a boy who takes his sword and sets out to kill creatures in the woods, succeeds in killing one, and brings the head back for his dad to see: "Jabber_?"

109. What is the full title of the 1873 adventure novel by Jules Verne about an Englishman named Phileas Fogg and his French servant who makes a bet with his fellow club members that he can circle the Earth in a certain amount of days: "Around the World in 80 _?"

110. What is the name of the 1873 speech by Susan B. Anthony after being fined one hundred dollars for casting an illegal ballot in the 1872 presidential election: "Women's Right to the _?"

111. What is the full title of the 1876 novel by Mark Twain about a mischievous, young boy and his adventures growing up near the Mississippi River: The Adventures of Tom _?"

112. What is the full title of the 1877 autobiographical memoir by English author Anna Sewell, narrated from the perspective of a horse from the time he was a carefree colt on an English farm to his hard life pulling cabs in London, to his happy retirement in the country, and reveals how he was treated by several different masters over the course of his life: "Black _?"

113. What is the full title of the 1877 novel by Russian author Leo Tolstoy set in 19th century Russia about a woman named Anna who is miserable and bored in her marriage, and so begins a friendship with the Count Vronsky: "Anna K_?"

114. What is the full title of the 1879 three-act play by Norwegian playwright Henrik Ibsen about a housewife named Nora Helmer who becomes disillusioned with her husband Torvald, who merely regards her as his *little caged song bird*: "A Doll's _?"

115. What is the name of the 1880 novel by Johanna Spyri about a young girl raised by her grandfather in the Swiss Alps of Switzerland? "H_?"

116. What is the full title of the 1880 novel by Lew Wallace that relates the adventures of the Jewish prince of Jerusalem Judah Ben-Hur, and his choice to convert to Christianity after realizing that he is wrong in wanting to seek revenge on his childhood friend Messala, who had wrongly imprisoned he and his family: "Ben-Hur: A Tale of the _?"

117. What is the full title of the 1881 novel by American author Mark Twain that tells the story of commoner Tom Canty who lives with his father in London, and Prince Edward, the son of King Henry VIII, who decide to switch clothes one day, and how each experiences the life of the other for a time before resuming their rightful places: "The Prince and the _?"

118. What is the title of the 1881 novel by Henry James that tells the story of an American woman named Isabel Archer who inherits a lot of money, travels to Europe to find herself, marries an artist named Gilbert Osmond who does not truly love her, and in the end finds some solace when she is able to reconnect with her cousin and her soul mate Ralph: "The Portrait of a _?"

119. What is the full title of the 1883 novel by Italian author Carlo Collodi, about an animated marionette carved by a wood carver named Geppetto, and the nose that grows when the puppet tells a lie: "The Adventures of _?

120. What is the full title of the 1883 novel by Howard Pyle about an English outlaw and his men who rob from the rich and give to the poor: "The Merry Adventures of Robin _?"

121. What is the full title of the 1883 novel by Scottish author Robert Lewis Stevenson, that relates the tale of sailor Jim Hawkins who is drawn to the world of pirates when he finds Captain Flint's map in a chest, and competes with Long John Silver to be the first to find the valuable booty on Skeleton Island in the West Indies: "Treasure __?"

122. What is the name of the poem by Ella Wheeler Wilcox first published in 1883 in "The New York Sun," that was inspired when the author empathized with the loneliness of a sorrowful widow, with the opening lines, *laugh, and the world laughs with you, weep, and you weep alone*: "S_?"

123. What is the full title of the 1884 novel by Mark Twain that relates the adventures of the main character and his friend Jim, a runaway slave, as they journey on a raft along the Mississippi River: "The Adventures of Huckleberry _?"

124. What is the title of the 1884 short story by French author Guy de Maupassant about how the lives of Madame Mathilde Loisel and her husband who borrow a precious piece of jewelry for a social event, lose the piece of jewelry, and for years after try to raise the several thousand French francs necessary to replace it, only to find out that this lost piece of jewelry was a paste imitation: "The N_?"

125. What is the full title of the 1885 adventure novel by H. Ryder Haggard about an African adventurer, Allen Quartermain, who leads a dangerous expedition in his quest to locate a lost treasure: "King Solomon's _?"

126. What is the name of the 1885 poem by Robert Louis Stevenson from the collection "A Child's Garden of Verses," about a about a child's interest in the dark image created by the sound that follows him around: "The S _?"

127. What is the full title of the 1886 adventure novel by Robert Louis Stevenson about David Belfour and his adventures as he sets out to claim his rightful inheritance, and escape an uncle who is plotting to cheat him out of it: "Kid_?"

128. What is the title of the 1886 novella by Leo Tolstoy that tells the story of the death of a court justice named Ivan in 19th century Russia, the illness that slowly led to his slow and painful death, how he looks back on his life with regret, the greed and personal gain that consume the thoughts of his family and friends, and how in the end, he experiences acceptance and peace as he leaves one world for another: "The Death of Ivan _?"

129. What is the title of the 1892 collection of twelve short stories by Arthur Conan Doyle featuring a detective named Sherlock and his faithful assistant Dr. Watson: "The Adventures of Sherlock _?"

130. What is the full title of the 1894 by Rudyard Kipling that is a collection of fables using animals to tell a story and to teach a lesson: "The Jungle _?"

131. What is the full title of the 1895 war novel by Stephen Crane, set during the American Civil War that centers on Henry Fleming, a private in the Union Army who flees from battle in the field, but later seeks to be wounded as proof of his bravery, and to cover up his cowardice: "The Red Badge of _?"

132. What is the full title of the 1898 science fiction novel by H.G. Wells that tells of the adventures of an un-named protagonist, his brother Surray, and life on Earth after it has been invaded by Martians: "The War of the _?"

133. What is the name of the 1899 short novel by Joseph Conrad that centers on the life of ivory transporter Charles Marlow and his journey down the Congo River in Africa, his search for a man named Kurtz,

the corruption of the trading company at different stations in the dense jungle of the Congo, and the mistreatment of the native people in the pursuit of the valuable ivory: "Heart of _?"

134. What is the full title of the 1900 novel by F. Frank Baum about a girl name Dorothy who makes friends with a scarecrow, a tin man, and a cowardly lion as she tries to find her way back home to Kansas along a yellow brick road, but has a wicked witch from the West in her way: "The Wonderful Wizard of _?"

135. What is the title of the 1900 novel by Joseph Conrad that tells the story of a British seaman named Jim, a man who struggles to come to terms with his past because he had abandoned his ship called the Patna, and his navigation privilege is taken away from him: "Lord _?"

136. What is the name of the 1901 autobiography of Booker T. Washington that relates his experiences as a young slave during the Civil War, the challenges he faced in getting an education, and his goal to establish vocational schools for aspiring African-Americans like the Tuskegee Institute in Alabama he founded: "Up From _?"

137. What is the full title of the 1902 novel by Beatrix Potter about a curious bunny that tries over and over to sneak into Mr. McGregor's vegetable garden: "The Tale of Peter _?"

138. What is the name of the 1902 novel by Scottish author J.M. Barrie about the adventures of a boy who never ages and can fly on the small island of Neverland, his best fairy friend Tinkerbell, and his interactions with mermaids, fairies, pirates, Native Americans, and children: "Peter _?"

139. What is the full title of the 1902 horror short story by W.W. Jacobs tells the tale of how a family friend introduces the White family to the powers of a part of a monkey that can grant its owner three wishes, but those wishes may come at a high price: "The Monkey's _?"

140. What is the name of the short story in the "Just So Stories" collection published in 1902 by Rudyard Kipling, about a leopard named Sheldon and how he got the markings on his body: "How the Leopard Got His _?"

141. What is the full title of the 1903 autobiography by the deaf and blind writer Helen Keller that tells the story of her early life and her relationship with her teacher Anne Sullivan: "Helen Keller: The Story of My _?"

142. What is the full title of the 1903 novel by Howard Pyle about an English King, a lady named Guinevere, and several knights that include Sir Lancelot: "King Arthur and his Knights of the Round _?

143. What is the full title of the 1903 children's novel by Kate Douglas Wiggin about Rebecca Randall, one of seven children, who is sent to live with her two strict aunts on an English farm, and ultimately inherits the land and farm from her aunts and is able to help support the Randall family: "Rebecca of Sunnybrook _?"

144. What is the full title of the 1903 novel by Jack London about a dog named Buck that is stolen from his domestic home in California, sent to Yukon Territory, Canada to work as a sled dog during the 19th century Gold Rush, and has to learn how to survive the harsh Canadian wilderness: "The Call of the _?"

145. What is the full title of the 1905 historical novel by Baroness Emma Orczy set during the French Revolution in which an English aristocrat enters France and tries to save innocent people from certain death, and leaves a leaves a red flower behind as his calling card: "The Scarlet _?"

146. What is the full title of the 1906 novel by Jack London, set in Yukon Territory, Canada during the Klondike Gold Rush, about a wild wolf-dog that is raised to be vicious, is later tamed by a gold-hunter named Scott, and eventually becomes a domesticated dog: "White _?

147. What is the name of the 1906 novel by American author and politician Upton Sinclair that portrays the lives and of immigrants in the United States, and touches on themes of social inequality, poverty, corruption, and poor working conditions and wages: "The J_?"

148. What is the name of the 1906 short story written by O. Henry about a young English couple who have very little money at Christmas time, so the lady sells her long tresses to buy her husband a chain for his grandfather's watch, and the husband sells his pocket watch to buy beautiful combs for his wife: "The Gift of the _?"

149. What is the name of the 1907 fantasy novel by Edith Nesbit about three children, Jerry, Jimmy, and Cathy, who discover a tunnel that leads them to a fairy-tale castle, a princess, and the magical powers of a ring they find inside the castle: "The Enchanted _?"

150. What is the full title of the 1908 novel by Canadian author Lucy Maud Montgomery about a red-haired orphan girl named Anne Shirley that is sent to live with a family on a farm on Prince Edward Island, and how she charms the lives of everyone she meets there: "Anne of Green _?"

151. What is the title of the 1908 novel by Kenneth Grahame about the friendship of a mole, a rat, a toad, and a badger, and their adventures near a river in the English countryside: "The Wind and the _?"

152. What is the title of the 1908 novel by English author E. M. Forster that tells the story of a girl named Lucy Honeychurch who is courted by an English man named George Emerson whom she meets while staying at a pension with her cousin that overlooks a courtyard in Italy, and must choose between this man whom she truly loves and her prim and proper fiancée named Cecil back in England: "A Room With a _?"

153. What is the name of the 1908 short story by Jack London about a man and his husky who brave the bitter, winter cold while on the Yukon trail in Alaska, goes to great lengths to save himself and his dog from frostbite and hypothermia, and struggles to escape his imminent death by building something to warm them: "To Build a _?"

154. What is the name of the poem by Rudyard Kipling published in 1910 essentially giving advice and motivation to his son John: "I_?"

155. What is the full title of the 1911 novel by Frances Hodgson Burnett about an orphaned British girl born in India, who returns to England to live with her wealthy uncle in a castle, and the magical things that take place after she works to bring the neglected yard back to life: "The Secret _?"

156. What is the title of the 1912 play by George Bernard Shaw that is named for a Greek character, tells the story of professor Henry Higgins who makes a bet that he can train a flower girl named Eliza

Doolittle to pretend she is a duchess at an ambassador's garden party, and was the inspiration for the 1956 musical, *My Fair Lady*: "P_?"

157. What is the full title of the 1913 novel by Eleanor H. Porter about an orphan girl who goes to live in Vermont with her wealthy but strict aunt, and manages to transform the entire town to a happy place through her sunny disposition and "The Glad Game:" "Polly_?"

158. What is the name of the 1916 four stanza poem written by Robert Frost with the famous final lines, *I took the one less traveled by, and that has made all the difference*: "The Road Not _?"

159. What is the name of the 1916 novel by Irish author James Joyce that tells the story of Stephan Dedalus growing up in Ireland, from the time he was a young boy to his young adult life trying to fit it in while in college, and his decision to leave Ireland to become an artist: "A Portrait of the Artist as a Young _?"

160. What is the full title of the 1920 novel by Hugh Lofting about a poor country doctor from England who learns to talk to animals with the help of his parrot Polynesia, travels to Africa to help sick monkeys, acquires some treasures from a pirate ship on his way home, and is able to retire with his earnings from his animals in a travelling circus: "Doctor _?"

161. What is the title of the 1922 novel by Irish author James Joyce that is set in Dublin, Ireland, follows the paths of the two main characters over the course of one day on June 16, 1907, a middle-aged Jewish man named Leopold Bloom, and a young scholar named Stephen Daedalus, and is told over 18 episodes: "U_?"

162. What is the full title of the 1922 book by Margery Williams about a stuffed bunny that is given to a little boy as a Christmas present, and realizes its dream when it becomes real through the love of its owner: "The Velveteen _?"

163. What is the full title of the 1922 poem by Robert Frost describing the feelings of rider pausing to watch the snow falling in the woods, and contains the memorable last line, *and miles to go before I sleep*: "Stopping by Woods on a Snowy _?"

164. What is the title of the 1923 Newbery award- winning book by Hugh Lofting set in South America, about a doctor who meets Tommy Stubbins who learns how to speak to animals, and who helps the doctor in his quest to find a naturalist named Long Arrow: "The Voyages of Doctor _?"

165. What is the name of the 1924 collection of poems by the America poet that is a collection of 597 poems and was published long after her death in 1886: "The Poetry of Emily _?"

166. What is the name of the 1924 short story by Richard Connell about a big game hunter named Rainsford who finds himself on a remote Caribbean island after falling from his boat, and is forced by the aristocrat and game-hunter General Zaroff to participate in a human man-hunt over three days or die, with only a knife, a bag of food and a three hour head start: "The Most Dangerous _?"

167. What is the name of the 1924 novel by E.M. Forster set in India when it was ruled by the British that profiles the often tense relationships between Indians and Anglos: "A Passage to _?"

168. What is the name of the 1924 novella by Herman Melville about a young sailor named Billy on a merchant ship in 1797, accused of conspiracy to mutiny by a fellow sailor named Claggart whom he unintentionally kills when confronted by him, his guilty sentence, and the legacy of hope he left behind in spite of it all: "Billy _?"

169. What is the name of the 1925 novel by F. Scott Fitzgerald about the rich and glitzy lifestyles and elaborate parties of Jay, Tom, Daisy, and others living in upscale Long Island in the summer of 1922: "The Great _?"

170. What is the full title of the 1926 book by A.A. Milne about the adventures of a honey-loving teddy bear, and his friends Tigger, Piglet, Owl, Kanga, Roo, Rabbit, and Eeyore: "Winnie-the-_?"

171. What is the full title of the 1926 novel by American author Ernest Hemingway set right after World War I that tells the story of Jake Barnes and Lady Brett Ashley and their journey from Paris to Pamplona, Spain to watch the running of the bulls during the summer Festival of San Fermín: "The Sun Also _?"

172. What is the name of the fictional book series created by Edward Stratemeyer and first published in 1927 under the collective pseudonym Franklin W. Dixon, about teenage brothers and amateur detectives Frank and Joe who find themselves involved in many adventures and mysteries: "The Hardy __?"

173. What is the name of the 1927 novel by Virginia Woolf that follows the Ramsey family and their visits to their summer home off the coast of Scotland, the challenges when faced with the realities of war, sickness, and death, and how the surviving members of the family finally experience a true connection when visiting the summer house after ten years and finally taking the long-promised journey to the lighted beacon: "To the _?"

174. What is the full title of the 1929 novel by Erich Maria Remarque that describes the physical and mental stress of German soldiers during World War I, and their challenges in integrating themselves back into society upon returning home from the front lines: "All Quiet on the Western _?"

175. What is the full title of the 1929 novel by William Faulkner about the once wealthy Compson family, and the challenges they face after losing their money, their faith, family members, and the respect of their neighbors in Jefferson, Mississippi: "The Sound and the _?"

176. What is the full title of the 1929 novel by Ernest Hemingway set during World War I in Italy that centers on an ambulance driver named Frederic Henry and his love for an English nurse named Catherine Barkley whom he meets after he is wounded: "A Farewell to _?"

177. What is the full title of the 1930 book by Watty Piper about a determined little train engine that struggles, but manages to pull a train loaded with toys to the other side of a mountain for expecting children: "The Little Engine that _?"

178. What is the name of the 1930 fictional mystery series published under the pseudonym Carolyn Keene, about a 16-year-old amateur detective who spends a lot of her time solving mysteries, sometimes along with her friends Bess Marvin, George Fayne, and her boyfriend Ned Nickerson: "Nancy __?"

179. What is the full title of the 1930 novel by William Faulkner that is narrated by 15 different characters, and tells the story of the death of Addie Bundren and the efforts of her family to follow her wishes and have her buried in the Mississippi town of Jefferson: "As I Lay _?"

180. What is the name of the 1930 novel by Dashiel Hammett about a detective named Samuel Spade who is hired to locate the non-existent sister of Miss Wonderly, his investigation into the mysterious death of his partner Miles Archer, his pursuit to find a jewel-encrusted bird statue in order to prove his own innocence, and his discovery that Miss Wonderly herself was the real murderer of his partner: "The Maltese _?"

181. What is the title of the 1931 novel by Pearl S. Buck that tells the story of a hard-working Chinese farmer named Wang Lung, his wife O-lan, his five children, the struggles they face in buying and maintaining farm land from his family that land in their village of Anhwei, feeding their children, and in leaving behind a legacy: "The Good E_?"

182. What is the full title of the 1932 novel by Laura Ingalls Wilder that is an autobiography of her early childhood memories and pioneer life in the woods of Pepin, Wisconsin: "Little House in the Big _?"

183. What is the full title of the 1932 novel by Laura Ingalls Wilder that tells about the journey of the Ingalls family from the big woods of Wisconsin to their new home they build on the prairie, and the many challenges that come with building a house, befriending Indians, planting crops, digging a well, and surviving harsh winters and prairie fires: "Little House on the _?"

184. What is the name of the 1932 novel by Aldous Huxley set in London about an ideal society hundreds of years into the future, where science has perfected the human race: "Brave New _?"

185. What is the full title of the 1932 novel by Charles Nordhoff and James Norman about a mutiny or rebellion against the commanding officer Lieutenant William Bligh of a British Royal Navy ship in 1789: "Mutiny on the _?"

186. What is the title of the 1933 story by A.A. Milne that tells the story of a young elephant who leaves the jungle, visits the city, and upon his return is appointed king: "The Story of B_?"

187. What is the full title of the 1934 novel by P.R. Travers about an English nanny with magical powers, who flies to the Banks household with her umbrella and her carpetbag to care for Jane, Michael, and twins John and Barbara: "Mary _?"

188. What is the full title of the 1934 crime novel by James M. Cain about a man named Frank Chambers, a drifter who starts working at a California diner where he meets a waitress he ends up falling in love with, and how they plot to murder her husband to get him out of the way: "The Postman Always Rings _?"

189. What is the title of the 1934 crime novel by Agatha Christie featuring the detective Hercule Poirot who investigates the murder of a wealthy man named Ratchett, an acquaintance he met on a train he boarded in Constantinople Istanbul, discovers that everyone on the train had a motive for murdering him, and is convinced in the end, that all 12 suspects as well as the conductor himself had a hand in his stabbing as revenge for a previous murder Ratchett, alias Cassetti had committed: "Murder on the Orient _?"

190. What is the full title of the 1935 novel by Enid Bagnold about a fourteen-year-old girl named Velvet Brown who trains her horse and ultimately wins the Grand National Steeplechase horse race, and how she prefers to emphasize the skill and accomplishment of the horse and not the rider in winning the race: "National _?"

191. What is the name of the 1936 children's book by Munro Leaf and illustrated by Robert Lawson, about a bull that prefers to stay in his meadow and smell the flowers, rather than fight a Spanish matador in a bull ring: "The Story of F_?"

192. What is the name of the poem by Langston Hughes first published in 1936 that talks about how the American dream of freedom and equality has never been fully realized by many African Americans and other minority groups, but ends with the glimmer of hope that the dream will come true one day soon: "Let America Be America _?"

193. What is the name of the 1936 historical novel and love story set during the Civil War by Margaret Mitchell depicting the lives of southern belle Scarlett O'Hara on her Georgia plantation called Tara, her relationship with Rhett Butler and Ashley Wilkes, and her journey to re-establish her life: "Gone with the _?"

194. What is the full title of the 1937 fantasy novel by J R.R. Tolkien that tells the story of Bilbo Baggins, his quest to win a share of the treasure that is being guarded by a dragon, and his many encounters with wizards, dwarves, trolls, goblins, dragons, spiders, and eagles: "The H _?"

195. What is the title of the 1937 novel by African American author Zora Neale Hurston, that tells the story of an African American woman named Janie Crawford, as told in a flashback to her best friend Pheoby, revealing what her life has been like from the time she was a powerless, young girl, to the present time in her adult life where she finally feels in control of her destiny: "Their Eyes Were Watching _?"

196. What is the title of the 1937 memoir by Danish author Isak Dinesen, the pen name of Karen Blixen, that is a reflection of seventeen years of the author's life living on a coffee plantation in Ngog Hills near Nairobi, Kenya: "Out of _?"

197. What is the title of the 1937 novella written by John Steinbeck that tells the story George Milton and Lennie Small, migrant farm workers in California who travel from place to place during the American Depression, share the ambition of someday owning their own ranch, and the tragic ending when George kills his friend Lennie for the sole purpose of sparing him the slow death he would have suffered had he been killed by the lynch mob: "Of Mice and _?"

198. What is the name of the 1938 folktale by Esphyr Slobodkina about a hat salesman with a moustache who wears his entire inventory of hats on his head, awakens from his nap in a tree to find that all of his hats except for his own have been stolen by monkeys, and how the monkeys proceed to imitate the salesman's gestures: "Caps for Sale: A Tale of a Peddler, Some Monkeys, and their Monkey _?"

199. What is the name of the 1938 novel by T.H. White that tells of the life of King Arthur in medieval England and the lessons he learns through Merlyn, proving at the end that he is the rightful King of England: "The Sword in the _?"

200. What is the name of the 1938 play by American playwright Thornton Wilder that tells the story of the citizens of a small town called Grover's Corners, with the players performing scenes without scenery or props from the town's history between 1901 and 1913: "Our _?"

201. What is the full title of the 1938 children's book by Richard and Florence Atwater that relates the story of a poor house painter Mr. Popper and his family who happens to receive first one penguin, and then another, and soon find themselves overwhelmed when the creatures take over their house: "Mr. Popper's _?"

202. What is the name of the 1938 novel by Marjorie Kinnan Rawlings that tells the story of a poor farming family in Florida and their only son, Jody Baxter, who adopts the fawn of a doe that his father shoots, but the deer becomes a nuisance when it continuously eats the crops and the young boy is faced with a hard choice, and in the end this choice contributes to his coming-of-age: "The Y_?"

203. What is the full title of the 1939 book, part of a series by the Austrian author Ludwig Bemelmans, about a girl who is staying at a boarding house in Paris, and the doll house she receives from her father while recovering after having her appendix removed: "Madel_?"

204. What is the full title of the 1939 novel by Irish author James Joyce, regarded as one of the most difficult literary works in the English language that centers on the Earwicker family living in a city near Dublin, Ireland, and their efforts to disprove a rumor that was spread about HCE, the father: "Finnegan's _?"

205. What is the name of the 1939 speech of a New York Yankees player who addressed the fans at Yankee Stadium, and let them know that he was retiring from baseball after being diagnosed with a fatal disease: "The Farewell Speech of Lou _?"

206. What is the name of the 1939 novel by John Steinbeck that tells the story of Tom Joad and his migrant farming family who are forced to leave their farm in Oklahoma because of draught, their difficult journey moving the family west with the promise of jobs, and the living conditions in California given the tension between the migrants and the landowners: "The Grapes of _?"

207. What is the name of the 1940 Newbery award-winning children's book by James Daugherty about the adventurous life of a pioneer and frontiersman named Daniel, and the trail he blazed through the Appalachian mountains from North Carolina into Kentucky where he founded the village of Boonsborough.: "Daniel _?"

208. What is the title of the 1940 book based on an old Russian Folk tale that was made popular in a Little Golden Book by Margot Zemach about a hen who worked hard to plant and harvest wheat, and to bake bread, and all her friends like sleepy Cat, noisy Little Duck, and lazy Dog who only wanted to help *eat* the bread: "The Little Red _?"

209. What is the title of the 1940 novel by Eric Knight about the journey of a dog after he is sold to a wealthy man 300 miles away, and the eventual reunion of the collie and his twelve-year-old owner Joe Carraclough: "Lassie Come _?"

210. What is the title of the 1940 children's book by Dorothy Kunhardt, named for a rabbit, and is an interactive book that encourages touching different textures: "Pat the _?"

211. What is the name of the first 1940 speech by the British Prime Minister Winston Churchill, who in his speech, emphasized that the fight against Adolf Hitler and the Nazis of Germany was paramount to the survival of Great Britain itself: "Blood, Toil, Tears, and _?"

212. What is the title of the 1940 novel by Ernest Hemingway about an American soldier named Robert Jordan who, fighting alongside other Spanish Republicans, and is given the task of blowing up a bridge during the attack on Segovia, Spain during the Spanish Civil War: "For Whom the Bell _?"

213. What is the title of the 1940 novel by American author Richard Wright that tells the story of Bigger Thomas, a twenty-year-old African-American living in poverty in Chicago, his attempt to cover up his murder of Mary, the daughter of the wealthy family he is working for, and the challenges he faces in trying to understand white people and the world he lives in right up to the time of his own execution: "Native _?"

214. What is the full title of the 1941 story, and part of a series of children's books by H.A. Rey, about a monkey and his adventures after meeting the man with a yellow hat: "Curious _?"

215. What is the full title of the 1941 story by Walter Farley that relates the story about a wild, black Arabian horse and his young owner Alec Ramsey who are stranded on a desert island after their ship sinks, and how Alec trains the horse to race with the help of a professional trainer after they are rescued: "The Black _?"

216. What is the name of the December 8, 1941 speech given by Franklin D. Roosevelt to Congress the day after the Japanese attack of Pearl Harbor, describing it to them as *a date which will live in infamy*: "Pearl Harbor Address to the _?"

217. What is the full title of the 1942 story by Janette Sebring Lowry about a little dog that does everything different than his brothers and sisters, and ends up the only one going to bed without any dessert: "The Pokey Little _?"

218. What is the name of the 1942 children's series by Gertrude C. Warner about four orphaned children, Henry, Jesse, Violet, and Benny, who live in an abandoned old train car and encounter many adventures and mysteries, but later move in with their wealthy grandfather but keep the train car and use it as a playhouse: "The Boxcar __?"

219. What is the name of the 1942 picture book by Margaret Wise Brown about a rabbit who wants to run off and his mom who promises to run after him if he does: "The Runaway _?"

220. What is the title of the 1942 picture book by Virginia Lee Burton about a country house on a hill, and the residents who live there who are eventually crowded out over time because of city development as the roads, lights, and apartments become closer and closer: "The Little H_?"

221. What is the full title of the 1943 Newbury award-winning novel by Esther Forbes set in colonial Boston, about a promising silversmith apprentice who suffers a burn to his hand, is later introduced to the Sons of Liberty, and ends up participating in the Battles of Lexington, Concord, and the Boston Tea Party: "Johnny T _?"

222. What is the full title of the 1943 fable by Antoine de Saint-Exupery that tells the story of an aviator forced to land in the Sahara desert, meets someone from the planet Asteroid 612, and over the next 8 days while repairing his plane, learns about all the places this person has visited: "The Little P _?"

223. What is the title of the 1943 novel by Albert Camus about a North African named Meursault, a man portrayed as detached and unemotional, who murders a man whom he recognizes in the French province of Algiers, but comes to terms with his indifference toward the world right before he is to die: "The S_?"

224. What is the full title of the 1944 children's book by Eleanor Estes about a Polish girl named Wanda Petronski who attends a school in Connecticut, and is teased by her classmates for wearing the same blue dress every day, but claims that she has several more dresses at home: "The Hundred _?"

225. What is the title of the 1944 Newbery award-winning novel by Robert Lawson set in the countryside near Danbury, Connecticut about a group of animals that are excited that some new folks are moving into an abandoned house, and wonder how things will change and if there will be a new garden in their future: "Rabbit H_?"

226. What is the full title of the 1944 play by Tennessee Williams based on the lives of Tom Wingfield, his mother Amanda, and his two sisters Rose and Laura, and their economic, mental, and emotional struggles as they try to adapt to a life without a husband and a father in the south: "The Glass _?"

227. What is the title of the 1945 Newbery award-winning book by Lois Lenski set in Florida, that tells the story of the feuding Boyer family who raise strawberries, and the Slater family who raise cattle, and what happens when Shoestring Slater's pony ruins the strawberries at Birdie Boyer's farm: "Strawberry _?"

228. What is the full title of the 1945 fictional character featured in a series of books by the Swedish author Astrid Lindgren about the adventures of a nine year old mischievous girl whose red pigtails stick out from both sides of her head, her pet monkey and her pet horse: "Pippi _?"

229. What is the full title of the 1945 children's novel by E.B. White about a little mouse who lives in New York City with his parents, his older brother George, Snowbell the cat, and his best friend Margalo, a bird, who he sets out to save when it disappears from its nest: "Stuart _?"

230. What is the name of the 1945 satirical novel by George Orwell about a group of mistreated pigs and other animals who decide to revolt against humans, and come to realize that are not better off for trying to run a farm by themselves in order to promote progress and equality: "Animal _?"

231. What is the name of the 1946 Newbery award novel by Carolyn Sherwin Bailey about a doll made from an apple tree twig, her head made from a hickory nut, lives in a corncob doll house, and how she adapts with the animals when her family leaves her behind one winter: "Miss H _?"

232. What is the title of the 1946 political novel by Robert Penn Warren, a title that was taken from the nursery rhyme "Humpty Dumpty" that tells the story of the governorship of William Stark, a man named Jack Burdon who arrives to work for him, and the political corruption of the American South during the Depression in the 1930's: "All the Kings's _?"

233. What is the full title of the 1947 book by Margaret Wise Brown about a rabbit that says goodnight to everything around him: "Goodnight _?"

234. What is the full title of the 1947 Newbery award-winning book by William Pene du Bois that relates the story of Professor Sherman who sets off on a journey in a hot air balloon and ultimately crashes on the volcanic island of Krakatoa and the greedy society of the twenty families who live there: "The Twenty-One _?"

235. What is the full title of the 1947 series featuring a lady who lives in an upside-down house and has a chest full of magical cures to be used on children with bad habits: "Mrs. Piggle _?"

236. What is the title of the 1947 novel by American author John Steinbeck about a pearl diver named Kino who goes to great lengths to sell a precious pearl he has found in order to pay the doctor to treat his son Coyotito, only to be pushed to kill in his quest to preserve the pearl and in the end, tosses the pearl back into the ocean after losing the son he tried so hard to protect: "The P_?"

237. What is the name of the diary published by her father in 1947, relating the events of Anne Frank, one of the most famous Jewish victims of the Holocaust, written during the two years she was hiding in an attic in German-occupied Amsterdam during World War II: "Diary of a Young _?"

238. What is the title of the 1947 novel by English author Malcolm Lowry that tells the story of Geoffrey Fermin, a British consul living in a small Mexican town near the volcanos Popocatepetl and Iztaccihuatl, and the arrival of his ex-wife Yvonne and his half-brother Hugh on November 2, 1938, the Mexican Day of the Dead, to rescue him from the bad choices he is making: "Under the _?"

239. What is the name of the 1947 novel by Albert Camus that tells the story of doctor Rieux and his co-workers and their battle against a contagious bacterial disease inflicting the people in the Algerian city of Oran, a disease that grows to epidemic proportions, and the suffering and quarantine that result: "The P_?"

240. What is the title of a 1948 children's book by Ruth Stiles Gannett about a boy named Elmer who runs away to an island and rescues a huge fire-producing lizard: "My Father's _?"

241. What is the title of the 1948 short story by Shirley Jackson about a Bill Hutchinson's wife Tessie who picks the fateful piece of paper in a controversial drawing, sealing her fate to be stoned by the people as an act of sacrifice in order to ensure a good crop: "The L_?"

242. What is the title of the 1948 novel by Alan Paton that centers on a black Anglican priest named Stephen Kumolo who initially travels to the city of Johannesburg to help his sister Gertrude, but while there searches for his son Absalom and learns that his son will be executed because he has murdered Arthur Jarvis, the son of Kumolo's neighbor James Jarvis, leaving both fathers having to come to terms with the death of their sons: "Cry, the Beloved _?"

243. What is the title of the 1949 Newbery award-winning children's book by Marguerite de Angeli set in England during the Middle Ages, that tells the story of a boy named Robin who is sent away by his father to become a knight, his brother Luke who takes him to a monastery to care for him after Robin hurts his legs, and the advice he receives from his brother when faced with a challenge: "The Door in the _?"

244. What is the title of the 1949 novel by George Orwell that tells of the story of Winston Smith and the citizens of Oceania who are living under the complete control of an oppressive political party, and Smith's struggle to break free from *Big Brother* and the powerful control of this totalitarian society: "19_?"

245. What is the title of the 1949 play by the American playwright Arthur Miller that centers around an unstable and unsuccessful traveling businessman named Willy Loman living in Brooklyn with his family, his efforts to find success in his professional life and fulfillment in his personal life, and his desire to steer both of his sons Biff and Harold into the business field: "Death of a _?"

246. What is the name of the 1950 Newbery award-winning book by Elizabeth Yates about an African prince who is captured by slave traders and brought to America to become a slave, masters a trade in the town of Jaffrey, New Hampshire, and becomes a respected citizen of the community: "Amos Fortune, Free _?"

247. What is the full title of the 1950 fantasy novel by C.S. Lewis about the adventures of four children, Peter, Susan, Edmund, and Lucy in the imaginary land of Narnia, after Lucy climbs into a wardrobe and discovers a magical forest: "The Lion, the Witch, and the _?"

248. What is the full title of the 1950 book by Beverly Cleary, the first in a series of books, about a young boy named Henry and his dog Ribsy: "Henry _?"

249. What is the full title of the 1951 novel by British author Roald Dahl about a boy name James who loses his parents, lives with his two strict aunts, and has new adventures with a Grasshopper and an Earthworm after he climbs into a peach that had grown to an enormous size after he accidentally spills magic crystals on the dying peach tree: "James and the Giant _?"

250. What is the name of the 1951 Newbery award-winning children's book by Eleanor Estes set in Connecticut in 1919, about a dog belonging to Jerry Pye that he paid for with his hard-earned money, and how the entire neighborhood of Cranbury came together to find his dog after he went missing: "Ginger P_?"

251. What is the full title of the 1951 novel by J.D. Salinger about a sixteen-year-old boy named Holden Caulfield from New York City, and how he deals with the challenges of identity and alienation as he makes his way through life: "Catcher in the _?"

252. What is the name of the 1951 war novel by James Jones that deals with the struggles of a company of soldiers in Hawaii before World War II, and the challenges of Private Robert E. Lee Pruitt with his superior officers: "From Here to_ ?"

253. What is the title of the 1952 Newbery award-winning children's book by Ann Nolan Clark set in South American that tells the story of an Incan boy named Cusi who lives in the mountains of Peru and tends to the llamas with a herder named Chuto, and learns of the traditions of his Inca ancestors: "Secret of the A_?"

254. What is the full title of the 1952 Newbery honor novel by E.B. White about a pig named Wilbur, his friendship with a spider named Charlotte who saves his life, and a rat named Templeton, all living on the Zuckerman farm: "Charlotte's _?"

255. What is the full title of the 1952 fantasy novel by Mary Norton about the Clock family, a family of little people who live underneath the kitchen, who *borrow* from big people living in an old country house: "The B _?"

256. What is the name of the 1952 poem by Chilean author Pablo Neruda published in a collection of poems entitled, "The Captain's Verses," telling of his feelings after he was exiled from his homeland of Chile: "If You Forget _?"

257. What is the title of the 1952 Pulitzer-prize winning novel by Ernest Hemingway about an aging fisherman named Santiago, his struggle to catch a huge Marlin, an ordeal taking three days, catching the 18 foot fish that would feed several people, only to be unsuccessful in bringing it back whole when it is eaten to the bone by sharks: "The Old Man and the _?"

258. What is the title of the 1952 novel by John Steinbeck set in the Salinas Valley in California that tells the story of two intertwined families, the Trasks and the Hamiltons, and loosely parallels the fall of Adam and Eve, and the sibling rivalry of Cain and Abel: "East of _?"

259. What is the title of the 1953 Newbery award-winning children's novel by Joseph Krumgold that centers on the life of a 12-year-old Hispanic-American boy named Miguel whose wish of visiting the Sangre de Cristo Mountains with his father and grandfather comes true mainly because his brother is called away by the draft: "And Now M_?"

260. What is the full title of the 1953 semi- autobiography by James Baldwin that describes the role of the Christian church in the lives of African-Americans, and suggests the existence of racism in the United States: "Go Tell It on the _?"

261. What is the name of the 1953 *Little Golden Book* by Garth Williams that describes young dogs, cats, pigs, rabbits, cows, sheep, ducks, and chickens that live on a farm: "Baby Farm _?"

262. What is the name of the 1953 *Little Golden Book* by Marian Potter that tells the story of the back car of a train who wants to be as popular as the front engine of the train and have all the children wave to him, but in the end is the hero after saving the train from rolling down a hill: "The Little Red _?"

263. What is the title of the 1953 play by Arthur Miller that is a fictionalized reenactment of the Salem witch trials taking place in Massachusetts Bay in the late 1600's: "The C_?"

264. What is the title of the 1954 Newbery award-winning children's novel by Meindert DeJong, about student named Lina and her classmates who come to discover why there are no storks in their fishing village of Shora, and conclude that Storks could nest on the steep roofs of their houses if the houses had wagon wheels perched on top of them: "The Wheel on the _?"

265. What is the full title of the 1954 fantasy novel by J.R.R. Tolkien that tells the epic journey of Hobbit Frodo Baggins possessing a powerful lost ring, and teams with dwarfs and elves crossing Middle Earth, in their quest to destroy the Ring of terror belonging to the Dark Lord: "The Lord of the _?"

266. What is the title of the 1955 Newbery award-winning children's novel by Jean Lee Latham about the son of a ship captain named Nathanial Bowditch who works for a time as an indentured servant on a ship, learns navigation skills on his own and through his schooling, and eventually creates a new and more accurate sailing navigation source that he eventually uses as he becomes the captain of his own ship after graduating Harvard: "Carry On, Mr. B_?"

267. What is the full title of the 1955 non-fiction book by Walter Lloyd that chronicles the devastating events of the sinking of the Titanic on April 15th, 1912: "A Night to _?"

268. What is the name of the 1955 children's book by Crockett Johnson about a mischievous four-year-old boy who has the power to create his own world just by drawing it: "Harold and the Purple _?"

269. What is the name of the 1955 novel by Vladimir Nabokov about a literature professor named Humbert who comes to live in a New England town and becomes infatuated with a young girl named Dolores and follows her everywhere: "Loli_?"

270. What is the title of the 1956 Newbery award-winning children's novel by Virginia Sorenson that centers around Marly's family who moves to the country to make things easier for her father who is suffering from the stress of the war, become friends with their neighbors Mr. and Mrs. Chirs, and return their kindness when Marly and her family help them gather maple syrup during sugaring time after Mr. Chris falls ill: "Miracles on Maple H_?"

271. What is the full title of the 1956 novel by Gene Zion about a family dog named Harry that does not like taking baths, runs away after burying the bath brush, and becomes so dirty that his own family does not recognize him when he returns home: "Harry the Dirty _?"

272. What is the full title of the 1956 children's novel by Fred Gipson that tells the story of a yellow mongrel dog who comes to stay with Travis Coates and his family at a ranch, how Travis eventually becomes attached to him, and the dog's fate at the end of the story after it is bitten by a rabid wolf: "Old _?"

273. What is the title of the 1957 Newbery award-winning historical novel by Harold Keith set west of the Mississippi during the American Civil War, that tells the story of a sixteen-year-old named Jefferson Davis Bussey, how he eventually fights for both the North and the South, and his discovery that the Union is smuggling new rifles to Indian forces of the Confederate General Stand Watie: "Rifles for_?"

274. What is the full title of the 1957 book by Theodore Geisel under the pen name Dr. Seuss, about a tall cat wearing a red bow tie and a tall red and white striped hat: "The Cat in the _?"

275. What is the full title of the 1957 book by Dr. Seuss about a grouchy Grinch with a heart two sizes too small, who decides to keep Christmas from coming to Whoville by stealing all the presents and food with his sleigh and his dog Max, but in the end understands the true meaning of the holiday: "How the Grinch Stole _?"

276. What is the pen name of Theodore Geisel whose birthday, March 2nd is the celebrated date for "Read Across America Day:" Dr. Seuss or Dr. Doolittle?

277. What is the title of the 1958 Newbery award-winning children's novel by Elizabeth George Speare about a free-spirited sixteen-year-old colonial girl named Kit who comes to live with relatives in

Connecticut, and finds solace in the meadows near a pond where she meets a witch named Hannah: "The Witch of Blackbird _?"

278. What is the title of the 1958 novella by Truman Capote that tells the story of Holiday Golightly living in a brownstone apartment in New York, her one year friendship with the unnamed narrator who lives in the flat above her, and her goal of marrying a rich man: "Breakfast at _"

279. What is the title of the 1959 Newbery award-winning children's novel by Joseph Krumgold set in New Jersey in the 1950's, that tells the story of twelve-year-old Rusch and his friendship with a European hermit named John who is given his name because he grows onions living near a town named Serenity, the town that wants to build a modern house to replace his simple hut, and Andy's wish to run away with him in order to be left alone: "Onion _?"

280. What is the full title of the 1959 novel by Jean Craighead George about a 12-year-old named Sam who runs away from his family's crowded New York apartment to the Catskill Mountains at his great-grandfather's abandoned farm, how he manages to survive a severe snowstorm and the harshness of the wilderness, and how he comes to realize that he needs both his family and the land to truly be happy in life: "My Side of the _?"

281. What is the name of the 1959 novel by John Knowles told from the point of view of Gene Forrester many years later, recalling his time as a sixteen-year-old student attending Devon boarding school in New Hampshire in 1942 during World War II, and reflecting on the friendship and rivalry he once shared with his roommate Finney, including his untimely death in the operating room as a result of a falling down the school's marble stairway: "A Separate _?"

282. What is the name of the 1960 rhyming children's book by Dr. Seuss about a girl and a boy and all the creatures they have as pets: "One Fish, Two Fish, Red Fish, Blue _?"

283. What is the name of the 1960 rhyming book by Dr. Seuss where "Sam-I-Am" tries to convince an unknown character to taste a specific breakfast plate: "Green Eggs and _?"

284. What is the name of the 1960 Newbery award-winning children's novel by Scott O'Dell that tells the story of a young, courageous girl named Karana, and based on the true story of Juana Maria, a Nicoleño Indian, who is left alone on an isolated island off the California coast for 18 years: "Island of the Blue __?"

285. What is the full title of the 1960 novel by Harper Lee about the injustice of prejudice with the story of Scout Finch, her brother Jem, a mysterious neighbor named Boo Radley, and her attorney father Atticus who faces a backlash after defending a black man who is wrongly accused of a crime: "To Kill a _?"

286. What is the full title of the 1960 book by Joy Adamson about how she and her husband George raised three orphaned lion cubs, the youngest of which they named Elsa, and how they eventually released her into the Kenya wilderness: "Born _?"

287. What is the full title of the 1961 novel by Scottish author Sheila Burnford that relates the story of a bull terrier, a Labrador, and a Siamese cat who travel 300 miles through the harsh Canadian wilderness

in search of their masters, and even though they are tired, weak, and hungry, they eventually reunite with their owners: "The Incredible _?"

288. What is the full title of the 1961 novel by the English author Roald Dahl about an orphaned English boy name James who finds himself inside a huge fruit along with a few friends, the adventures that ensue as it rolls through air, land, and water, and how James lives out his life in New York City in what was once part of this huge fruit: "James and the Giant _?"

289. What is the name of the children's novel originally published in 1961 by P.D. Eastman about a group of dogs who operate cars and scooters and ultimately have a dog party: "Go, Dog._?"

290. What is the full title of the 1961 novel by Wilson Rawls about a boy named Billy Coleman who buys and trains two Redbone Coonhounds in the Ozarks, how the dogs learn to excel at coon hunting, and how Billy finds peace when he sees a special plant growing over the graves of his beloved dogs, a plant that according to Indian legend, can only be planted by an angel: "Where the Red Fern _?"

291. What is the full title of the 1961 adventure novel filled with literary puns by Norton Juster about a boy named Milo who receives a magic tollbooth and uses his toy car to drive through it and arrives at a castle where Princess Rhyme and Princess Reason reside: "The Phantom T_?"

292. What is the name of the 1961 speech by President John F. Kennedy when he said to the American people, *ask not what your country can do for you, ask what you can do for your country*: "The Inaugural _?"

293. What is the name of the 1961 novel by Joseph Heller that is set in 1943 during World War II, and follows the events of an Air Force squadron under Captain John Yossarian and their efforts to fulfill their air mission off the coast of Italy, and their quest to return home safely: "Catch_?"

294. What is the full title of the 1962 Caldecott award-winning picture book by Ezra Jack Keats about an African-American boy named Peter who is excited to go outside and explore the neighborhood after the first major snowfall of the season: "The Snowy _?"

295. What is the full title of the 1962 science fiction fantasy Newbery award-winning novel by Madeleine L'Engle about Meg and Charles Wallace and their friend Calvin, their journey into space on a mission to find the Wallace children's father who has mysteriously disappeared, and the evil forces they find themselves up against: "A Wrinkle in _?"

296. What is the name of the 1962 series of children's books by Stan and Jan Berenstain about an animal family that include Papa, Mama, Brother, Sister, and Honey where some lesson is learned at the end: "The Berenstain _?"

297. What is the title of the 1962 novel by Ken Kesey and set in an Oregon mental institution, about an unstable man named Randle McMurphy who bands together with other patients against the totalitarian rule of nurse Ratched, along with other conflicts that emerge within the ward: "One Flew Over the Cuckoo's _?"

298. What is the title of the 1963 Newbery award-winning children's novel by Emily Cheney Neville, that centers on a fourteen-year-old boy named David Mitchell living in New York, his friendship with an

elderly neighbor name Kate and her many cats, and the cat he adopts that brings adventure and meaning into his life: "It's Like This, C_?"

299. What is the full title of the 1963 Caldecott Medal-winning picture book by Maurice Sendak about a boy named Max who dresses up in a wolf suit, is sent to his room without supper for misbehaving, becomes the "king" of the animals on the island he has sailed to in his bedroom that has magically transformed into a forest and an ocean, and wakes up to find a hot supper waiting for him: "Where the Wild Things _?"

300. What is the name of the children's book series first published in 1963 by Norman Bridwell about a puppy who becomes the birthday present and beloved pet of Emily Elizabeth, a puppy that grows to over 25 feet tall: "Clifford the Big Red _?"

301. What is the name of the public speech given by civil rights activist Martin Luther King Jr. in 1963 in Washington, D.C. on the steps of the Lincoln Memorial, and with a crowd of over 250,000, calling for an end to racism and discrimination in America, and outlining his hopes for freedom and equality: "I Have a _?"

302. What is the title of the 1964 Newbery award-winning children's novel by Maia Wojciechowska that centers on twelve-year-old Manolo Olivar, the son of a famous Spanish bullfighter named Juan who was killed by a bull when Manolo was very young, how Manolo comes to terms with the high expectation of the people of Spain to follow in his father's footsteps, and his realization that his true calling is not as a matador in a bullring, but as a doctor in a hospital: "Shadow of a _?"

303. What is the full title of the 1964 novel by Roald Dahl about a boy named Charlie Bucket who finds a golden ticket inside a candy bar, visits a candy factory run by Willie Wonka and singing Oommpa Loompas, and experiences all that the factory has of offer along with his grandpa Joe and four other children named Veruca, Violet, Mike, and Augustus: "Charlie and the Chocolate _?"

304. What is the full title of the 1964 children's book by Jeff Brown about a boy who is flattened by a bulletin board that falls on top of him while he is sleeping, can slide under locked doors, can be flown as a kite by his brother Arthur, and can be mailed in an envelope until the day his is re-inflated by his brother by a bicycle pump: "Flat _?"

305. What is the full title of the 1964 novel by Louise Fitzhugh about an eleven-year-old named Harriet, her friends Sport, Janie, and Rachael, and how she goes on to write stories about all the people along her spy route: "Harriet the _?"

306. What is the full title of the 1964 fantasy novel by Lloyd Alexander that tells of the adventures of an Assistant Pig-Keeper named Taran who lives with the enchanter Dallben, and his quest to escape ordinary farm life and become a hero: "The Book of T _?"

307. What is the full title of the 1964 children's picture book written by Shel Silverstein that tells the story of a young boy and his relationship with an apple tree through the years of his life: "The Giving _?"

308. What is the name of the 1964 speech by the anti-apartheid South African Nelson Mandela right now facing trial because of his opposition to the government in power: "I am Prepared to _?"

309. What is the title of the 1965 Newbery award-winning children's novel by Elizabeth Borton de Treviño about a half-African slave named Juan who works for and learns to paint himself from his master, the famous Spanish artist Diego Velázquez: "I, Juan de _?"

310. What is the full title of the 1965 fantasy novel by Lloyd Alexander that continues the story of Taran, the Assistant Pig Keeper, and his attempt to capture the Magical Cauldron from Arawn Death Lord: "The Black _?"

311. What is the full title of the 1965 novel by Beverly Cleary about Ralph the mouse living at the Mountain View Inn and the toy motorcycle belonging to a new guest named Keith that eventually becomes Ralph's to keep: "The Mouse and the _?"

312. What is the title of the book first published in 1965 by Charles M Schulz and based on the Christmas special, about a boy named Charlie Brown who is trying to understand the real meaning of a holiday, and celebrates the season with Lucy, Linus, and Snoopy and the gang: "A Charlie Brown _?"

313. What is the title of the of the world's best-selling 1965 science fiction novel by Frank Herbert that is set in the distant future in the year 10191, where space travel and life in the universe are dependent upon a spice called melange that only exists on the planet Arrakis, and the desire by many to control this planet: "D_?"

314. What is the name of the 1966 Newbery award-winning novel by Irene Hunt about a seven-year-old girl named Julie who goes to live with her Aunt Cordelia after her mother dies, following her life from ages seven to seventeen from elementary school through high school: "Up a Road _?"

315. What is the full title of the 1967 Newbery award-winning novel by E L. Konigsburg about a girl name Claudia Kinkaid who convinces her brother to run away with her and hide out at the Metropolitan Museum of Art in New York City, and the mystery of the famous statue they name "Angel," that leads them to the owner who allows them to search her records in order to discover the secret about the famous statue: "From the Mixed-Up Files of Mrs. Basil E. _?"

316. What is the name of the 1967 children's picture book by Bill Martin, Jr. and Eric Carle with animals of different colors that helps the reader associate colors with objects: "Brown Bear, Brown Bear, What Do You _?"

317. What is the title of the 1967 novel by Columbian author Gabriel García Márquez that tells the story of the Buendía family over seven generations in the mythical Macondo, the city founded by the family patriarch José Arcadia Buendía, and the quest for peace and truth over the span of one hundred years: "One Hundred Years of _?"

318. What is the title of the 1967 novel by Chaim Potok that tells the story of two boys named Reuven Malter and Danny Saunders who meet at a baseball game and become friends, the challenges the boys and their fathers face living Brooklyn, New York at the end of World War II, and the challenges that come with trying to live a devoted Jewish life: "The C _?"

319. What is the name of the 1968 Newbery award-winning fantasy novel by Lloyd Alexander that follows an Assistant Pig Keeper named Taran, who joins forces with his countrymen in the land of Prydain to defeat Arawn Death-Lord in order to rule the kingdom: "The High K_?"

320. What is the full title of the 1968 book by Don Freeman about a teddy bear that is on a display shelf in a store, how he searches the store at night for his missing button, and the girl named Lisa that buys him the next day with money from her piggy bank, takes him home, and sews a button on the strap of his overalls: "Cord_?"

321. What is the full title of the 1968 book by Beverly Cleary about a mischievous girl who manages to create trouble wherever she goes in her kindergarten class: "Ramona the _?"

322. What is the name of the 1969 Newbery award-winning novel by William H. Armstrong about a young boy living with his poor African-American sharecropper family and their dog, their fight for their survival, the reunion of the family and the dog, and the satisfaction that is felt by the young boy because he has learned to read: "Sound_?"

323. What is the full title of the 1969 picture book by Eric Carle about an insect who eats an enormous amount of unusual food, grows big and fat, and later emerges as a beautiful butterfly: "The Very Hungry _?"

324. What is the full title of the 1969 autobiography by Maya Angelou from her early years into adulthood, as she becomes transformed from a victim of racism, to a mature, dignified and capable woman: "I Know Why the Caged Bird _?"

325. What is the title of the 1969 novel by Kurt Vonnegut about the experiences of soldier Billy Pilgrim during World War II, and the effects of the bombing of Dresden, Germany: "Slaughterhouse _?"

326. What is the title of the 1970 Newbery award-winning novel by Betsy Byars that tells the story of fourteen-year-old Sara Godfrey growing up with her brother and sister, their Aunt Willie, and her search for her mentally challenged brother Charlie after he goes missing: "Summer of the S _?"

327. What is the name of the 1970 first book in a series written and illustrated by Arnold Lobel that relate the adventures of two amphibians through a series of short stories: "Frog and Toad are __?"

328. What is the full title of the 1970 novel by E.B. White that tells the story of Louis, a Trumpeter Swan that is born without a voice who learns to play a musical trumpet to earn money and to win the attention of Serena: "The Trumpet of the _?"

329. What is the name of the 1971 Newbery award-winning book by Robert C. O'Brian that relates the story of a widow mouse named Frisby and her four children, and how she manages to move her family and save her farm from a farmer's plow with the help of highly intelligent laboratory rats: "Mrs. Frisby and the Rats of N _?"

330. What is the full title of the 1971 children's book by Barbara Robinson that relates the story of Imogene, Claude, Ralph, Leroy, Ollie, and Gladys Herndon and their participation in a church holiday play: "The Best Christmas Pageant __?"

331. The is the name of the 1971 book by Dr. Seuss that tells about the state of the environment and a creature that speaks for the trees to protect them from the Once-ler: "The Lor_?"

332. What is the name of the 1972 Newbery award-winning children's novel by Jean Craighead George about a young girl named Julie who runs away from her Alaskan village, her acceptance by a pack of Arctic dogs, and her struggle to reconcile her old life with the Eskimos and her new one in the wilderness: "Julie of the _?"

333. What is the name of the 1972 adventure novel by English author Richard Adams about a group of rabbits including Hazel and Fiver, who engage in several adventures as they seek to establish their new warren on a hill in England: "Watership _?"

334. What is the full title of the 1972 book by Judith Viorst about a boy named Alexander who has an extremely bad day from the moment he wakes up and trips on his skateboard, to the time he goes to bed when his nightlight burns out and vows to move to Australia: "Alexander and the Terrible, Horrible, No Good, Very Bad D_?"

335. What is the name of the 1973 Newbery award-winning children's book by Paula Fox about a boy named Jesse Bollier who is kidnapped and forced to play his fife flute aboard a slave ship called *The Moonlight* for shackled slaves, and how he is affected by the inhumanity and savagery of the African slave trade: "The Slave D_?"

336. What is the title of the 1974 Newbery award-winning children's novel by Virginia Hamilton about a young boy named M.C. Higgins living on Sara's Mountain in the Appalachians with his family, the struggler he feels with regard to leaving the mountain because of the danger of sliding subsoil from mining explosions, and remaining in their home because it is the home of his great-grandmother who had escaped slavery and settled at the base of this mountain: "M.C. Higgins, the _?"

337. What is the full title of a 1974 collection of poems and drawings by Shel Silverstein that include a poem about a story about a boy that transforms into a TV set, and a girl that eats a whale: "Where the Sidewalk _?"

338. What is the name of the 1975 Newbery award-winning fantasy novel by Susan Cooper about a boy named Will Stanton who goes to live with his Welsh aunt while recovering from an illness, his quest to locate the magic golden harp with his friend Bran Davies and his dog Cafall because the harp is the last artifact needed to awaken the Sleepers, the warriors that are needed by the Light in order to defeat the king of the mountain and the Dark: "The Grey K _?"

339. What is the full title of the 1975 fantasy novel by Natalie Babbitt about ten-year-old Winnie Foster, the secret she discovers about the Tuck family who are living an eternal life after drinking from a magic spring, and a stranger that arrives who wants to take Winnie back to her home and sell the spring water: "Tuck _?"

340. What is the name of the 1976 Newbery award-winning novel by Mildred D. Taylor that reveals what life is like in the South in the 1930's after the American Civil War for a strong and proud African American family including nine-year-old Cassie Logan and her three brothers, the white Simms family, and themes of land-ownership, prejudice, and racism: "Roll of Thunder, Hear Me __?"

341. What is the full title of the 1976 autobiographical novel by African-American author Alex Haley that tells the story of Kunta Kinte, who grew up in Gambia, Africa, was captured and sold into slavery to American in 1767, following his harsh life through many generations including the author's, a seventh generation descendent of Kunta Kinte: "Roots: The Saga of an American F _?"

342. What is the name of the series of children's game books of 1977 by Edward Packard that are written in the second person where the reader is actually the protagonist of the story, and makes choices throughout the book that ultimately determine the outcome of the plot: "Choose Your Own _?"

343. What is the full title of the 1977 Newbery award-winning novel by Katherine Patterson about two friends, Jesse and Leslie, the imaginary world they create near a creek, and the memorial that Jesse builds in honor of Leslie after she accidentally drowns when the rope that she is swinging on breaks: "Bridge to __?"

344. What is the title of the 1977 novel by American author Toni Morrison, named for a Biblical King and the name of the great-grandfather of the main character, that tells story of an African American man named Macon "Milkman" Dead III growing up in Michigan, and includes accounts of the migration of slaves to Africa and to other parts of the United States: "Song of S_?"

345. What is the title of the 1978 Newbery award-winning novel by Ellen Raskin about the sixteen heirs of millionaire Sam Westing who come to hear the will which is actually a puzzle, divides the heirs into eight pairs, gives each pair specific clues, and promises his fortune of $200 million dollars made from his company Westing Paper Products to the person solving his murder: "The Westing _?"

346. What is the full title of the 1978 book by Judi Barrett where a grandfather narrates a story to his grandchildren about a town called Chewandswallow whereby all the residents are provided all their meals by raining food, and how an unexpected storm forces them to move to another town where they must learn to get their food in the usual way: "Cloudy with a Chance of _?"

347. What is the name of the 1978 children's picture book by English author Raymond Briggs is a wordless story about a young boy and his wintertime creation who share a magical time together: "The Snow_?"

348. What is the name of the 1978 collection of 32 short poems by Maya Angelou that are centered on the theme of hopefulness and rising above adversity: "And Still I _?"

349. What is the title of the 1979 Newbery award-winning historical novel by Joan Blos, written in the form of a journal, that provides a detailed account of the daily life of Catherine Hall living in New England with her sister and her widowed father between 1830 and 1832, with particular emphases on the events of her father's remarriage, the sudden death of her best friend, and her assistance to an escaped slave: "The Gathering of Days: A New England Girl's _?"

350. What is the name of the 1979 children series by James and Deborah Howe about the Monroe family and the bunny they find at a feature of *Dracula*, a bunny that sucks the juice out of vegetables: "Bunni_?"

351. What is the name of the German fantasy novel first published in 1979 by Michael Ende about a boy named Bastian Balthazar Bux who discovers a book in an antique store, and is transported into a fantasy world as he magically becomes part of the book while reading it: "The Neverending _?"

352. What is the name of the 1979 novel by American author William Styron that tells a multi-dimensional story of a southern author named Stingo and his relationship with a Polish refugee named Sophie, where he ultimately learns of the unbearable choice she was forced to make with regard to her two children while imprisoned at the Auschwitz concentration camp in Germany: "Sophie's _?"

353. What is the name of the children's 1980 book by Nadine Bernard Wescott that is based on a cumulative song that gets worse and worse after an old lady swallows a fly: "I Know an Old Woman Who Swallowed a _?"

354. What is the name of the 1981 Newbery winning and Caldecott Honor children's picture book written by Nancy Willard that is a collection of fifteen poems describing the events over a day and a half of a child's visit to William Blake's Inn, and its residents that include a Rabbit, a Rat, a Tiger, a King of Cats, and a Wise Cow: "A Visit to William Blake's Inn: Poems for Innocent and Experienced T _?"

355. What is the name of the 1981 Newbery award-winning novel by Katherine Patterson that centers on the relationships of the Bradshaw family, especially daughter Sara Louise who is always trying to escape the shadow of her prettier twin sister Caroline, and how she finally comes full circle after having twins of her own: "Jacob Have I _?"

356. What is the full title of the 1981 children's Newbery honor book by Beverly Cleary about a mischievous third grade student named Ramona and her sister Beezus in junior high: "Ramona Quimby, Age _?"

357. What is the name of the 1981 children's fantasy Caldecott Medal-winning picture book by Chris Van Allsburg that tells the story of Peter and Judy Shephard that find a jungle adventure game in a park, and after they take it home to play it, discover that all the dangers in the game like lions and monsoons suddenly come to life: "Juman_?"

358. What is the name of the 1981 children's collection of poems by Shel Silverstein, with each poem accompanied by an illustration: "A Light in the _?"

359. What is the title of the 1982 children's Newbery award-winning novel by Cynthia Voigt that tells the story of Dicey, Sammy, Maybeth, and James Tillerman who are living with their widowed grandmother on a farm in Maryland while their mother is at a psychiatric hospital in Boston, how they adjust in their new school and with their new friends, and how in the end, they come to terms with their mother's death: "Dicey's _?"

360. What is the name of the 1982 novel by Alice Walker that centers on Celie, a poor African-American girl living in Georgia who communicates her thoughts in her letters to God, the abuse she suffers at the hands of her father, the complex relationships with Sofia and a local singer named Shug Avery, her discovery that her children are alive, and the eventual reunion with her sister Nettie after believing that she had died: "The Color _?"

361. What is the title of the 1983 Newbery award-winning novel by Beverly Cleary that centers on the letters that Leigh Botts writes to his favorite author, Boyd Henshaw, and in his correspondence with the author, Leigh reveals his feelings regarding his parents' divorce, his tense relationship with his father, adjusting to a new school, and a mysterious student who keeps stealing his lunch, and in the

end comes to understand that there are some circumstances in his life that he cannot change: "Dear Mr. H_?"

362. What is the title of the 1984 Newbery award-winning fantasy novel by Robin McKinley that centers on Aerin Dragon-Killer and her journey from the shy daughter of the King of Damar, to the queen seeking to protect her people from Northerners, and her quest to rebuild the kingdom: "The Hero and the C _?"

363. What is the full name of the 1985 Newbery award-winning children's book by Patricia MacLachlan about a farmer whose wife has died, writes an ad in a newspaper for a wife and mother of his children Anna and Caleb, and the lady from Maine who answers his ad: "Sarah, Plain and __?"

364. What is the full title of the 1985 children's Caldecott Medal-winning picture book written and illustrated by Chris Van Allsburg about a young boy who boards a train headed for the North Pole, and while there, chooses a bell from a reindeer's harness as his gift, loses it on the train on the way home, and receives it under the tree as a gift from Santa, a bell that only he and his sister can hear: "The Polar _?"

365. What is the name of the 1985 children's series authored by Joanna Cole and illustrated by Bruce Degen that center around science teacher Mrs. Frizzle, and the exotic field trips she takes her class on in order to experience science first hand: "The Magic School _?"

366. What is the name of the 1985 children's book by Laura Numeroff that is a circular story about a little boy who gives a sweet treat to a mouse, and it asks then for a glass of milk and many more things: "If You Give a Mouse a _?"

367. What is the title of the 1986 Newbery award-winning children's novel by Sid Fleischman that centers on the events of the spoiled Prince Horace, or Prince Brat as he is sometimes called, an orphaned boy named Jemmy who that takes any punishment in place of the prince, and their challenges after they run away for a time and trade places: "The Whipping B_?"

368. What is the name of the novel series by Ann M. Martin beginning in 1986 that centers on Kristy Thomas, Mary Ann Spier, Claudia Kishi, and Stacey McGill, Connecticut middle school students who form a club to help parents with their child care needs: "The Babysitters _?"

369. What is the name of the January 28, 1986 speech by President Ronald Reagan after the space accident that occurred the day before in which all seven astronauts died, where he reassured all Americans, *the future doesn't belong to the fainthearted, it belongs to the brave*: "Address to the Nation on the Challenger _?"

370. What is the title of the 1987 Newbery award-winning biography by Russell Freedman that tells of the life of Abraham Lincoln through stories and photographs beginning with his childhood, his marriage to Mary Todd Lincoln, his Presidency, and his assassination: "Lincoln: A_?"

371. What is the name of the 1987 children's book written and illustrated by Graeme Base that contain detailed animal illustrations for each letter of the alphabet, a short poem for each letter, and a hidden picture of the author as a young boy for each illustration: "Anim_?"

372. What is the full title of the 1987 survival novel by Gary Paulson about thirteen-year-old Brian Robeson, and how he survives the harsh Canadian wilderness after his plane crashed with little more than the clothes on his back and the tool he managed to save: "Hat_?"

373. What is the full title of the 1987 Caldecott Medal-winning picture book by Jane Yolen that tells the story of a father and daughter who encounter a Great Horned Owl while out one cold, snowy evening: "Owl _?"

374. What is the name of the 1987 speech by President Ronald Reagan at the Brandenburg Gate near Berlin, Germany where he challenged the Soviet Union leader Mikhail Gorbachev with the words: "Mr. Gorbachev, tear down this _?"

375. What is the name of the 1987 novel by American author Toni Morrison that centers around a former slave named Sethe who had killed her young daughter and had tried to kill her other three daughters when people from her former plantation arrived to return them to the plantation in Ohio, and a woman, presumed to be the ghost of her murdered daughter, who returns to Sethe's house at 124 Bluestone Road Cincinnati years later and haunts it: "Be_?"

376. What is the title of the 1987 Newbery award-winning novel by Paul Fleishman that is a collection of fourteen children's poems intended to be read aloud by two people, with insects as the theme: "Joyful Noise: Poems for Two V_?"

377. What is the name of the 1988 children's novel by Roald Dahl about a gifted, young girl with magical powers who uses these powers against the strict headmistress at her school: "Matil_?"

378. What is the full title of the 1989 historical fiction Newbery award-winning novel by Louis Lowry, and centers on the escape of ten-year-old Annemarie Johansen's Jewish family from Copenhagen in Nazi-occupied Denmark during the Holocaust: "Number the _?"

379. What is the full title of the 1989 book by Bill Martin, Jr. and John Archambault about lower-case letters who climb a coconut tree, and the capital or upper-case letters that come to their aid after the small letters fall to the ground: "Chicka Chicka Boom _?"

380. What is the name of the 1989 children's picture book by Jon Scieszka and Lane Smith that is a variation of "Three Little Pigs" from the Wolf's point of view, as he tries to borrow a cup of sugar from three pigs to make his grandmother a birthday cake, and is finally thrown in jail trying to pound down the door of the pig living in the house made of bricks: "The True Story of the Three Little _?"

381. What is the name of the 1989 children's book by Jan Brett about a Ukrainian child named Nikki who loses one of his white articles of clothing that his grandmother had made for him, and the different animals like the mole, fox, rabbit, bear, and mouse that take up residence inside of it until Nicki finally finds it in the snow: "The M_?"

382. What is the title of the 1990 Newbery award-winning novel by Jerry Spinelli that follows an orphaned boy named Jeffrey Lionel Magee who winds up in Two Mills, Pennsylvania, and becomes known as somewhat of a legend in the town that is racially divided because of his athleticism and his efforts to unite the people: "Maniac M_?"

383. What is the name of the 1990 children's book, the last one published by Dr. Seuss, about a protagonist that travels through various places, suggesting all the places there are to experience and discover: "Oh, the Places You Will _?"

384. What is the name of the 1991 Newbery award-winning novel by Phyllis Reynolds Naylor about a young boy named Marty Preston and the abused beagle dog he rescues from his neighbor, and his torment because he has to lie and steal to keep him: "Shi_?"

385. What is the name of the 1991 children's picture book by David Wiesner that is named for a day of the week, and centers around frogs that rise out of a pond on lily pads and descend on the residents of a nearby town: "T_?"

386. What is the title of the 1992 Newbery award-winning novel by Cynthia Rylant about an orphaned child named Summer who finally finds happiness when she goes to live with her Aunt May and Uncle Ob in the Appalachian mountains, and the grief that she and her Uncle Ob experience after her Aunt May dies suddenly: "Missing _?"

387. What is the name of the children's horror fiction novels first published in 1992 by R.L. Stine that include stories about kids that find themselves in scary situations like "Welcome to Dead House," the first novel: "Goose_?"

388. What is the name of the 1992 children's book by Jon Scieszka that is a collection of tales making fun of the original tale like *The Ugly Duckling* and *The Gingerbread Man* as told by Jack from *Jack and the Beanstalk*: "The Stinky Cheese Man and Other Fairly Stupid _?"

389. What is the name of the 1993 Newbery award-winning novel by Lois Lowry that tells the story of twelve-year-old Jonas and other citizens that have to follow strict rules and give up many freedoms in order to live in a perfect, utopian society, but in the end, the society is revealed to be just the opposite because the people are not given basic freedoms, freedoms necessary for a happy life: "The G_?"

390. What is the title of the 1994 Newbery award-winning novel by Sharon Creech that centers on thirteen-year-old Salamanca Hiddle's car journey with her grandparents from Idaho to Ohio, telling them the story of the disappearance of her friend Phoebe's mother, a story that closely resembles the truth about her own mother's disappearance: "Walk Two M_?"

391. What is the name of the 1994 children's book by British author Sam MacBratney about two Nutbrown hares that try to outdo each other in stating how much one cares for the other: "Guess How Much I Love _?"

392. What is the title of the 1995 Newbery award-winning novel by Karen Cushman that tells the story of a homeless girl named Brat who adopts the name Alyce, becomes an apprentice to a midwife, and eventually overcomes obstacles and gains the confidence to find her own place in the world: "The Midwife's A_?"

393. What is the full title of the 1995 fantasy novel by Philip Pullman that relates the journey of Lyra to the Arctic in order to look for her missing friend Roger, and her imprisoned uncle Lord Asriel: "The Golden _?"

394. What is the name of the 1996 Newbery award-winning novel by E.L. Konigsburg about the life challenges of a paraplegic sixth grade teacher named Mrs. Eva Olinski, along with four of her students Noah, Nadia, Julian, and Ethan who compete in academic competitions calling themselves "The Souls," and the life lessons they all learn about the importance of hard work, family, and friends: "The View from S_?"

395. What is the title of the 1996 book by Andrew Clements about a student named Nick who invents a new word for a pen, a word that earns him national recognition: "Frin_?"

396. What is the name of the 1997 Newbery award-winning novel by Karen Hesse that tells the story in free verse format about an Oklahoma farming family during the Dust Bowl years of 1934 and 1935, focusing primarily on the challenges faced by the main character Billie Jo Kelby that include the burning accident of her mother, and the physical and mental health of the father: "Out of the D_?"

397. What is the full title of the debut 1997 novel of J.K. Rowling about a boy who discovers that he is a wizard, and experiences many new adventures at the Hogwarts School of Witchcraft and Wizardry, and how he succeeds in stopping Lord Voldemort: "Harry Potter and the Sorcerer's _?"

398. What is the full title of the 1997 novel by Dav Pilkey, the first in a series, about 4th graders Harold Hutchins and George Beard who make a comic strip with a made-up superhero: "The Adventures of Captain _?"

399. What is the name of the 1997 children's rhyming book by Deborah Guarino and Steve Kellog about a little llama that asks his friends if their moms are llamas too: "Is Your Mama a _?"

400. What is the title of the children's book series first published in 1997 by Kate McMullan about a boy named Wiglaf and his two friends Erica Von Royale and Angus du Pangus who attend a special school to learn the art of killing dragons: "Dragon Slayers' A_?"

401. What is the name of the series of realistic fiction books first published in 1997 by Jeff Kinney that serve as journals of the main character named Greg Hefley that tell the story of his daily adventures and challenges during his middle school years: "Diary of a Wimpy _?"

402. What is the name of the 1998 Newbery award-winning novel by Louis Sachar about a boy named Stanley who is caught for stealing a pair of sneakers, sentenced to 18 months at Camp Green Lake, and has to dig a hole in the desert only to find out that the warden was actually seeking to find the treasure left behind by the outlaw Kissing Kate Barlow: "H_?"

403. What is the title of the 1999 Newbery award-winning novel by Christopher Paul Curtis about a ten-year-old boy named Bud Caldwell living in an orphanage in Flint, Michigan in 1936 during the Great Depression, his relationship with his foster brother Todd, his longing to find his jazz musician father, and the journey he takes west with his friend Bugs: "Bud, Not _?"

404. What is the full title of the children series first published in 1999 by Lemony Snicket that follows the adventures of Violet, Klaus, and Sunny Baudelaire after their parents' death in a fire, and wherever they go are followed by misfortune: "A Series of Unfortunate _?"

405. What is the title of the 1999 children's book by Marcus Pfister about a about a sea animal with beautiful blue, green, purple, and silver scales who finds friendship with other sea animals when he learns to share: "The Rainbow F_?"

406. What is the title of the 2000 Newbery award-winning historical fiction novel by Richard Peck about fifteen-year-old Mary Alice Dowdel who leaves Chicago to go and live with her grandma in a farming community for one year, her adjustment to her new school and participation in the school's Christmas Pageant, and the boy, Royce McNabb, that she meets and eventually marries after her return to her Grandma's house in the countryside: "A Year Down Y_?"

407. What is the name of the 2000 children's picture book by Doreen Cronin about a herd of Farmer Brown's cows who find a typewriter and write letters to Farmer Brown stating their demands: "Click, Clack, Moo: Cows that _?"

408. What is the name of the 2000 fictional character and book by the same name written and illustrated by Ian Falconer about a pig who loves to sing, go to the beach, paint on walls, and build sand castles: "Oliv__?"

409. What is the full title of the 2000 novel by Pam Muñoz Ryan about a young Mexican girl, the daughter of wealthy Mexican landowners, who travels to California with her mother by train after her father was killed by bandits, and her life and the lives of other immigrants working at a farm in Depression-era America: "Esperanza _?"

410. What is the name of the 2000 children's novel by Kate DiCamillo about a ten-year-old girl named India Opal that lives with her preacher father in Florida, finds a big dog in the supermarket and names him after it, and collects stories to one day tell her mother who is not living with them at the present time: "Because of Winn-_?"

411. What is the title of the 2001 Newbery award-winning novel by Linda Sue Park that tells the story of a twelve-year-old Korean orphaned boy named Tree-ear, his fascination with pottery, his relationship with a potter named Min, his journey to transport Min's vases to Songdo after Min is granted a commission from Emissary Kim based on one broken piece or shard, and realizing his dream of making his own pottery: "A Single S_?"

412. What is the title of the 2002 Newbery award-winning novel by Avi set in 1377 England about a thirteen-year-old boy known as Asta's Son accused of a crime he did not commit, is declared a "wolf's head" meaning he may be shot by anyone at any time, and his journey through the countryside where in the end he is forced to defend himself to save his life, taking with him only the name of Crispin and his mother's cross of lead: "Crispin: The Cross of L_?"

413. What is the name of the 2002 children's books based on the Nickelodeon series like "Dora's Backpack" about the adventures of a young Latina girl named Dora and her monkey named Boots: "Dora the _?"

414. What is the title of the 2003 Newbery award-winning fantasy novel by Kate DiCamillo that is divided into four chapters, each told from the perspective of a different character, and follows the adventures of Despereaux Tilling, a castle mouse that sets out to save a beautiful human princess: "The Tale of Despereaux: Being the Story of a Mouse, a Princess, Some Soup, and a Spool of _?"

415. What is the title of the 2004 Newbery award-winning novel by Cynthia Kadohata about the life of a Japanese-American girl name Katie who has moved to an apartment in Georgia after her family's store is forced to go out of business, how she comes to terms with the death of her sister Lynn after a long illness, and her feelings when she hears the voice of her sister in the waves on a California beach at the end speaking their sister-created phrase meaning shiny and sparkling: "Kira-_?"

416. What is the full title of the 2004 novel by Judy Blume about nine-year-old Peter Hatcher who feels overshadowed by his spoiled two year old brother named Farley but nicknamed Fudge who gets away with everything, even swallowing his pet turtle Dribble: "Tales of a Fourth Grade __?"

417. What is the title of the 2005 Newbery award-winning novel by Lynn Rae Perkins that follows the lives of teenagers Debbie, Hector, Patty, Lenny, and Phil, revealing how their lives cross after spending one summer together in their small town of Seldem, and how each becomes more mature and confident by the end of that summer: "Criss_?"

418. What is the title of the 2006 Newbery award-winning novel by Susan Patron that centers on a ten-year-old girl named Lucky living in a California desert town named Hard Pan, how she runs away to the desert when she finds what she thinks are travel papers belonging to Brigitte, her father's first wife who has come to live with them after the death of her mother, and how after being found in the desert with two of her friends, learns that the papers were actually adoption papers: "The Higher Power of L_?"

419. What is the name of the 2006 book by Eric Carle that has pictures that can be both seen and felt, about an insect that works hard to spin her web, while other farm animals continuously try to distract her: "The Very Busy S_?"

420. What is the title of the 2007 Newbery award-winning children's book by Laura Amy Schilz that is written as a series of monologues along with two dialogues by different members of a medieval village in 1255 that include lords, ladies, millers, monks, and peasants: "Good Masters! Sweet Ladies! Voices from a Medieval V _?"

421. What is the title of the 2008 Newbery winning fantasy novel by Neil Gaiman where each of the eight chapters tells a story, beginning with a person as a small toddler who later assumes the name of Nobody, and his adventures and encounters as he grows up in a graveyard: "The Graveyard _?"

422. What is the name of the fantasy book series first published in 2008 by Stephanie Meyer about Isabella Swan who movies from Arizona to Washington and finds her life in danger after meeting a 104-year-old vampire named Edward Cullen: "Twi-?"

423. What is the full title of the 2008 trilogy science fiction series by Suzanne Collins from the voice of Katniss Everdeen in the nation of Panem, the Capitol that exercises political control over the entire nation, and the boys and girls that are selected by a lottery in each of the districts to compete in mortal battle: "The Hunger _?"

424. What is the title of the 2009 Newbery award-winning novel by Rebecca Stead about Miranda Sinclair living in New York City, who receives a mysterious note informing her to write down the location of her spare key and to document future events, events that include her mum's appearance on *The*

$20,000 Pyramid, when her best friend Sal suddenly stops talking to her, and the appearance of a laughing man: "When You Reach _?"

425. What is the full title of the 2010 Newbery award-winning children's novel by Clare Vanderpool about a girl named Abilene who is sent to live with a friend of her father's in Manifest, Kansas in 1936, what she learns about a boy named Jinx dating back to 1917 from the fortune teller Miss Sadie, supported with letters and news clippings found in a box, and how Abilene makes the connection of how the old life and times of Manifest somewhat fit into her current life and times: "Moon Over M_?"

426. What is the title of the 2011 Newbery award-winning autobiographical novel by Jack Gantos that tells of a boy named Jack living in Norvelt, Pennsylvania who as a punishment for firing his father's Japanese sniper rifle, has to help his neighbor Miss Volker write obituaries and her history column, and discovers that he has a great interest in historical events that he never learned about in school: "Dead End in N_?"

427. What is the title of the 2012 Newbery award-winning children's book by Katherine Applegate about a gorilla named Ivan living in a glass-walled cage at the Exit 8 Big Top Mall and Video Arcade, and how he changes his perspective of life somewhat after meeting Ruby, a baby elephant: "The One and Only I_?"

428. What is the name of the book published in 2013 by Norwegian authors Ylvis and Christian Lochstoer and illustrator Svein Nyhus, based on a popular YouTube video that tells how the cat goes meow, the dog goes woof, and the mouse goes squeak: "What Does the Fox _?"

429. What is the title of the 2014 Newbery Medal winner by Katie DiCamillo about the adventures of a young girl named Flora who loves to read comics, and her relationship with a squirrel: "Flora and Ulysses: The Illuminated _?"

430. What is the title of the 2014 Caldecott Medal winner illustrated by Brian Floca about a family's weeklong train trip from Omaha, Nebraska to Sacramento, California in 1868: "Lo_?"

431. What is the name of the reference book, first published in 1955 and every year thereafter, that contains a collection of world records, and is one of the best-selling books of all time: "G__?"

432. What is your favorite book?

433. What is the title of the 2015 Caldecott Medal winner by Dan Santat about Beekle, and imaginary friend who embarks on a journey looking for his human: "The Adventures of __?"

434. What is the title of the 2016 Caldecott Medal winner written by Lindsay Mattick that tells the story of the friendship shared between a real bear and a soldier: "Finding __?"

435. What is the title of the 2017 Caldecott Medal winner by Javaka Steptoe that tells the story of a young artist named Jean Michel Basquiat: "Radiant __?"

436. What is the name of the 2017 Newbery Medal fantasy book by Kelly Barnhill about a young girl raised by a witch, a swamp monster, and a Perfectly Tiny Dragon who must unlock the magical powers that were given to her as a baby: "The Girl Who Drank the __"?

APPENDICES – Answers to Questions

APPENDIX 1: Chapter 1 – Language Arts

Language Arts – Pre-School

1. Says name
2. Says first name
3. Says letters in first name
4. Says letters in last name
5. Says middle name
6. Says last name
7. Says age
8. Names person older
9. Names person younger
10. Names person of same age
11. Says birth date
12. Says current month
13. Says today's day of the week
14. Says tomorrow's day
15. Says yesterday's day
16. Can express feelings
17. Speaks in sentences
18. Converses with adult
19. Asks a question
20. Expresses how feeling today
21. Orders yesterday's activities
22. Listens carefully when being book is read aloud
23. Answers questions about book
24. Can re-tell a story
25. Shows correct direction to read a book
26. Recites a nursery rhyme
27. Rhymes two and shoe
28. Finishes poem, "Rain,Rain"
29. Finishes poem, "Diddle Diddle Dumpling"
30. Finishes poem, "Wee Willie Winkie"
31. Finishes poem, "Peter,Peter"
32. Finishes poem, "To market,to market"
33. Sings "Kookaburra"
34. Sings "Pop Goes the Weasel"
35. Sings "John Jacob"
36. Sings "Happy Birthday"
37. Sings "Twinkle Twinkle"
38. Sings "Rock-A-Bye Baby"
39. Sings "Row, Row, Row your Boat"
40. Sings "Old MacDonald"
41. Sings "Here we go round."
42. Sings/Dances "Ring around the Rosie"
43. Sings/Motions "This Little Piggy"
44. Sings/Motions "Eensey, Weensey Spider"
45. Sings/Motions "Five Little Monkeys"
46. Sings/Motions "I'm a Little Teapot"
47. Sings/Motions "Heads, Shoulders..."
48. Sings/Claps "B-I-N-G-O"
49. Sings/Claps "If You're Happy"
50. "Goldilocks and the Three Bears"
51. Red
52. Three
53. Wolf
54. Straw, sticks, and bricks
55. Pigs live in brick house happily ever after
56. Names a story
57. Draws a straight line
58. Scissors
59. Knows how to use scissors
60. Quiet, walk, observe safety rules
61. Follows rules for board game
62. Says a familiar board game
63. Says favorite toy
64. Says favorite food
65. Chew with mouth closed; use napkin etc.
66. Please
67. Thank you
68. You're welcome.
69. Hello Mr. __
70. Hello Mrs. __
71. Says if hot or cold today
72. Says if it is day or night
73. Morning
74. Night/Evening
75. Afternoon
76. Correctly states time of day
77. Breakfast
78. Lunch
79. Supper/Dinner
80. Correctly states current season
81. States gender
82. Knows number of siblings and names them
83. Says pets and their names
84. Feed/Water/Groom/Vet/Take outside etc.
85. Legs
86. Mouth
87. Hand
88. Shows left hand
89. Shows right hand
90. States correct hand
91. Can dress self
92. Can zip

93. Can button
94. Can tie shoes
95. Nose
96. Ears
97. Eyes
98. Feet
99. Points and names parts of body
100. Green
101. Names green things
102. Blue
103. Names blue things
104. States eye color
105. States hair color
106. Red
107. Names red things
108. Yellow
109. Names yellow things
110. Names orange things
111. Names black things
112. Names white things
113. Names pink things
114. Names purple things
115. States color of room, etc.
116. Sings alphabet
117. Words
118. Points to the cover of this book
119. Points to back of book
120. Points out page in book
121. "Pretends" to read book
122. Can turn pages
123. Car, bike, train, plane, bus, boat, etc.
124. Ambulance/Rescue Squad
125. Dump truck
126. Tow truck
127. Bus/Car
128. Fire truck
129. Water/Milk/ Oil
130. Boat/Ship
131. Motorcycle
132. Yes
133. Train/Monorail/Subway
134. Airplane/Jet
135. Tractor
136. Hammer, wrench, screw driver, etc.
137. Cow, pig, chicken, etc.
138. Elephant, Giraffe, Tiger, etc.
139. Whale, shark, octopus, etc.
140. Deer, bear, raccoon, etc.
141. Butterfly, fly, ant, ladybug, etc.
142. Dog, cat, bird, rabbit, etc.
143. Tiger, zebra, etc.
144. Dolphins, fish, etc.
145. Bird, eagle, bats, etc.
146. Deer, sheep, buffalo, moose, etc.
147. Dogs, cats, wolves, etc.
148. Tigers, lions, bears, cats, etc.
149. Wolf, bat, dog, tiger, etc.
150. Giraffe
151. Elephant
152. Imitates bird sound "Tweet-tweet"

153. Imitates dog sound "Woof"
154. Imitates cat sound "Meow"
155. Imitates frog sound "Ribbit"
156. Imitates horse sound
157. Growls like a bear
158. Imitates monkey sound
159. Imitates cow sound "Moo"
160. Squawks like a chicken
161. Quacks like a duck
162. Elephant
163. Mouse
164. States who is taller
165. House
166. Points up
167. Down
168. Mentions items in bedroom
169. Out
170. Points to front of book
171. Back
172. Mentions items on bed
173. Off
174. Says if TV on or off
175. Mentions items under bed
176. Over
177. Points to top of page
178. Bottom
179. Points to middle of page
180. States middle name
181. Points to bottom of page
182. Top
183. Happy
184. Day
185. In front of
186. Below
187. Big/large
188. High
189. Under
190. Less
191. Different
192. Names person same size
193. Names something besides bed
194. Names something inside dresser
195. Names something outside house
196. Right side up
197. Names a hot food (soup)
198. Names a cold food (ice cream)
199. Names fast animal (cheetah)
200. Names slow animal (turtle)
201. Different
202. Reads word "a"
203. Reads word "and"
204. Reads word "away"
205. Reads word "big"
206. Reads word "blue"
207. Reads word "can"
208. Reads word "come"
209. Reads word "down"
210. Reads word "find"
211. Reads word "for"
212. Reads word "funny"

213. Reads word "go"
214. Reads word "help"
215. Reads word "here"
216. Reads word "I"
217. Reads word "in"
218. Reads word "is"
219. Reads word "it"
220. Reads word "jump"
221. Reads word "little"
222. Reads word "look"
223. Reads word "make"
224. Reads word "me"
225. Reads word "my"
226. Reads word "not"
227. Reads word "one"

228. Reads word "play"
229. Reads word "red"
230. Reads word "run"
231. Reads word "said"
232. Reads word "see"
233. Reads word "the"
234. Reads word "three"
235. Reads word "to"
236. Reads word "two"
237. Reads word "up"
238. Reads word "we"
239. Reads word "where"
240. Reads word "yellow"
241. Reads word "you"

Language Arts – Kindergarten

242. German word
243. Children's Garden
244. Sings alphabet
245. Says other "a" words.
246. Says other "b" words
247. Says other "c" words
248. Says other "d" words
249. Says other "e" words
250. Says other "f" words
251. Says other "g" words
252. Says other "h" words
253. Says other "i" words
254. Says other "j" words
255. Says other "k" words
256. Says other "l" words
257. Says other "m" words
258. Says other "n" words
259. Says other "o" words
260. Says other "p" words
261. Says other "q" words
262. Says other "r" words
263. Says other "s" words
264. Says other "t" words
265. Says other "u" words
266. Says other "v" words
267. Says other "w" words
268. Says other "x" words
269. Says other "y" words
270. Says other "z" words
271. Images of bones or teeth
272. Cat, bat, etc.
273. c-a-t
274. d-a-d
275. Glad, mad, dad, etc.
276. Finishes "Hickory Dickory"
277. Finishes "Diddle Diddle"
278. Finishes "Little Bo Peep"
279. Finishes "Little Boy Blue"
280. Finishes "Ba Ba Black Sheep"
281. Finishes "One, Two…"

282. Finishes "Rain, rain..."
283. Finishes "It's raining..."
284. Finishes "Roses are Red"
285. Finishes "Jack and Jill"
286. Finishes "Jack Be Nimble"
287. Finishes "Little Miss Muffet"
288. Finishes "Mary had a lamb"
289. Finishes "Old Mother Hubbard"
290. Finishes "Old King Cole"
291. Finishes "Three Blind Mice"
292. Finishes "Three Little Kittens"
293. Finishes "There was an old woman"
294. Finishes "Star light, star bright"
295. Words
296. Sentences
297. Paragraphs
298. Books, newspapers, etc.
299. Stories, letters, cards, etc.
300. States correct writing hand
301. Computer keyboard
302. "Ask Me Smarter"
303. Says title of favorite book
304. Author
305. Draws pictures
306. False
307. True
308. False
309. Yes
310. Non-fiction
311. Books, magazines, computers, etc.
312. Use library card
313. Due date
314. Media Specialist/Librarian
315. Overdue
316. Yes
317. Non-fiction
318. Fiction
319. Preparing a food or dish
320. Winter
321. Autumn/Fall

163

322.	Spring		370.	Says word "ate"
323.	Summer		371.	Says word "be"
324.	Puppy		372.	Says word "black"
325.	Kitten		373.	Says word "brown"
326.	Heavy		374.	Says word "but"
327.	Light		375.	Says word "came"
328.	After school		376.	Says word "did"
329.	States time of day		377.	Says word "do"
330.	Round		378.	Says word "eat"
331.	Twelve		379.	Says word "for"
332.	States clock short hand number		380.	Says word "get"
333.	States clock long hand number		381.	Says word "good"
334.	Noon		382.	Says word "have"
335.	Midnight		383.	Says word "he"
336.	Calendar		384.	Says word "into"
337.	Seven		385.	Says word "like"
338.	Names days of week		386.	Says word "must"
339.	Saturday and Sunday		387.	Says word "new"
340.	States objects to right of bed		388.	Says word "no"
341.	States objects to left of bed		389.	Says word "now"
342.	States objects between bed and door		390.	Says word "on"
343.	Names object far away		391.	Says word "our"
344.	Names object close by		392.	Says word "out"
345.	Song		393.	Says word "please"
346.	Chooses song to sing		394.	Says word "pretty"
347.	Says a famous story		395.	Says word "ran"
348.	Identifies familiar stories		396.	Says word "ride"
349.	Fables		397.	Says word "saw"
350.	States familiar fable		398.	Says word "say"
351.	Longest		399.	Says word "she"
352.	Bigger		400.	Says word "so"
353.	Best		401.	Says word "soon"
354.	The worst		402.	Says word "that"
355.	Quietly		403.	Says word "there"
356.	Hopefully		404.	Says word "they"
357.	Gold		405.	Says word "this"
358.	Silver		406.	Says word "too"
359.	Copper		407.	Says word "under"
360.	Sorry		408.	Says word "want"
361.	And dogs		409.	Says word "was"
362.	Leap		410.	Says word "well"
363.	There's a way		411.	Says word "went"
364.	Best friend		412.	Says word "what"
365.	Do onto you		413.	Says word "white"
366.	Says word "all"		414.	Says word "who"
367.	Says word "am"		415.	Says word "will"
368.	Says word "are"		416.	Says word "with"
369.	Says word "at"		417.	Says word "yes"

Language Arts – 1st Grade

418.	Says and spells first name		425.	H-a-t
419.	Says middle name		426.	Says –an words
420.	Says and spells last name		427.	Says –at words
421.	26		428.	Says –ap words
422.	Cites a word for each letter		429.	Says –ab words
423.	A-E-I-O-U		430.	Says –ad words
424.	Consonants		431.	Says –am words

432.	Says –ack words	492.	ng
433.	Says –and words	493.	s
434.	Says –ash words	494.	ed
435.	Says –ail words	495.	er
436.	Says –ain words	496.	est
437.	Says –air words	497.	ly
438.	Says –ate words	498.	Short
439.	Says –ake words	499.	Long
440.	Says –ale words	500.	Short
441.	Says –ame words	501.	Long
442.	Says –ay words	502.	Short
443.	Says –all words	503.	Long
444.	Says –aw words	504.	Silent
445.	Says –ar words	505.	Short
446.	Says –ark words	506.	Long
447.	Says –art words	507.	Birth-day
448.	Says –ank words	508.	Compound
449.	Says –int words	509.	Compound
450.	Says –ed words	510.	Foot-ball
451.	Says –en words	511.	Sometimes, somewhere, etc.
452.	Says –et words	512.	Can and not
453.	Says –eck words	513.	Apostrophe
454.	Says –ell words	514.	It and is
455.	Says –est words	515.	I'm
456.	Says –in words	516.	I'll
457.	Says –ip words	517.	We'll
458.	Says –it words	518.	Are and not
459.	Fun, bun, etc.	519.	The t's or th's
460.	Fight, bite, sight, etc.	520.	The q's
461.	Look, took, etc.	521.	u
462.	Free, see, me, etc.	522.	Ant, cat, and dog
463.	Test, west, etc.	523.	Ball
464.	Deep, weep, etc.	524.	Period
465.	Claps to "Twinkle, Twinkle"	525.	Question mark
466.	Nursery rhymes	526.	Exclamation point
467.	Fairy tales	527.	Capital
468.	No	528.	Yes
469.	The Three Little Pigs	529.	Lower case
470.	Fables	530.	Action word
471.	Identifies written works	531.	Thing
472.	Identifies visual media	532.	Yes
473.	H-o-p	533.	Ran
474.	H-o-p-e	534.	Park
475.	F-r-o-g	535.	Yes
476.	S-t-o-p	536.	Pretty
477.	T-r-i-p	537.	Says adjective(s)
478.	S-h-i-p	538.	Names a fiction story
479.	S-e-a	539.	Names a non-fiction story
480.	S-e-e	540.	Cinderella, Sleepy Beauty, etc.
481.	B-o-o-k	541.	Title
482.	T-r-e-e	542.	Author
483.	C-o-w	543.	Illustrator
484.	F-a-n, etc.	544.	Table of Contents/chapters
485.	c	545.	Depends on format
486.	a	546.	Publishes book to buy
487.	t	547.	2015
488.	ch	548.	Yes
489.	th	549.	Yes
490.	wh	550.	Points out text
491.	sh	551.	No

552. Describes cover
553. Call number
554. Summarizes plot of Goldilocks
555. Forest, cottage, etc.
556. Tasted porridge/cereal
557. Sat in three chairs
558. House in woods; small, medium, big
559. Little girl with golden hair
560. Fantasy
561. Says favorite story
562. Sequences events of Goldilocks story
563. Prince
564. Glass slipper
565. The Ball
566. Midnight
567. Clothes and carriage will turn back
568. Glass Carriage
569. Opinion
570. A fact
571. Butterflies fly, etc.
572. Gives opinion about butterflies
573. Gives opinion about something
574. Looked
575. Looking
576. Looks
577. Look
578. Listened
579. A caption
580. Is
581. Are
582. Am
583. Are
584. Has
585. Have
586. Have
587. Have
588. Are
589. T-o
590. T-w-o
591. T-o-o
592. Dogs
593. Cat
594. Witches
595. Beaches
596. Baby
597. Out
598. Dry
599. Near/close
600. Hot
601. Fast/Quick
602. Whisper
603. Sweet
604. New
605. Full
606. Win
607. Rich
608. Day
609. Weak
610. Wild

611. Back
612. Pretty
613. Beginning or start
614. Morning
615. Evening
616. Before
617. After
618. Away
619. Flowers
620. Try and try again
621. Perfect
622. Merrier
623. Home
624. Says today's date
625. Says yesterday's day
626. Names days of week
627. Names 12 months of year
628. Says birth date
629. Says word "after"
630. Says word "again"
631. Says word "an"
632. Says word "any"
633. Says word "as"
634. Says word "ask"
635. Says word "by"
636. Says word "could"
637. Says word "every"
638. Says word "fly"
639. Says word "from"
640. Says word "give"
641. Says word "giving"
642. Says word "has"
643. Says word "had"
644. Says word "her"
645. Says word "him"
646. Says word "his"
647. Says word "how"
648. Says word "just"
649. Says word "know"
650. Says word "let"
651. Says word "live"
652. Says word "may"
653. Says word "of"
654. Says word "old"
655. Says word "once"
656. Says word "open"
657. Says word "over"
658. Says word "put"
659. Says word "round"
660. Says word "some"
661. Says word "stop"
662. Says word "take"
663. Says word "thank"
664. Says word "them"
665. Says word "then"
666. Says word "think"
667. Says word "walk"
668. Says word "were"
669. Says word "when"

Language Arts – 2nd Grade

670. Yes
671. Yes
672. Yes, can print all letters
673. Says words (adios, crepe, frankfurter, etc.)
674. Articulates books of liking
675. Can sound out words
676. Looking at pictures, etc.
677. Yes, can identify main ideas
678. Yes
679. Can re-tell story
680. Can sequence events in a story
681. Can identify genre
682. Yes, can imagine story
683. Yes
684. Compares and contrasts 2 stories
685. Find information
686. Books, internet, etc.
687. Dictionary
688. Alphabetical
689. Sand, show, sound, stop
690. Same, sand
691. Yes
692. Says books and magazines read
693. Says name of local paper
694. No
695. Long
696. Short
697. Short
698. Long
699. Spells was
700. Spells were
701. Spells says
702. Spells said
703. Spells who
704. Spells why
705. Spells light
706. Spells right
707. Spells bedroom
708. Spells sometimes
709. Spells sailboat
710. Spells happy
711. Spells silly
712. Spells pretty
713. Spells know
714. Spells wrong
715. Opposite
716. Loud
717. The same
718. Large, huge, etc.
719. Little, tiny, etc.
720. Homonym
721. Key lock
722. You are right or correct
723. A prefix
724. A suffix
725. The suffix
726. Smallest

727. Slowly
728. Ageless, fearless, timeless, etc.
729. Adorable, comfortable, invisible, etc.
730. Refund, reuse, review, etc.
731. Unsafe, unbelievable, etc.
732. Punctuation
733. Quotation
734. Sleeping
735. Climbed
736. Finished; Uses word in sentence
737. Did
738. Ate
739. Read
740. Wore
741. Dried
742. Saw
743. Came
744. He was
745. They were
746. Went
747. Found
748. Said
749. Describes last book read
750. Has written letter
751. An end
752. Table of Contents
753. Index
754. Says yes or no
755. Anne Frank, et al
756. To record thoughts
757. Yes
758. Can identify sentence
759. Can write a sentence
760. Can write a question
761. Can write exclamatory sentence
762. Can write letter
763. Can write thank you note
764. Can write report
765. Can write story
766. Can write poem
767. For gift, kind gesture, party, etc.
768. Can draft ideas on paper
769. Re-write and modify
770. Check for errors
771. Yes
772. No, copyright infringement
773. Can write upper and lower case letters
774. Can write report on book
775. Books, internet, atlases, etc.
776. Informational book organized alphabetically
777. Can identify all parts of book
778. Recognizes genres with examples
779. Biography
780. The illustrator
781. The author
782. Encyclopedia
783. Can turn on computer

784. Identifies keyboard, monitor, and mouse
785. Yes, keyboarding important
786. Can conduct basic search
787. No
788. Cites inappropriate use of internet
789. Can do basic computer search in library
790. Can load basic software
791. Reads word "always"
792. Reads word "around"
793. Reads word "because"
794. Reads word "been"
795. Reads word "before"
796. Reads word "best"
797. Reads word "both"
798. Reads word "buy"
799. Reads word "call"
800. Reads word "cold"
801. Reads word "does"
802. Reads word "don't"
803. Reads word "fast"
804. Reads word "first"
805. Reads word "five"
806. Reads word "found"
807. Reads word "gave"
808. Reads word "goes"
809. Reads word "green"

810. Reads word "it's"
811. Reads word "made"
812. Reads word "many"
813. Reads word "off"
814. Reads word "or"
815. Reads word "pull"
816. Reads word "read"
817. Reads word "right"
818. Reads word "sing"
819. Reads word "sit"
820. Reads word "sleep"
821. Reads word "tell"
822. Reads word "their"
823. Reads word "these"
824. Reads word "those"
825. Reads word "upon"
826. Reads word "us"
827. Reads word "use"
828. Reads word "very"
829. Reads word "wash"
830. Reads word "wish"
831. Reads word "work"
832. Reads word "would"
833. Reads word "write"
834. Reads word "your"

Language Arts – 3rd Grade

835. Yes
836. Yes
837. Reads silently
838. Reads aloud
839. Sounds out new and unfamiliar words
840. 26
841. A, E, I O, U (sometimes y)
842. Yes
843. Makes "th" sound
844. Makes "st" sound
845. Makes "bl" sound
846. Makes "gr" sound
847. Makes "sc" sound
848. Says "br" word
849. Says "cr" word
850. Says "dr" word
851. Says "fr" word
852. Says "gr" word
853. Says "pr" word
854. Says "tr" word
855. Says "bl" word
856. Says "cl" word
857. Says "fl" word
858. Says "gl" word
859. Says "pl" word
860. Says "sl" word
861. Says "sc" word
862. Says "sk" word
863. Says "sm" word

864. Says "sn" word
865. Says "sp" word
866. Says "st" word
867. Says "sw" word
868. Says "scr" word
869. Says "squ" word
870. Says "str" word
871. Says "spr" word
872. Says "spl" word
873. Yes
874. Deputy
875. Primary
876. Alphabetical
877. u
878. Yes
879. Yes
880. Hard "c"
881. Hard "c"
882. Hard "c"
883. Says hard "c" words
884. Soft "c"
885. Soft "c"
886. Soft "c"
887. Says soft "c" words
888. Yes
889. Hard "g"
890. Hard "g"
891. Hard "g"
892. Soft "g"

893.	Soft "g"	953.	Yes
894.	Soft "g"	954.	Spells beige
895.	Yes	955.	Spells chief
896.	Yes, Y can be both	956.	Spells piece
897.	Yes	957.	Spells science
898.	Consonant	958.	Spells receive
899.	Vowel	959.	Spells thief
900.	Vowel	960.	Compound words
901.	An	961.	Spells everything
902.	An umbrella	962.	Spells yourself
903.	An honor	963.	Spells butterfly
904.	A cat	964.	Spells somewhere
905.	An owl	965.	Spells sailboat
906.	A bird	966.	Spells grandfather
907.	An elephant	967.	Names compound words
908.	A chest	968.	Yes
909.	Find definition, syllables, etc.	969.	Recognizes base of word
910.	Alphabetical	970.	Listen
911.	Can look up word in dictionary	971.	Dependent
912.	Can identify right meaning of word	972.	The beginning
913.	Declare, defend, destroy, device	973.	Recognizes prefix
914.	Hum	974.	un
915.	Lima bean	975.	re
916.	"X"	976.	mis
917.	Can have multiple definitions	977.	un
918.	Nail net	978.	in
919.	Coast cocoa	979.	pre
920.	Crate credit	980.	mis
921.	Yes	981.	re
922.	Syllables	982.	inconsiderate
923.	Yes	983.	dis
924.	Two syllables	984.	im
925.	Three syllables	985.	un
926.	One syllable	986.	ly
927.	Two syllables	987.	Base or root word
928.	Four syllables	988.	Pretty
929.	Yes, can blend syllables	989.	Yes
930.	Table	990.	End
931.	Monkey	991.	Yes, they are common suffixes
932.	Can divide words	992.	Plays
933.	Tur-tle	993.	Played
934.	Snow-board-ing	994.	Playing
935.	Pop-u-la-tion	995.	ous
936.	Yes, spelling is important	996.	less
937.	No	997.	ful
938.	The "g" and "h" silent	998.	less
939.	Spells half	999.	ily
940.	The letter "l"	1000.	ful
941.	Spells tough	1001.	less
942.	The letters "gh"	1002.	or
943.	Spells hop	1003.	ist
944.	Spells hope	1004.	er
945.	Yes, final "e" silent	1005.	ist
946.	Long	1006.	ian
947.	Spells pail	1007.	ian
948.	Spells pale	1008.	Same thing
949.	Spells quit	1009.	Large, huge
950.	Spells queen	1010.	Intelligent, bright
951.	u	1011.	Mistake
952.	c	1012.	Dangerous

1013.	Rich	1073.	There
1014.	Finished	1074.	Their
1015.	Walk	1075.	They're
1016.	Careful	1076.	Yes
1017.	Afraid, terrified	1077.	Seize
1018.	Helper, aid	1078.	Seas
1019.	Large, big	1079.	Sees
1020.	Sob	1080.	Cent or sent
1021.	Rich	1081.	Claws
1022.	Moist	1082.	Tail
1023.	The opposite	1083.	Vain
1024.	Narrow	1084.	Peak
1025.	Rough	1085.	Flare
1026.	Easy	1086.	Poll
1027.	Full	1087.	Earn
1028.	Destroy	1088.	Bow
1029.	Shallow	1089.	Wrote
1030.	Sweet	1090.	Bred
1031.	Under	1091.	Tense
1032.	Friend, comrade	1092.	Air
1033.	Light	1093.	Pair
1034.	Rich	1094.	Towed
1035.	Easy and soft	1095.	Fare
1036.	Wild	1096.	Fair
1037.	Wide	1097.	Blew
1038.	Asleep	1098.	Blue
1039.	Least	1099.	Waist
1040.	Dry	1100.	Waste
1041.	Break	1101.	Principal
1042.	Yes	1102.	Principle
1043.	Right: Turn right, you're right	1103.	Threw; through
1044.	Yes	1104.	Meet; meat
1045.	Container; sport	1105.	Won; one
1046.	Measurement; outdoor space	1106.	Yes
1047.	Insect; verb for airborne	1107.	Can identify genres
1048.	Crouch down; animal	1108.	Yes
1049.	Container; verb for ability	1109.	Tall tales
1050.	Baseball position; container for liquid	1110.	Folktale
1051.	Jewelry;: phone signal; circular marking	1111.	Fairy tale
1052.	Baseball stick; nocturnal animal	1112.	Made-up
1053.	C, a speech	1113.	Myths
1054.	A, location of a building	1114.	Yes
1055.	B, the writing on the envelope	1115.	Yes
1056.	Yes	1116.	Cover, pictures, etc.
1057.	Yes	1117.	Yes
1058.	Yes	1118.	Yes
1059.	Yes	1119.	Yes
1060.	Flour	1120.	Yes
1061.	Peace	1121.	Yes
1062.	Cent and sent	1122.	Plain lady marries prince
1063.	Yes	1123.	Cinderella, prince, wicked family
1064.	By	1124.	Home and prince's castle
1065.	Bye	1125.	Lady transforms into princess etc.
1066.	Buy	1126.	Yes
1067.	Yes	1127.	Fact
1068.	To	1128.	Opinion
1069.	Too	1129.	Fact can be proven
1070.	Two	1130.	Personal judgment
1071.	Yes	1131.	Yes
1072.	Write	1132.	Identifies paragraph

1133. Five
1134. Yes, can identify sentence parts
1135. Person, place, or thing
1136. Performs the action
1137. Walked
1138. Walk, run, jump, danced, etc.
1139. Park
1140. Zoo, Kansas, Sam, computer, etc.
1141. Mrs. Smith
1142. Dr. Smith, Chicago, Mozart, etc.
1143. Yes
1144. Is
1145. Have
1146. Substitutes for a noun
1147. Maya
1148. She
1149. He
1150. It
1151. I, you, he, she, it, we, they, etc.
1152. Describes a verb
1153. Slowly
1154. ly
1155. Never
1156. Quickly, easily, here, out, now, very
1157. Too
1158. Also
1159. To
1160. Two
1161. Indent
1162. Topic sentence
1163. Identifies punctuation mark
1164. Apostrophe
1165. John's books
1166. I-t apostrophe s
1167. It is
1168. Isn't
1169. Don't
1170. I'll
1171. They're
1172. Yes
1173. Yes, can write cursive
1174. Yes
1175. Drafting
1176. Revising
1177. Editing
1178. Find and correct errors
1179. Yes
1180. Publishing
1181. Idiom
1182. Easy to do
1183. Words
1184. Choosers
1185. Romans do
1186. Pod
1187. Leg
1188. Beans
1189. Dogs
1190. Cap
1191. Do onto you
1192. Upper case

1193. Subject
1194. Alex
1195. Predicate
1196. Eats ice cream
1197. Purred softly
1198. First word
1199. Yes
1200. Wisconsin
1201. Yes
1202. Yes
1203. Yes
1204. Cat
1205. Wife
1206. Tooth
1207. Goose
1208. Penny
1209. Dogs
1210. Turtles
1211. Echoes
1212. Potatoes
1213. Tomatoes
1214. Heroes
1215. Boxes
1216. Families
1217. Pennies
1218. Qualities
1219. Halves
1220. Leaves
1221. Thieves
1222. Wolves
1223. Selves
1224. Knives
1225. Lives
1226. Fish
1227. Deer
1228. Sheep
1229. Men
1230. Women
1231. Persons/People
1232. Children
1233. Mice
1234. Feet
1235. Teeth
1236. Oxen
1237. Copy
1238. Geese
1239. Fly
1240. Katie
1241. Arizona
1242. Thanksgiving Day
1243. Names specific river
1244. Names specific city
1245. Names specific athlete
1246. Names specific president
1247. Names specific street
1248. Names specific month
1249. Names specific holiday
1250. Names specific ocean
1251. Names specific artist
1252. Leaves

1253.	Noun	**1313.**	Drink
1254.	Cites nouns	**1314.**	Describes a noun
1255.	Yes	**1315.**	Curly
1256.	Describes an action	**1316.**	Pretty
1257.	Drove	**1317.**	Blonde
1258.	Lake	**1318.**	Proper adjective
1259.	Cites action verbs	**1319.**	American, Spanish, French, etc.
1260.	Verbs of being	**1320.**	Descriptive adjectives
1261.	Am	**1321.**	Adjectives
1262.	Is	**1322.**	Adjectives
1263.	Are	**1323.**	Adjectives
1264.	Was	**1324.**	Adjectives
1265.	Were	**1325.**	Taste adjectives
1266.	Has	**1326.**	Touch adjectives
1267.	Have	**1327.**	Adjectives
1268.	Present	**1328.**	Fun, crowded, tasty, etc.
1269.	Past	**1329.**	Demonstrative adjective
1270.	Future	**1330.**	Pretty, big, city, etc.
1271.	Played	**1331.**	Young, red, new, etc.
1272.	Cried	**1332.**	Little, old, chocolate, etc.
1273.	Went	**1333.**	These
1274.	Ate	**1334.**	Those
1275.	Bought	**1335.**	This house
1276.	Made	**1336.**	That tree over there
1277.	Felt	**1337.**	An adjective
1278.	Heard	**1338.**	Bigger
1279.	Thought	**1339.**	Biggest
1280.	Saw	**1340.**	Taller, tallest
1281.	Kept	**1341.**	Happier, happiest
1282.	Brought	**1342.**	More peaceful, the most peaceful
1283.	Was	**1343.**	Friendlier, friendliest
1284.	Did	**1344.**	Better, best
1285.	Knew	**1345.**	Worse, the worst
1286.	Broke	**1346.**	More, the most
1287.	Began	**1347.**	Littler, the littlest
1288.	Had	**1348.**	Farther, the farthest
1289.	Paid	**1349.**	Simile
1290.	Gave	**1350.**	Bone
1291.	Cut	**1351.**	Pie
1292.	Told	**1352.**	Bat
1293.	Spoke	**1353.**	Bee
1294.	Sent	**1354.**	Feather
1295.	Took	**1355.**	Wind
1296.	Met	**1356.**	Apple
1297.	Taught	**1357.**	Elephant
1298.	Left	**1358.**	An adverb
1299.	Found	**1359.**	Swiftly
1300.	Read	**1360.**	No
1301.	Flew	**1361.**	Yes
1302.	Got	**1362.**	Adverbs of frequency
1303.	Swam	**1363.**	Yes
1304.	Say	**1364.**	Adverbs of place
1305.	Shake	**1365.**	Adverbs of purpose
1306.	Ring	**1366.**	Adverbs of time
1307.	Stand	**1367.**	Preposition
1308.	Find	**1368.**	Yes
1309.	Blow	**1369.**	Under
1310.	Give	**1370.**	Uses correct prepositions
1311.	Freeze	**1371.**	Takes place of a noun
1312.	Sleep	**1372.**	She

1373. She
1374. He
1375. They
1376. We
1377. I
1378. John and I
1379. Yes
1380. John invited me
1381. Yes
1382. To me
1383. Mine; my
1384. Hers; her
1385. His; his
1386. Yours; your
1387. Ours; our
1388. Theirs; their
1389. Yes
1390. Interjection
1391. Ouch
1392. Hooray
1393. Oh my
1394. Conjunction
1395. But
1396. And
1397. If
1398. Contraction
1399. Didn't
1400. Letter
1401. I'd
1402. I'll
1403. Wouldn't
1404. They've
1405. Haven't
1406. You're
1407. Would not
1408. Will not
1409. Declarative
1410. Interrogative
1411. Declarative
1412. Interrogative
1413. Is
1414. Are
1415. Yes
1416. Yes
1417. Yes
1418. Printing
1419. Ideally yes
1420. Yes
1421. Yes
1422. Yes
1423. Yes
1424. A sentence
1425. Yes
1426. Studied; good grade
1427. Flat tire; tow truck
1428. Period
1429. Comma
1430. Comma
1431. After singing and dancing
1432. After city name

1433. Question mark
1434. Exclamation point!
1435. Quotation marks
1436. Before do and after cream
1437. All in marks except, said Brittney
1438. Apostrophe
1439. Yes
1440. Before
1441. Marcos's bike
1442. Jack's
1443. After
1444. The singers' voices
1445. You're
1446. Abbreviation
1447. Period
1448. St.
1449. Ave.
1450. Dr.
1451. Varies
1452. U.S.
1453. Washington D.C.
1454. Oct.
1455. Ave.
1456. Bat, sat, rat, mat, etc.
1457. Pig
1458. Bet, get, set, jet, etc.
1459. Sight, fight, might, bright, etc.
1460. Bold, fold, gold, told, etc.
1461. Beat, feat, heat, meat, etc.
1462. A) how, low
1463. Disappointed
1464. Yes
1465. Yes
1466. Growled
1467. Amazed
1468. Sad
1469. Hid
1470. Dangerous
1471. Paragraph
1472. Indent
1473. Topic sentence
1474. Topic sentence
1475. Supporting sentences
1476. First, second, then, last, etc.
1477. Yes
1478. Names a story
1479. Can tell a story
1480. Can predict ending
1481. Yes
1482. Yes
1483. Snow White, Seven Dwarfs, Queen
1484. Castle, Forest
1485. Snow White hides in home with Dwarfs to escape wicked Queen.
1486. Snow White living with Dwarfs, etc.
1487. Magic mirror, poison apple, Dwarf names
1488. To gain information
1489. A fact
1490. An opinion
1491. How they are similar

1492. How they are different
1493. Cites what currently reading
1494. Names genre
1495. Fiction
1496. Non-fiction
1497. Yes
1498. Dewey Decimal System
1499. Non-fiction
1500. Call numbers
1501. Encyclopedia, atlas, dictionary, etc.
1502. Historical fiction
1503. Different
1504. Yes
1505. Yes
1506. Biography
1507. Autobiography
1508. Yes
1509. Poetry
1510. Prose
1511. Myth
1512. Yes
1513. Science fiction
1514. Legend
1515. A folktale
1516. Yes
1517. Fable
1518. Fables
1519. Names fables
1520. Aesop
1521. Fiction
1522. Yes
1523. Yes
1524. Yes
1525. Yes
1526. Yes
1527. Greeting
1528. Yes
1529. Yes
1530. Middle of envelope
1531. Upper left corner
1532. Upper right corner
1533. Yes
1534. Occasion, time, date, etc.
1535. Yes
1536. Birthday gift, etc.
1537. Yes
1538. Applying for job, etc.
1539. Yes
1540. Point of view
1541. Yes
1542. Internet, Encyclopedia, etc.
1543. Reference materials
1544. Yes
1545. Yes
1546. Yes
1547. Casual
1548. Formal
1549. Yes
1550. Newbery award
1551. Draws pictures

1552. Caldecott
1553. Plays, dramas
1554. Yes
1555. Dialogue
1556. Modifying in order to improve it
1557. Yes
1558. Speech
1559. Yes
1560. Yes
1561. Hello, my name is
1562. Yes
1563. Name, number, etc.
1564. Paraphrasing
1565. Paraphrases a story
1566. Summarizing
1567. Yes
1568. Graph
1569. Yes
1570. Restaurant, café
1571. Yes
1572. Find out date of event
1573. An outline
1574. Reference
1575. Yes
1576. Dictionary
1577. A thesaurus
1578. Large, huge, etc.
1579. Atlas
1580. Maps, borders, etc.
1581. Almanac
1582. Phone book
1583. Encyclopedia, Internet, etc.
1584. Almanac
1585. The Internet
1586. Yes
1587. Daily news and events
1588. Indicates what article is about
1589. Yes
1590. Yes
1591. A caption
1592. Yes
1593. Yes
1594. Indicates what book is about
1595. Chapters
1596. Table of Contents
1597. Index
1598. Glossary
1599. Index
1600. Yes
1601. Informational text
1602. Lists informational topics
1603. Yes
1604. Functional text
1605. Directions, recipes, etc.
1606. Reads word "about"
1607. Reads word "better"
1608. Reads word "bring"
1609. Reads word "carry"
1610. Reads word "clean"
1611. Reads word "cut"

1612. Reads word "done"
1613. Reads word "draw"
1614. Reads word "drink"
1615. Reads word "eight"
1616. Reads word "fall"
1617. Reads word "far"
1618. Reads word "full"
1619. Reads word "got"
1620. Reads word "grow"
1621. Reads word "hold"
1622. Reads word "hot"
1623. Reads word "hurt"
1624. Reads word "if"
1625. Reads word "keep"
1626. Reads word "kind"
1627. Reads word "laugh"
1628. Reads word "life"
1629. Reads word "long"

1630. Reads word "much"
1631. Reads word "myself"
1632. Reads word "never"
1633. Reads word "only"
1634. Reads word "own"
1635. Reads word "pick"
1636. Reads word "seven"
1637. Reads word "shall"
1638. Reads word "show"
1639. Reads word "six"
1640. Reads word "small"
1641. Reads word "start"
1642. Reads word "ten"
1643. Reads word "today"
1644. Reads word "together"
1645. Reads word "try
1646. Reads word "warm"

Language Arts – 4th Grade

1647. Language arts
1648. Yes, can read silently
1649. Yes, can read aloud
1650. Yes, can summarize
1651. Names short story
1652. Names chapter book
1653. Names poem
1654. No
1655. Stanza
1656. Refrain
1657. Prose
1658. Sonnet
1659. Fourteen
1660. William Shakespeare
1661. Names play
1662. Yes
1663. At the beginning
1664. At the end
1665. Find page number of topic
1666. A glossary
1667. The preface
1668. The appendix
1669. Yes
1670. Syllables; part of speech, etc.
1671. Hello, et al
1672. Yes, can predict
1673. Can sequence events
1674. Yes
1675. Yes
1676. Yes
1677. Yes
1678. Both have wicked stepmothers, etc.
1679. Yes
1680. Sleeping Beauty was a royal and put under a curse; Cinderella was a commoner who lived with step-family and went to a Ball, etc.
1681. Cause and effect

1682. Pluto is the farthest planet is cause, Pluto is the coldest planet is the effect.
1683. Fiction
1684. Non-fiction
1685. A fable
1686. Aesop
1687. A tall tale
1688. Drama
1689. A biography
1690. A legend
1691. Yes
1692. Yes
1693. An English legend
1694. A myth
1695. A Greek myth
1696. A ballad
1697. A limerick
1698. Satire
1699. An allegory
1700. Epic
1701. Literary elements
1702. Foreshadowing
1703. Hyperbole
1704. A simile
1705. A metaphor
1706. A metaphor
1707. Alliteration
1708. Onomatopoeia
1709. Personification
1710. Deep
1711. Fall
1712. Cabinet
1713. Hatchet
1714. Meet
1715. Basket
1716. Hatch
1717. Words

1718. Right
1719. To him or her
1720. Believing
1721. None
1722. Waste
1723. Place
1724. Moon
1725. Cure
1726. Pours
1727. Live
1728. Thin
1729. Drink
1730. Etcetera
1731. RSVP
1732. Yes
1733. Yes
1734. Yes
1735. Yes
1736. Yes
1737. Yes
1738. Bibliography
1739. Author, title, publisher, date, etc.
1740. Last name
1741. Yes
1742. Yes
1743. Can write a thank you note
1744. Yes
1745. Yes
1746. Yes
1747. Writing
1748. Rough draft
1749. Topic sentence
1750. Concluding sentence
1751. Yes
1752. Prose
1753. Yes
1754. Yes
1755. Yes
1756. Cites persuasive essay
1757. Cites informative essay
1758. Cites entertaining essay
1759. Yes
1760. Internet, Encyclopedia, etc.
1761. An encyclopedia
1762. A thesaurus
1763. A dictionary
1764. An atlas
1765. An online encyclopedia
1766. Yes
1767. Yes
1768. Apposition
1769. Eight
1770. Verb
1771. Noun
1772. Cheetah
1773. Adjective
1774. Smart
1775. Pronoun
1776. He
1777. He

1778. She
1779. It
1780. They
1781. Personal pronouns
1782. Possessive pronouns
1783. Verb
1784. Jumped
1785. Yes
1786. Adverb
1787. Quickly
1788. Well
1789. Preposition
1790. Prepositions
1791. Beside
1792. On
1793. Prepositional phrases
1794. Conjunction
1795. And
1796. But
1797. Interjection
1798. Wow!
1799. Yes
1800. Yes
1801. Jack
1802. Loves Ice Cream
1803. A fragment
1804. A fragment
1805. I or we, etc.
1806. Run-on sentence
1807. I went to Chicago. It is a big city.
1808. Lisa and Michael made cookies.
1809. Am
1810. Is
1811. Are
1812. Lives
1813. Was
1814. A declarative
1815. An interrogative
1816. Exclamatory
1817. Imperative
1818. A declarative
1819. Period
1820. An interrogative
1821. Question mark
1822. Pose the words as a question
1823. Say the words as a statement
1824. An exclamatory sentence
1825. Exclamation point
1826. Imperative
1827. An imperative
1828. Comma
1829. After the number 7
1830. After yes
1831. After Orlando
1832. Before
1833. Before
1834. After bones
1835. Commas
1836. After cookies and brownies
1837. A comma

1838. A semi-colon
1839. A colon
1840. A colon
1841. A comma
1842. A colon
1843. A colon
1844. Apostrophe
1845. Friend's
1846. After
1847. Girls'
1848. Dog's
1849. Apostrophe
1850. Letter
1851. We're
1852. A
1853. O
1854. Don't
1855. I'd
1856. They're
1857. She is
1858. I will
1859. You are
1860. Did not
1861. Will not
1862. Quotation marks
1863. Yes
1864. Before I, after tonight
1865. A synonym
1866. Clean, etc.
1867. Friend, etc.
1868. Try, etc.
1869. Woman, etc.
1870. Different, unknown, etc.
1871. Glad, etc.
1872. Antonym
1873. Succeed
1874. False
1875. Expensive
1876. Cloudy
1877. Solid
1878. Shy
1879. Dry
1880. Far
1881. Under
1882. Rough
1883. Smooth
1884. A prefix
1885. Not
1886. Im
1887. Not possible
1888. In
1889. Not visible
1890. Non
1891. Not fiction
1892. Wrong
1893. Mis
1894. Wrongly behave
1895. Before
1896. pre
1897. Before the game

1898. in
1899. en
1900. In danger
1901. End of a word
1902. ly
1903. ly
1904. ily
1905. y
1906. Full of
1907. ful
1908. Capable of
1909. able
1910. ible
1911. Verb into noun
1912. Agreement
1913. Achieve
1914. Stem word
1915. Deny
1916. A palindrome
1917. An idiom
1918. Hard time
1919. Says word "action"
1920. Says word "actually"
1921. Says word "alive"
1922. Says word "although"
1923. Says word "amount"
1924. Says word "area"
1925. Says word "blood"
1926. Says word "cause"
1927. Says word "central"
1928. Says word "century"
1929. Says word "charcoal"
1930. Says word "chart"
1931. Says word "check"
1932. Says word "club"
1933. Says word "colony"
1934. Says word "company"
1935. Says word "condition"
1936. Says word "court"
1937. Says word "deal"
1938. Says word "death"
1939. Says word "describe"
1940. Says word "design"
1941. Says word "disease"
1942. Says word "eleven"
1943. Says word "equal"
1944. Says word "experience"
1945. Says word "factor"
1946. Says word "favorite"
1947. Says word "figure"
1948. Says word "hospital"
1949. Says word "include"
1950. Says word "increase"
1951. Says word "known"
1952. Says word "least"
1953. Says word "length"
1954. Says word "loud"
1955. Says word "measure"
1956. Says word "molecule"
1957. Says word "natural"

1958. Says word "necessary"
1959. Says word "noun"
1960. Says word "oxygen"
1961. Says word "phrase"
1962. Says word "property"
1963. Says word "radio"
1964. Says word "receive"
1965. Says word "replace"
1966. Says word "rhythm"
1967. Says word "serve"
1968. Says word "similar"
1969. Says word "southern"
1970. Says word "squirrel"
1971. Says word "straight"

1972. Says word "subtle"
1973. Says word "suffix"
1974. Says word "surely"
1975. Says word "though"
1976. Says word "thought"
1977. Says word "touch"
1978. Says word "twice"
1979. Says word "used"
1980. Says word "usually"
1981. Says word "view"
1982. Says word "weight"
1983. Says word "wheat"
1984. Says word "whom"
1985. Says word "young"

Language Arts – 5th Grade

1986. Genres
1987. Fiction and Non-Fiction
1988. Children's literature
1989. Fantasy
1990. Mystery
1991. Horror
1992. Romance
1993. A thriller
1994. A biography
1995. An autobiography
1996. A speech
1997. Non-Fiction
1998. Drama
1999. Poetry
2000. Fable
2001. Fantasy
2002. Science Fiction
2003. Realistic Fiction
2004. Folklore
2005. Historical Fiction
2006. Horror
2007. Tall tale
2008. Legend
2009. Mythology
2010. Non-Fiction
2011. An essay
2012. Non-Fiction
2013. Fiction
2014. A ballad
2015. A narrative poem
2016. A lyric poem
2017. Free verse
2018. A stanza
2019. Rhyme scheme
2020. Stress
2021. Meter
2022. Iambic pentameter
2023. A couplet
2024. A limerick
2025. A cinquain
2026. A quatrain

2027. Haiku
2028. Homer
2029. A play
2030. Yes
2031. No
2032. A famous poet
2033. Robert Frost
2034. Ralph Waldo Emerson
2035. Walt Whitman
2036. Gwendolyn Brooks
2037. Emily Dickenson
2038. William Blake
2039. Lewis Carroll
2040. John Keats
2041. Henry David Thoreau
2042. Edgar Allan Poe
2043. Lord Byron
2044. John Milton
2045. Elizabeth Barrett Browning
2046. Maya Angelou
2047. A sonnet
2048. A short story
2049. An article
2050. A novel
2051. An interview
2052. Fiction and Non-Fiction
2053. Print, eBooks, etc.
2054. Visually impaired, elderly, etc.
2055. Dewey Decimal System
2056. Author
2057. Playwright
2058. Title
2059. Sub-title
2060. Illustrator
2061. Chapters
2062. Table of Contents
2063. Glossary
2064. Index
2065. Copyright
2066. Publisher
2067. Bibliography

2068.	Yes	2128.	Sound
2069.	Dictionary	2129.	Light
2070.	Thesaurus	2130.	Much, many
2071.	Atlas	2131.	First, earliest form
2072.	Almanac	2132.	Mind, soul
2073.	GPS	2133.	Distant, far
2074.	Yes	2134.	Heat, hot
2075.	An acronym	2135.	Three
2076.	Acronyms	2136.	Year, annual
2077.	Names acronyms	2137.	Before
2078.	Yes	2138.	Water
2079.	The plot	2139.	Two
2080.	The conflict	2140.	Hundred
2081.	The setting	2141.	Ten
2082.	The characters	2142.	Speak, say
2083.	The protagonist	2143.	Dual, two
2084.	The antagonist	2144.	Good fate
2085.	Point of view	2145.	Heir
2086.	First person	2146.	Work
2087.	Third person	2147.	Great, large
2088.	The theme	2148.	Less, small
2089.	Author's purpose	2149.	Ship
2090.	Author's style	2150.	All
2091.	The Newbery Award	2151.	After, behind
2092.	Caldecott Medal	2152.	Before, previous
2093.	The Nobel	2153.	First
2094.	The Pulitzer	2154.	Four
2095.	Best seller	2155.	United
2096.	By genre	2156.	Vision, see
2097.	Translation	2157.	Life
2098.	Written	2158.	Etymology
2099.	Spoken	2159.	Yes
2100.	English, Spanish, etc.	2160.	African
2101.	No	2161.	Arabic
2102.	Spanish	2162.	Australian
2103.	Monolingual	2163.	Chinese
2104.	Bilingual	2164.	Dutch
2105.	Multi-lingual	2165.	East Indian
2106.	Mandarin Chinese	2166.	French
2107.	English	2167.	German
2108.	Spanish	2168.	Hebrew
2109.	Yes	2169.	Irish
2110.	Yes	2170.	Italian
2111.	7,000 languages	2171.	Japanese
2112.	English	2172.	Native American
2113.	linguistics	2173.	Hawaiian
2114.	Yes	2174.	Russian
2115.	Yes	2175.	Polish
2116.	Air	2176.	Spanish
2117.	Star	2177.	Turkish
2118.	Book	2178.	Hello
2119.	Life	2179.	Goodbye
2120.	Universe	2180.	Please
2121.	Circle or ring	2181.	Thank you
2122.	Earth	2182.	Yes
2123.	Water	2183.	No
2124.	Measure	2184.	Cat
2125.	Large, bit	2185.	Cow
2126.	Small, short	2186.	Dog
2127.	Single, one	2187.	Frog

2188. Horse
2189. Pig
2190. Snake
2191. A la carte
2192. A la mode
2193. Au revoir
2194. Bon appétit
2195. Bonjour
2196. Bon voyage
2197. Cul de sac
2198. En route
2199. Faux pas
2200. Hors d'oeuvre
2201. Laissez-faire
2202. On an invitation
2203. Respond to event
2204. Carpe diem
2205. Bona fide
2206. Et cetera
2207. Mea culpa
2208. Status quo
2209. Vice versa
2210. Prefix
2211. Against
2212. Between
2213. Together
2214. Middle
2215. Before
2216. After
2217. Not
2218. Partial
2219. Suffix
2220. –ly
2221. Slowly
2222. Happily
2223. –ist
2224. –ish
2225. –ness
2226. –ion and -er
2227. Rather
2228. Yes
2229. Indent
2230. Capitalize it
2231. Yes
2232. Yes
2233. Yes
2234. Yes
2235. Yes
2236. Yes
2237. Yes
2238. Period
2239. Question mark
2240. Exclamation point
2241. Comma
2242. Comma
2243. After number
2244. After the city or town
2245. Appositive
2246. Sara Smith
2247. My Goldendoodle

2248. Colon
2249. Colon
2250. Italics
2251. Either one
2252. Italicize
2253. Before Star, after Banner
2254. Parts of speech
2255. Noun and verb (predicate)
2256. Noun
2257. Tree, teacher, store, etc.
2258. Proper noun
2259. Jim, Phoenix, etc.
2260. Washington, D.C.
2261. Common noun
2262. New York
2263. Store, phone, she, etc.
2264. A pronoun
2265. Shorter
2266. Yes
2267. Me, my, or mine
2268. Depends on how it is used
2269. Yes
2270. Cases
2271. Nominative case she
2272. Nominative case they
2273. Nominative
2274. Objective
2275. My sister and I
2276. Ryan and me
2277. I, she, he, they, we, etc.
2278. An adjective
2279. Blue and expensive
2280. Red bike, windy path, etc.
2281. Big, smart, loud, etc.
2282. Verb
2283. Run, see, played, is, etc.
2284. Yes
2285. Ate
2286. Will eat
2287. Eats
2288. Adverb
2289. Slowly
2290. No
2291. Soon
2292. Very
2293. Well
2294. Quietly, fast, easily, very, etc.
2295. Carefully set down
2296. Quickly, loudly, carefully, etc.
2297. When
2298. Where
2299. To what extent
2300. Worse
2301. Tallest
2302. Least
2303. Many
2304. Best
2305. A conjunction
2306. Conjunctions
2307. So you should…

2308. But, and, so, etc.
2309. A preposition
2310. In, on, under, between, etc.
2311. An interjection
2312. Yikes!
2313. What!
2314. Hey, ouch, oh my, etc.
2315. The direct object
2316. Murals
2317. Murals
2318. Slaves
2319. Slaves
2320. Yes
2321. The indirect object
2322. Zach
2323. Zach
2324. Friends
2325. His friends
2326. Indirect object
2327. Paul
2328. Made
2329. Pizza
2330. Yes
2331. Baby
2332. Baby
2333. Baby
2334. Yes
2335. Singular
2336. Plural
2337. He teaches science.
2338. The deer ran
2339. Fly
2340. Was
2341. Likes
2342. Like
2343. Active
2344. Passive voice
2345. Active
2346. Active voice
2347. Passive
2348. A fragment
2349. A run-on
2350. A complete sentence
2351. A fragment
2352. A run-on
2353. Add the word "so" after bake
2354. The predicate
2355. Directed traffic at intersection
2356. Cried
2357. Carried …to mom
2358. After
2359. Garbage
2360. In the brisk wind were flying
2361. Yes
2362. Says short story topic
2363. Yes
2364. Yes
2365. Says report topic
2366. Says essay topic
2367. The introduction

2368. The body
2369. The conclusion
2370. The thesis statement
2371. Literal
2372. No
2373. Literal
2374. Figurative
2375. Literal
2376. Figurative
2377. Oxymoron
2378. Jumbo shrimp
2379. Oxymorons
2380. Imagery
2381. Hyperbole
2382. Hyperbole
2383. Says a hyperbolic phrase
2384. A simile
2385. A simile
2386. A simile
2387. A metaphor
2388. She is a mule.
2389. Her face was…
2390. A blanket
2391. A symbol
2392. Statue of Liberty, flag etc.
2393. The 50 states
2394. Love
2395. Danger; poison
2396. Yes
2397. Two paths in life
2398. Personification
2399. Personification
2400. Onomatopoeia.
2401. Drip, drizzle, splash, etc.
2402. Snake
2403. Boom, bang, pop, etc.
2404. Sssssss…pop!
2405. Vroom vroom!
2406. Woof, growl, arf etc.
2407. Meow, purr, etc.
2408. Quack quack
2409. Tweet tweet
2410. Baa baa
2411. Ribbit ribbit
2412. Alliteration
2413. Alliteration
2414. Drama
2415. A playwright
2416. Comedy
2417. Tragedy
2418. Masks
2419. William Shakespeare
2420. The Globe Theater
2421. Shakespeare's plays
2422. Comedies
2423. Tragedies
2424. Several scenes
2425. A sonnet
2426. No
2427. No

2428.	Yes
2429.	Yes
2430.	Yes
2431.	A greeting
2432.	A heading
2433.	A personal letter
2434.	A business letter
2435.	Yes
2436.	A greeting
2437.	A closing
2438.	Best Regards, etc.
2439.	Yes
2440.	Spanish
2441.	Spanish
2442.	French
2443.	Yes
2444.	All
2445.	Deep
2446.	Well
2447.	Bush
2448.	Mouth
2449.	Parted
2450.	Neighbors
2451.	Lost
2452.	Best
2453.	Evil
2454.	Invention
2455.	Over
2456.	Shy
2457.	Black
2458.	Eating
2459.	Day
2460.	Thumb
2461.	Nine
2462.	Hot
2463.	Cat
2464.	Fiction
2465.	Wishes
2466.	You
2467.	Winks
2468.	Shoulder
2469.	Hatch
2470.	Crow
2471.	Lining
2472.	Between
2473.	Side
2474.	Stone
2475.	Barrel
2476.	Molehill
2477.	Earned
2478.	Lines
2479.	Thunder
2480.	Horns
2481.	Home
2482.	Wounds
2483.	Harry
2484.	Versa
2485.	Boils
2486.	Be
2487.	Touché

2488.	Says "ache"
2489.	Says "amphibian"
2490.	Says "antique"
2491.	Says "audience"
2492.	Says "bawl"
2493.	Says "beach"
2494.	Says "biceps"
2495.	Says "binoculars"
2496.	Says "boarder"
2497.	Says "break"
2498.	Says "canoes"
2499.	Says "capital"
2500.	Says "capitol"
2501.	Says "conversation"
2502.	Says "cylinder"
2503.	Says "deceive"
2504.	Says "decimal"
2505.	Says word "diagnose"
2506.	Says "diagonal"
2507.	Says "dialogue"
2508.	Says "drought"
2509.	Says "earthquake"
2510.	Says word "equal"
2511.	Says word "equator"
2512.	Says word "equivalent"
2513.	Says word "exclamation"
2514.	Says word "expedition"
2515.	Says word "expense"
2516.	Says word "extinguish"
2517.	Says word "extraordinary"
2518.	Says word "extrasensory"
2519.	Says word "extraterrestrial"
2520.	Says word "fir"
2521.	Says word "guard"
2522.	Says word "inquire"
2523.	Says word "judicial"
2524.	Says word "knight"
2525.	Says word "loose"
2526.	Says word "microphone"
2527.	Says word "mourn"
2528.	Says word "neighbor"
2529.	Says word "night"
2530.	Says word "paraphrase"
2531.	Says word "pause"
2532.	Says word "peace"
2533.	Says word "petition"
2534.	Says word "piece"
2535.	Says word "pour"
2536.	Says word "preamble"
2537.	Says word "prejudice"
2538.	Says word "prospector"
2539.	Says word "punctuation"
2540.	Says word "usually"
2541.	Says word "quail"
2542.	Says word "qualify"
2543.	Says word "quality"
2544.	Says word "quantity"
2545.	Says word "quarrel"
2546.	Says word "quiet"
2547.	Says word "quite"

2548. Says word "quotation"
2549. Says word "quotient"
2550. Says word "request"
2551. Says word "retract"
2552. Says word "route"
2553. Says word "sequence"
2554. Says word "sketch"
2555. Says word "sleigh"
2556. Says word "surround"
2557. Says word "thermometer"
2558. Says word "toe"
2559. Says word "unique"
2560. Says word "vertebrates"

2561. Says word "veto"
2562. Says word "wade"
2563. Says word "weighed"
2564. Says word "whether"
2565. Says word "view"
2566. Says word "whole"
2567. A pen name
2568. Own name
2569. Mark Twain
2570. Dr. Seuss
2571. The Bible
2572. Classics

APPENDIX 2: Chapter 2 – Notable Literary Works through the Ages

1. Iliad
2. Odyssey
3. Aesop
4. Golden egg
5. Fox
6. Mouse
7. Wolf
8. Hare
9. Mouse
10. Grasshopper
11. Lion
12. Andromache
13. King
14. Aeneid
15. Beowulf
16. Carta
17. Tales
18. Metamorphoses
19. Prince
20. Comedy
21. Juliet
22. Caesar
23. Hamlet
24. Othello
25. Mancha
26. Lear
27. Day
28. Bible
29. Torah
30. Stage
31. Proud
32. Lost
33. Progress
34. Boots
35. Hood
36. Nights
37. Crusoe
38. Travels
39. Goose
40. Built
41. Beast
42. Death
43. Sense
44. Independence
45. Tyger
46. Rose
47. Beanstalk
48. Daffodils
49. Faust
50. Sensibility
51. Robinson
52. Grimm brothers
53. Prejudice
54. Beauty
55. Emma
56. Frankenstein
57. Juan
58. Hollow
59. Winkle
60. Ivanhoe
61. Autumn
62. Urn
63. Tales
64. Mohicans
65. Dame
66. Bears
67. Clothes
68. Twist
69. Death
70. Pendulum
71. Heart
72. Carol
73. Duckling
74. Musketeers
75. Cristo
76. Raven
77. Girl
78. Tales
79. Amontillado
80. Fair
81. Eyre
82. Heights
83. Manifesto
84. Copperfield
85. Ways
86. Letter
87. Dick
88. Gables
89. Woman
90. Slavery
91. Cabin
92. Woods
93. Grass
94. Bovary
95. Cities
96. Worst of times
97. Ride
98. Expectations
99. Miserables
100. Address
101. Wonderland
102. Captain
103. Punishment
104. Women
105. Peace
106. Sea
107. Glass
108. Jabberwocky
109. Days
110. Suffrage
111. Sawyer
112. Beauty
113. Karenina
114. House
115. Heidi
116. Christ
117. Pauper
118. Lady
119. Pinocchio
120. Hood
121. Island
122. Solitude
123. Finn
124. Necklace
125. Mines
126. Shadow
127. Kidnapped
128. Ilyich
129. Holmes
130. Book
131. Courage
132. Worlds
133. Darkness
134. Oz
135. Jim
136. Slavery
137. Rabbit
138. Pan
139. Paw
140. Spots
141. Life
142. Table
143. Farm
144. Wild
145. Pimpernel
146. Fang
147. Jungle
148. Magi
149. Castle
150. Gables
151. Willows
152. View
153. Fire
154. If
155. Garden
156. Pygmalion
157. Pollyanna
158. Taken
159. Man
160. Dolittle
161. Ulysses
162. Rabbit
163. Evening
164. Dolittle
165. Dickenson

166. Game
167. India
168. Budd
169. Gatsby
170. Pooh
171. Rises
172. Boys
173. Lighthouse
174. Front
175. Fury
176. Arms
177. Could
178. Drew
179. Dying
180. Falcon
181. Earth
182. Woods
183. Prairie
184. World
185. Bounty
186. Babar
187. Poppins
188. Twice
189. Express
190. Velvet
191. Ferdinand
192. Again
193. Wind
194. Hobbit
195. God
196. Africa
197. Men
198. Business
199. Stone
200. Town
201. Penguins
202. Yearling
203. Madeline
204. Wake
205. Gehrig
206. Wrath
207. Boone
208. Hen
209. Home
210. Bunny
211. Sweat
212. Tolls
213. Son
214. George
215. Stallion
216. Nation
217. Puppy
218. Children
219. Bunny
220. House
221. Tremain
222. Prince
223. Stranger
224. Dresses
225. Hill

226. Menagerie
227. Girl
228. Longstocking
229. Little
230. Farm
231. Hickory
232. Men
233. Moon
234. Balloons
235. Wiggle
236. Pearl
237. Girl
238. Volcano
239. Plague
240. Dragon
241. Lottery
242. Country
243. Wall
244. 1984
245. Salesman
246. Man
247. Wardrobe
248. Huggins
249. Peach
250. Pye
251. Rye
252. Eternity
253. Andes
254. Web
255. Borrowers
256. Me
257. Sea
258. Eden
259. Miguel
260. Mountain
261. Animals
262. Caboose
263. Crucible
264. School
265. Rings
266. Bowditch
267. Remember
268. Crayon
269. Lolita
270. Hill
271. Dog
272. Yeller
273. Watie
274. Hat
275. Christmas
276. Dr. Seuss
277. Pond
278. Tiffany's
279. John
280. Mountain
281. Peace
282. Fish
283. Ham
284. Dolphins
285. Mockingbird

286. Free
287. Journey
288. Peach
289. Go
290. Grows
291. Tollbooth
292. Address
293. Catch-22
294. Day
295. Time
296. Bears
297. Nest
298. Cat
299. Are
300. Dog
301. Dream
302. Bull
303. Factory
304. Stanley
305. Spy
306. Three
307. Tree
308. Die
309. Pareja
310. Cauldron
311. Motorcycle
312. Christmas
313. Dune
314. Slowly
315. Frankweiler
316. See
317. Solitude
318. Chosen
319. King
320. Corduroy
321. Pest
322. Sounder
323. Caterpillar
324. Sings
325. Five
326. Swans
327. Friends
328. Swan
329. Nimh
330. Ever
331. Lorax
332. Wolves
333. Down
334. Day
335. Dancer
336. Great
337. Ends
338. King
339. Everlasting
340. Cry
341. Family
342. Adventure
343. Terabithia
344. Solomon
345. Game

346. Meatballs
347. Snowman
348. Rise
349. Journal
350. Bunnicula
351. Story
352. Choice
353. Fly
354. Travelers
355. Loved
356. 8
357. Jumanji
358. Attic
359. Song
360. Purple
361. Henshaw
362. Crown
363. Tall
364. Express
365. Bus
366. Cookie
367. Boy
368. Club
369. Disaster
370. Photo biography
371. Animalia
372. Hatchet
373. Moon
374. Wall
375. Beloved
376. Voices

377. Matilda
378. Stars
379. Boom
380. Pigs
381. Mitten
382. Magee
383. Go
384. Shiloh
385. Tuesday
386. May
387. Goosebumps
388. Tales
389. Giver
390. Moons
391. You
392. Apprentice
393. Compass
394. Saturday
395. Frindle
396. Dust
397. Stone
398. Underpants
399. Llama
400. Academy
401. Kid
402. Holes
403. Buddy
404. Events
405. Fish
406. Yonder
407. Type

408. Olivia
409. Rising
410. Dixie
411. Shard
412. Lead
413. Explorer
414. Thread
415. Kira
416. Nothing
417. Cross
418. Lucky
419. Spider
420. Village
421. Book
422. Twilight
423. Games
424. Me
425. Manifest
426. Norvelt
427. Ivan
428. Say
429. Adventures
430. Locomotive
431. Guiness
432. Names favorite book
433. Beekle
434. Winnie
435. Child
436. Moon

Bibliography

"Ducksters: Education Site for Kids and Teachers." *Ducksters: Education Site for Kids and Teachers*. N.p., n.d. Web. Accessed 2014. http://www.ducksters.com.

"ENCHANTED LEARNING HOME PAGE." *ENCHANTED LEARNING HOME PAGE*. N.p., n.d. Web. 10 Accessed 2014. http://www.enchantedlearning.com.

"Fact Monster from Information Please." *Fact Monster: Online Almanac, Dictionary, Encyclopedia, and Homework Help*. N.p., n.d. Web. Accessed 2014. http://www.factmonster.com.

Grade Level Help at Internet 4 Classrooms." *Grade Level Help at Internet 4 Classrooms*. N.p., n.d. Web. Accessed 2014. http://www.internet4classrooms.com.

Hirsch, E. D. *What Your First grader Needs to Know: Fundamentals of a Good First-Grade Education*. New York: Doubleday, 1991. Print.

Hirsch, E. D. *What Your Third Grader Needs to Know: Fundamentals of a Good Third-Grade Education*. New York: Doubleday, 1992. Print.

Hirsch, E. D. *What Your Fourth Grader Needs to Know: Fundamentals of a Good Fourth-Grade Education*. New York: Doubleday, 1992. Print.

Hirsch, E. D. *What Your Fifth Grader Needs to Know: Fundamentals of a Good Fifth-Grade Education*. New York: Doubleday, 1993. Print.

Hirsch, E. D., and John Holdren. *What Your Kindergartner Needs to Know: Preparing Your Child for a Lifetime of Learning*. New York: Doubleday, 1996. Print.

Hirsch, E. D. *What Your Second Grader Needs to Know: Fundamentals of a Good Second-Grade Education*. Rev. Ed. New York: Dell, 1998. Print.

Hirsch, E. D., and Linda Bevilacqua. *What Your Preschooler Needs to Know*. New York, NY: Bantam Dell, 2008. Print.

"K-12 Curriculum." *Cedarburg*. N.p., n.d. Web. June 2014. http://www.cedarburg.buildyourowncurriculum.com/public/Landing_Grades.aspx.

"Make an Amazing Timeline in Minutes." *Preceden: Timeline Maker & Timeline Generator*. N.p., n.d. Web. Accessed 2014. http://www.preceden.com.

"Native Indian Tribes." *Warpaths2piecepipes*. N.p., n.d. Web. Accessed 2014. http://www.warpaths2piecepipes.com.

"Typical Course of Study." *Typical Course of Study*. N.p., n.d. Web. 10 July 2014. http://www.worldbook.com/typical-course-of-study.

BIBLIOGRAPHY

"Online Dictionary | Thesaurus." *Online Dictionary*. N.p., n.d. Web. Accessed 2014.
    http://www.onlinedictionary.com.

"Practice Math & Language Arts." *IXL Math and English*. N.p., n.d. Web. Accessed 2014. http://www.ixl.com.

"The Great Idea Finder - Celebrating the Spirit of Innovation." *The Great Idea Finder - Celebrating the Spirit
    of Innovation*. N.p., n.d. Web. Accessed 2014. http://www.ideafinder.com.

"Top Ten Lists at TheTopTens." *Top Ten Lists at TheTopTens*. N.p., n.d. Web. Accessed 2014.
    http://www.thetoptens.com.

"Touropia - Travel, Tours and Top Tens." *Touropia*. N.p., n.d. Web. Accessed 2014. http://www.touropia.com.

"Wikepedia.com." *Wikepedia.com*. N.p., n.d. Web. 30 Accessed 2014. http://www.wikepedia.com.

www.ingramcontent.com/pod-product-compliance
Lightning Source LLC
Chambersburg PA
CBHW081654270326
41933CB00017B/3168